Design America

RANCH HOME *Plans*

The plans in our Design America Series have been created by many of the nation's top architects and designers. No matter what your taste, you're sure to find several homes you would be thrilled to call your own.

Design America Ranch Plans is a collection of best-selling one-story homes including atrium plans.

Plan #562-0279 on page 71

These plans cover a wide range of architectural styles in a popular range of sizes. A broad assortment is presented to match a wide variety of lifestyles and budgets. Each design page features floor plans, a front view of the house, interior square footage of the home, number of bedrooms, baths, garage size and foundation types. All floor plans show room and exterior dimensions.

Technical Specifications - Every effort has been made to ensure that these plans and specifications meet most nationally recognized building codes (BOCA, Southern Building Code Congress and others). Drawing modifications and/or the assistance of a local architect or professional designer are sometimes necessary to comply with local codes or to accommodate specific building site conditions.

Plan #562-0162 on page 274

Blueprint Ordering - Fast and Easy - Your ordering is made simple by following the instructions on page 9. See page 8 for more information on which types of blueprint packages are available and how many plan sets to order.

Your Home, Your Way - The blueprints you receive are a master plan for building your new home. They start you on your way to what may well be the most rewarding experience of your life.

CONTENTS

Design America Ranch Home Plans is published by Home Design Alternatives, Inc. (HDA, Inc.) 4390 Green Ash Drive, St. Louis, MO 63045. All rights reserved. Reproduction in whole or in part without written permission of the publisher is prohibited. Printed in U.S.A © 2001. Artist drawings shown in this publication may vary slightly from the actual working blueprints.

House shown on front cover is
Plan #562-DBI-2461 and is featured on page 113.
Photo Courtesy of Design Basics.

Our Blueprint Packages Offer...

Quality plans for building your future, with extras that provide unsurpassed value, ensure good construction and long-term enjoyment.

A quality home - one that looks good, functions well, and provides years of enjoyment - is a product of many things - design, materials, craftsmanship. But it's also the result of outstanding blueprints - the actual plans and specifications that tell the builder exactly how to build your home.

And with our BLUEPRINT PACKAGES you get the absolute best. A complete set of blueprints is available for every design in this book. These "working drawings," are highly detailed, resulting in two key benefits:

- *Better understanding by the contractor of how to build your home, and...*

- *More accurate construction estimates.*

When you purchase one of our designs, you'll receive all of the BLUEPRINT components shown here - elevations, foundation plan, floor plans, cross-sections and details. Other helpful building aids are also available to help make your dream home a reality.

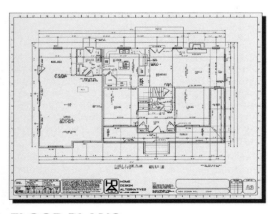

COVER SHEET

This sheet is the artist's rendering of the exterior of the home. It will give you an idea of how your home will look when completed and landscaped.

FOUNDATION PLAN

The foundation plan shows the layout of the basement, walk-out basement, crawl space, slab or pier foundation. All necessary notations and dimensions are included. See plan page for the foundation types included. If the home plan you choose does not have your desired foundation type, our Customer Service Representatives can advise you on how to customize your foundation to suit your specific needs or site conditions.

FLOOR PLANS

These plans show the placement of walls, doors, closets, plumbing fixtures, electrical outlets, columns, and beams for each level of the home.

EXTERIOR ELEVATIONS
These drawings illustrate the front, rear and both sides of the house, with all details of exterior materials and the required dimensions.

INTERIOR ELEVATIONS
Interior elevations provide views of special interior elements such as fireplaces, kitchen cabinets, built-in units and other special features of the home.

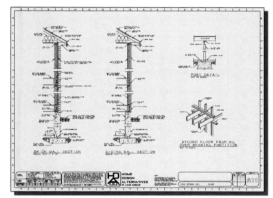

DETAILS
Details show how to construct certain components of your home, such as the roof system, stairs, deck, etc.

CROSS SECTIONS
Cross sections show detail views of the home as if it were sliced from the roof to the foundation. This sheet shows important areas such as load-bearing walls, stairs, joists, trusses and other structural elements, which are critical for proper construction.

Other Helpful Building Aids...

Your Blueprint Package will contain the necessary construction information to build your home. We also offer the following products and services to save you time and money in the building process.

Rush Delivery - Most orders are processed within 24 hours of receipt. Please allow 7 working days for delivery. If you need to place a rush order, please call us by 11:00 a.m. CST and ask for overnight or second day service.

Technical Assistance - If you have questions, call our technical support line at 1-314-770-2228 between 8:00 a.m. and 5:00 p.m. CST. Whether it involves design modifications or field assistance, our designers are extremely familiar with all of our designs and will be happy to help you. We want your home to be everything you expect it to be.

Material List - Material lists are available for many of our plans. Each list gives you the quantity, dimensions and description of the building materials necessary to construct your home. You'll get faster and more accurate bids from your contractor and material suppliers, and you'll save money by paying for only the materials you need. Refer to the Home Plan Index for availability.

Home Plans Index

Plan Number	Square Feet	Price Code	Page	Material List Available	Plan Number	Square Feet	Price Code	Page	Material List Available	Plan Number	Square Feet	Price Code	Page	Material List Available
562-0105	1,360	A	24	✓	562-0370	1,721	C	179	✓	562-0707	2,723	E	10	✓
562-0110	1,605	B	34	✓	562-0382	1,546	B	61	✓	562-0710	2,334	D	178	✓
562-0112	1,668	C	137	✓	562-0387	1,958	C	115	✓	562-0712	2,029	C	16	✓
562-0127	1,996	D	315	✓	562-0393	1,684	B	163	✓	562-0713	3,199	E	25	✓
562-0151	2,874	E	53	✓	562-0394	1,558	B	99	✓	562-0714	2,808	E	311	✓
562-0161	1,630	B	138	✓	562-0398	1,736	B	145	✓	562-0715	4,826	G	52	✓
562-0162	1,882	D	274	✓	562-0407	2,517	D	50	✓	562-0717	1,268	A	138	✓
562-0163	1,772	C	294	✓	562-0409	2,598	D	83	✓	562-0718	1,340	A	39	✓
562-0172	1,643	B	40	✓	562-0410	1,742	B	284	✓	562-0719	2,483	D	182	✓
562-0173	1,220	A	241	✓	562-0412	2,109	C	177	✓	562-0721	2,437	D	283	✓
562-0176	1,404	A	95	✓	562-0419	1,882	C	12	✓	562-0724	1,969	C	262	✓
562-0181	1,408	A	172	✓	562-0420	1,941	C	338	✓	562-0727	1,477	A	339	✓
562-0185	2,396	D	207	✓	562-0423	2,350	D	208	✓	562-0729	2,218	D	78	✓
562-0188	1,800	C	119	✓	562-0424	1,689	B	54	✓	562-0730	2,408	D	41	✓
562-0190	1,600	C	160	✓	562-0438	2,558	D	63	✓	562-0731	1,761	B	194	✓
562-0191	1,868	D	90	✓	562-0440	2,365	D	190	✓	562-0732	1,681	D	266	✓
562-0192	1,266	A	31	✓	562-0441	1,747	B	309	✓	562-0733	2,070	C	326	✓
562-0193	2,252	D	21	✓	562-0442	1,950	C	242	✓	562-0745	1,819	C	133	✓
562-0194	1,444	A	278	✓	562-0443	2,255	D	348	✓	562-0746	2,516	D	150	✓
562-0195	988	AA	183	✓	562-0447	1,393	B	214	✓	562-0794	1,433	A	258	
562-0198	1,416	A	233	✓	562-0450	1,708	B	17	✓	562-0796	1,599	B	289	
562-0200	1,343	A	106	✓	562-0477	1,140	AA	182	✓	562-0797	2,651	E	110	
562-0203	1,475	B	272	✓	562-0478	1,092	AA	117	✓	562-0798	2,128	C	334	✓
562-0212	1,707	C	97	✓	562-0484	1,403	A	11	✓	562-0799	1,954	C	204	✓
562-0214	1,770	B	180	✓	562-0485	1,195	AA	197	✓	562-0800	2,532	D	263	
562-0215	1,846	C	193	✓	562-0495	987	AA	230	✓	562-0803	3,366	F	293	
562-0216	1,661	B	159	✓	562-0500	1,134	AA	267	✓	562-1101	1,643	B	173	✓
562-0217	1,360	A	134	✓	562-0502	864	AAA	241	✓	562-1117	1,440	A	92	✓
562-0226	1,416	A	327	✓	562-0503	1,000	AA	175	✓	562-1118-1 & 2	1,550	B	72	✓
562-0227	1,674	B	69	✓	562-0505	1,104	AA	107	✓	562-1120-1 & 2	1,232	A	237	✓
562-0229	1,676	B	85	✓	562-0506	1,375	A	30	✓	562-1124	1,345	A	171	✓
562-0235	2,501	D	245	✓	562-0507	1,197	AA	301	✓	562-1216-1 & 2	1,668	B	64	✓
562-0237	1,631	B	147	✓	562-0510	1,400	A	42	✓	562-1220	1,540	B	226	✓
562-0241	829	AAA	273	✓	562-0515	1,344	A	134	✓	562-1223-1 & 2	3,108	E	328	✓
562-0244	1,994	D	15	✓	562-0516	2,015	C	297	✓	562-1227-1 & 2	1,042	AA	67	✓
562-0245	2,260	D	239	✓	562-0520	1,720	B	210	✓	562-1229-1 & 2	1,610	B	219	✓
562-0246	1,539	B	292	✓	562-0529	1,285	B	93	✓	562-1230-1 & 2	1,288	A	198	✓
562-0249	1,501	B	257	✓	562-0534	1,288	A	167	✓	562-1243-1 & 2	2,705	E	219	✓
562-0251	1,407	A	112	✓	562-0541	2,080	C	209	✓	562-1248	1,574	B	217	✓
562-0256	1,698	B	168	✓	562-0542	1,832	C	32	✓	562-1253	1,996	C	158	✓
562-0257	1,862	C	130	✓	562-0543	1,160	AA	295	✓	562-1260	2,190	C	353	✓
562-0263	3,003	E	192	✓	562-0547	720	AAA	139	✓	562-1263-1 & 2	2,155	C	344	✓
562-0264	1,689	B	28	✓	562-0582	800	AAA	249	✓	562-1265	2,530	D	203	✓
562-0262	2,070	C	265	✓	562-0583	1,000	AA	224	✓	562-1266	2,086	C	304	✓
562-0265	1,314	A	275	✓	562-0584	1,300	A	30	✓	562-1267-1 & 2	1,800	C	120	✓
562-0268	1,135	AA	74	✓	562-0585	1,344	A	102	✓	562-1273	1,730	B	175	✓
562-0269	1,428	A	154	✓	562-0587	1,120	AA	313	✓	562-1275-1 & 2	1,932	C	151	✓
562-0271	1,368	A	102	✓	562-0650	1,020	AA	131	✓	562-1276-1 & 2	1,533	B	191	✓
562-0273	988	AA	255	✓	562-0651	962	AA	146	✓	562-1285-1 & 2	1,540	B	82	✓
562-0276	950	AA	67	✓	562-0657	796	AAA	197	✓	562-1286-1 & 2	1,723	B	75	✓
562-0277	1,127	AA	305	✓	562-0659	1,516	B	276	✓	562-1310	1,704	B	101	
562-0279	1,993	D	71	✓	562-0660	1,321	A	66	✓	562-1324	1,907	C	251	
562-0280	1,847	C	193	✓	562-0661	1,712	B	215	✓	562-1329	1,364	A	106	✓
562-0281	1,624	B	94	✓	562-0676	1,367	A	215	✓	562-1336	1,364	A	167	✓
562-0282	1,642	B	75	✓	562-0678	1,567	B	23	✓	562-1400-1 & 2	1,102	AA	255	✓
562-0283	1,800	D	350	✓	562-0679	1,466	A	228	✓	562-1418	2,180	C	38	✓
562-0286	1,856	C	104	✓	562-0682	1,941	C	259	✓	562-1429	1,500	B	282	
562-0287	2,718	E	109	✓	562-0685	1,844	C	58	✓	562-AMD-1135	1,467	A	256	
562-0289	2,513	D	314	✓	562-0687	1,596	B	327	✓	562-AMD-1213	2,197	C	195	
562-0294	1,655	B	76	✓	562-0688	1,556	B	54	✓	562-AMD-1216	2,155	C	347	
562-0296	1,396	A	301	✓	562-0689	1,539	B	328	✓	562-AMD-1219	2,755	E	103	
562-0297	1,320	A	93	✓	562-0690	1,400	A	14	✓	562-AX-4315	2,018	C	174	
562-0315	2,481	D	127	✓	562-0693	1,013	AA	166	✓	562-AX-5378	1,897	C	112	
562-0316	1,824	C	43	✓	562-0694	1,285	A	171	✓	562-AX-5380	1,480	A	339	
562-0335	1,865	D	49	✓	562-0695	448	AAA	117	✓	562-AX-90303	1,615	B	169	
562-0336	2,467	D	149	✓	562-0696	676	AAA	213	✓	562-AX-91316	1,097	AA	271	
562-0338	2,397	E	144	✓	562-0697	924	AA	237	✓	562-AX-93308	1,793	B	261	
562-0339	2,287	E	227	✓	562-0698	1,143	AA	240	✓	562-AX-95367	1,595	B	234	
562-0340	2,153	C	337	✓	562-0699	1,073	AA	246	✓	562-AX-96355	1,699	B	165	
562-0342	2,089	C	199	✓	562-0700	416	AAA	74	✓	562-AX-97359	1,380	A	298	
562-0343	2,056	C	22	✓	562-0701	2,308	D	300	✓	562-AX-98364	2,585	D	189	
562-0348	2,003	D	335	✓	562-0702	1,558	B	91	✓	562-BF-1426	1,420	A	310	
562-0355	3,814	F	18	✓	562-0703	2,412	D	142	✓	562-BF-1711	1,770	B	272	
562-0357	1,550	B	27	✓	562-0705	2,758	E	13	✓	562-BF-1718	2,665	E	204	
562-0364	2,531	D	55	✓	562-0706	1,791	B	223	✓	562-BF-1828	1,828	C	60	

Home Plans Index

Plan Number	Square Feet	Price Code	Page	Material List Available	Plan Number	Square Feet	Price Code	Page	Material List Available	Plan Number	Square Feet	Price Code	Page	Material List Available
562-BF-1901	1,925	C	296		562-FB-969	2,311	D	299		562-JA-79298	2,229	D	51	
562-BF-2210	3,172	E	287		562-FB1119	1,915	C	192		562-JA-90199	1,801	C	82	
562-BF-2610	2,684	E	354		562-FB-1158	2,072	C	46		562-JA-90299	1,490	A	329	
562-BF-DR1109	1,191	AA	148		562-FD7018	1,417	A	345		562-JFD-10-1436-1	1,436	A	59	
562-BF-DR1311	1,984	C	217		562-FD7110	1,980	C	342		562-JFD-10-1456-2	1,456	A	233	
562-BF-DR1819	2,424	D	229		562-FD7397-L	2,470	D	105		562-JFD-10-1629-21	1,629	B	276	
562-CHP-1432-A-142	1,405	A	125		562-FD7627-L	2,030	C	269		562-JFD-10-1692-1	1,692	B	92	
562-CHP-1532-A-141	1,500	B	282		562-FD7852-L	2,506	D	247		562-JFD-10-1724-2	1,724	B	273	
562-CHP-1732-A-101	1,704	B	89		562-FD8110A	1,431	A	208		562-JFD-10-1840-2	1,840	C	343	
562-CHP-2233-A-36	2,263	D	133		562-FD8166-L	2,061	C	317		562-JFD-10-1842-2	1,842	C	148	
562-CHP-2243-A-29	2,246	D	185		562-FD8265-L	1,584	B	176		562-JFD-10-1875-1	1,875	C	45	
562-CHP-2443-A-38	2,481	D	29		562-FDG-7773	1,653	B	224		562-JFD-10-2096-2	2,096	C	123	
562-CHP-2443-A-67	2,450	D	187		562-FDG-8378-L	2,591	D	19		562-JFD-10-2178-2	2,178	C	222	
562-DB679	1,511	B	128		562-FDG-8425-L	2,434	D	323		562-JFD-10-2228-2	2,228	D	114	
562-DB1379	1,429	A	318		562-FDG-8469-L	2,911	E	123		562-JFD-10-2278-2	2,278	D	86	
562-DB1539	1,996	C	312		562-FDG-8526	2,370	D	333		562-JV-1236-742-B	1,978	C	330	
562-DB1767	1,604	B	212		562-FDG-8567-L	2,528	D	303		562-JV-1276-A	1,296	A	305	
562-DB1963	1,347	A	213		562-FDG-8673	1,604	B	212		562-JV-1293-A	1,293	A	28	
562-DB2212	1,735	B	108		562-FDG-8701-L	2,578	D	26		562-JV-1325-B	1,325	A	244	
562-DB2290	1,666	B	100		562-FDG-8729-L	2,529	D	201		562-JV-1389-A	1,389	A	122	
562-DB2377	1,636	B	250		562-GM-1253	1,253	A	295		562-JV-1389-B	1,411	A	140	
562-DB2537	1,580	B	235		562-GM-1333	1,333	A	166		562-JV-1617-A-SJ	1,617	B	216	
562-DB2761	1,341	A	39		562-GM-1406	1,406	A	110		562-JV-1635-A	1,635	B	324	
562-DB2778	2,456	E	286		562-GM-1474	1,474	A	200		562-JV-1646-A	1,646	B	136	
562-DB2818	1,651	B	132		562-GM-1507	1,507	B	162		562-JV-1675-A	1,675	B	58	
562-DB3006	1,806	C	96		562-GM-1550	1,550	B	33		562-JV-1716-A	1,716	B	336	
562-DB3010	1,422	A	336		562-GM-1562	1,562	B	48		562-JV-1769-B	1,769	B	118	
562-DBI-1748-19	1,911	C	164		562-GM-1572	1,572	B	243		562-JV-1781-B	1,781	B	158	
562-DBI-2206-24	2,498	D	141		562-GM-1842	1,842	C	77		562-JV-1840-A	1,840	C	47	
562-DBI-2461	1,850	C	113		562-GM-1849	1,849	C	68		562-JV-1869-A	1,869	C	36	
562-DBI-2652-25	2,512	D	341		562-GM-1892	1,892	C	268		562-JV-1896-A	1,896	C	128	
562-DBI-3019	1,479	C	346		562-GM-2158	2,158	C	253		562-JV-1982-A	1,982	C	342	
562-DBI-4208	2,057	C	346		562-GSD-1001	3,158	E	288		562-JV-1985-A	1,983	C	33	
562-DBI-4953-18	1,853	C	84		562-GSD-1017	3,671	F	188		562-JV-2012-A-SJ	2,012	C	290	
562-DBI-5003	2,750	E	103		562-GSD-1023-C	1,890	C	125		562-JV-2033-A	2,033	C	127	
562-DBI-24035-9P	1,395	A	214		562-GSD-1085	2,086	C	264		562-JV-2542-A	2,542	D	281	
562-DBI-24038-9P	2,126	C	161		562-GSD-1123	1,734	B	57		562-LBD-10-1B	1,087	AA	79	
562-DBI-24045-9P	1,263	A	146		562-GSD-1260	2,788	E	280		562-LBD-13-1A	1,310	A	231	
562-DDI-89-101	2,255	D	111		562-GSD-1748	1,496	A	302		562-LBD-15-4A	1,575	B	95	
562-DDI-90-103	1,871	C	70		562-GSD-2875	2,880	E	307		562-LBD-17-14A	1,725	B	47	
562-DDI-92-101	1,785	B	316		562-HDG-97001	1,872	C	70		562-LBD-17-7A	1,742	B	24	
562-DDI-92-103	960	AA	159		562-HDG-97006	1,042	AA	122		562-LBD-18-11A	1,890	C	248	
562-DDI-94-101R	2,327	D	19		562-HDG-98006	1,631	B	343		562-LBD-18-5A	1,862	C	44	
562-DDI-95-113	2,710	E	76		562-HDG-99004	1,231	A	139		562-LBD-19-15A	1,955	C	232	
562-DDI-95-114	1,018	AA	240		562-HDS-1758	1,783	B	238		562-LBD-19-16A	1,993	C	173	
562-DL-13663L	1,366	A	313		562-HDS-1834	1,834	C	62		562-LBD-26-21A	2,648	E	154	
562-DL-16053L1	1,605	B	155		562-HDS-1993	1,993	C	205		562-LBD-26-23A	2,678	E	256	
562-DL-16653L1	1,665	B	114		562-HDS-2010-2	2,010	C	231		562-LBD-27-26A	2,745	E	211	
562-DL-17104L1	1,710	B	198		562-HDS-2221-2	2,221	D	116		562-MG-9305	1,606	B	150	
562-DL-17353L1	1,735	B	254		562-HDS-2278	2,278	D	320		562-MG-97099	1,093	AA	230	
562-DL-17653L1	1,765	B	308		562-HDS-2322	2,322	D	246		562-MN1353	1,353	A	156	
562-DL-18803L1	1,880	C	98		562-HDS-2454	2,458	D	285		562-MN1538	1,538	B	322	
562-DL-19053L1	1,905	C	196		562-HDS-2551	2,551	D	121		562-MN1687	1,687	B	126	
562-DL-19603L2	1,960	C	170		562-HDS-2636	2,636	E	87		562-MN1764	1,764	B	306	
562-DL-20604L2	2,060	C	170		562-HDS-2731	2,731	E	181		562-MN1817	1,817	C	42	
562-DL-21644L1	2,164	C	291		562-HDS-2962	2,962	E	220		562-MN1941	1,941	C	319	
562-DL-21804L1	2,180	C	79		562-HDS-3556	3,556	F	332		562-MN1963	1,963	C	349	
562-DL-23804L2	2,380	D	325		562-JA5219	1,802	C	73		562-MN2439	2,439	D	129	
562-DL-23824L2	2,382	C	321		562-JA5269	2,042	C	124		562-N064	1,176	AA	116	✓
562-DL-25454L1	2,545	D	291		562-JA5359	1,730	B	260		562-N087	784	AAA	62	✓
562-DL-25604L2	2,560	D	65		562-JA5399	2,204	D	143		562-N114	792	AAA	31	✓
562-DL-29054L2	2,905	E	81		562-JA5469	1,663	B	88		562-N118	527	AAA	131	✓
562-DL-35355LS2	3,535	F	277		562-JA5509	1,984	C	218		562-N130	1,584	B	186	✓
562-ES-125-1 & 2	1,605	B	279	✓	562-JA-53394	1,763	B	340		562-N131	733	AAA	107	✓
562-FB-174	2,115	C	334		562-JA-61495	1,540	B	20		562-N286-1 & 2	1,408	A	85	✓
562-FB-543	1,945	C	331		562-JA-63295	2,049	C	225		562-N294-1 & 2	1,092	AA	267	✓
562-FB-599	2,236	D	157		562-JA-64396	2,196	C	101		562-N297-1 & 2	1,042	AA	249	✓
562-FB-743	1,978	C	235		562-JA-65796	1,370	A	156		562-N299-1 & 2	1,317	A	275	✓
562-FB-797	1,845	C	352		562-JA-65996	1,962	C	35		562-P-130-1 & 2	1,778	B	184	✓
562-FB-845	1,779	B	56		562-JA-67596	1,919	C	151		562-UDG-99003	1,425	A	152	
562-FB-902	1,856	C	135		562-JA-73897	1,794	B	289		562-UDG-99011	2,900	E	236	
562-FB-930	2,322	D	80		562-JA-74397	2,991	E	37		562-VL947	947	AA	206	
562-FB-933	2,193	C	153		562-JA-75197	3,034	E	270		562-VL1267	1,267	A	183	
562-FB-960	2,201	D	221		562-JA-77598	1,600	B	202		562-VL2069	2,069	C	292	
562-FB-968	2,403	D	252		562-JA-78798	1,806	C	351		562-VL2162	2,162	C	211	

What Kind Of Plan Package Do You Need?

Once you find the home plan you've been looking for, here are some suggestions on how to make your Dream Home a reality. To get started, order the type of plans that fit your particular situation.

Your Choices:

The One-set package - This single set of blueprints is offered so you can study or review a home in greater detail. But a single set is never enough for construction and it's a copyright violation to reproduce blueprints.

The Minimum 5-set package - If you're ready to start the construction process, this 5-set package is the minimum number of blueprint sets you will need. It will require keeping close track of each set so they can be used by multiple subcontractors and tradespeople.

The Standard 8-set package - For best results in terms of cost, schedule and quality of construction, we recommend you order eight (or more) sets of blueprints. Besides one set for yourself, additional sets of blueprints will be required by your mortgage lender, local building department, general contractor and all subcontractors working on foundation, electrical, plumbing, heating/air conditioning, carpentry work, etc.

Reproducible Masters - If you wish to make some minor design changes, you'll want to order reproducible masters. These drawings contain the same information as the blueprints but are printed on erasable and reproducible paper. This will allow your builder or a local design professional to make the necessary drawing changes without the major expense of redrawing the plans. This package also allows you to print as many copies of the modified plans as you need.

Mirror Reverse Sets - Plans can be printed in mirror reverse. These plans are useful when the house would fit your site better if all the rooms were on the opposite side than shown. They are simply a mirror image of the original drawings causing the lettering and dimensions to read backwards. Therefore, when ordering mirror reverse drawings, you must purchase at least one set of right reading plans.

OTHER GREAT PRODUCTS TO HELP YOU BUILD YOUR DREAM HOME

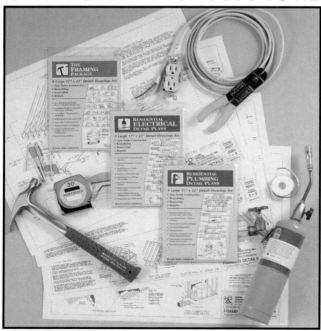

DETAIL PLAN PACKAGES:
FRAMING • ELECTRICAL • PLUMBING

Three separate packages offer homebuilders details for constructing various foundations; numerous floor, wall and roof framing techniques; simple to complex residential wiring; sump and water softener hookups; plumbing connection methods; installation of septic systems, and more. Each package includes three-dimensional illustrations and a glossary of terms. Purchase one or all three.
Cost: $20.00 each or all three for $40.00

THE LEGAL KIT

Avoid many legal pitfalls and build your home with confidence using the forms and contracts featured in this kit. Included are request for proposal documents, various fixed price and cost plus contracts, instructions on how and when to use each form, warranty statements and more. Save time and money before you break ground on your new home or start a remodeling project. All forms are reproducible. The kit is ideal for homebuilders and contractors.
Cost: $35.00

ORDER FORM

IMPORTANT INFORMATION TO KNOW BEFORE YOU ORDER YOUR HOME PLANS

❏ **Exchange Policies -** Since blueprints are printed in response to your order, we cannot honor requests for refunds. However, if for some reason you find that the plan you have purchased does not meet your requirements, you may exchange that plan for another plan in our collection. At the time of the exchange, you will be charged a processing fee of 25% of your original plan package price, plus the difference in price between the plan packages (if applicable) and the cost to ship the new plans to you. *Please note: Reproducible drawings can only be exchanged if the package is unopened, and exchanges are allowed only within 90 days of purchase.*

❏ **Building Codes & Requirements -** Our plans conform to most national building codes. However, they may not comply completely with your local building regulations. Some counties and municipalities have their own building codes, regulations and requirements. The assistance of a local builder, architect or other building professional may be necessary to modify the drawings to comply with your area's specific requirements. We recommend you consult with your local building officials prior to beginning construction.

Plan prices guaranteed through December 31, 2001.

BLUEPRINT PRICE SCHEDULE

BEST VALUE

Price Code	One-Set	SAVE $75.00 Five-Sets	SAVE $150.00 Eight-Sets	Material List*	Reproducible Masters
AAA	$195	$260	$290	$40	$390
AA	245	310	340	45	440
A	295	360	390	45	490
B	345	410	440	45	540
C	395	460	490	50	590
D	445	510	540	50	640
E	495	560	590	50	690
F	545	610	640	50	740
G	650	715	745	55	845
H	755	820	850	55	950

OTHER OPTIONS...

Additional Plan Sets*	$ 35.00	
Print In Mirror Reverse*	add $ 5.00	per set
Legal Kit	$ 35.00	

Detail Plan Packages: (Buy 2, get 3rd FREE)
Framing, Electrical & Plumbing $20.00 ea.
Rush Charges . . . .   Next Day Air $38.00
                                 Second Day Air $25.00

Available only within 90 days after purchase of plan package or reproducible masters of same plan.

ORDER FORM

Please send me Plan Number 562 - _____
Price Code _____
(See Home Plans Index)

❏ Reproducible Masters $ _____
❏ Eight-Set Plan Package $ _____
❏ Five-Set Plan Package $ _____
❏ One-Set Plan Package (no mirror reverse) $ _____
❏ ____ (Qty.) Additional Plan Sets ($35.00 each) $ _____
❏ Print ____ (Qty.) sets in Mirror Reverse (add $5.00/set) $ _____
❏ Material List (see index for availability) $ _____
❏ Legal Kit (see page 8) $ _____
Detail Plan Packages: (see page 8)
   ❏ Framing   ❏ Electrical   ❏ Plumbing $ _____
        SUBTOTAL $ _____
        SALES TAX (MO residents add 7%) $ _____
❏ Rush Charges $ _____
        SHIPPING & HANDLING $ 12.50
        TOTAL ENCLOSED (US funds only) $ _____

❏ Enclosed is my check or money order payable to HDA, Inc. (Sorry, no COD's)

Please note that plans are not returnable.

Mail to: HDA, Inc.
4390 Green Ash Drive
St. Louis, MO 63045-1219

I hereby authorize HDA, Inc. to charge this purchase to my credit card account (check one):

❏ MasterCard   ❏ VISA   ❏ DISCOVER NOVUS   ❏ AMERICAN EXPRESS Cards

My card number is _____

The expiration date is _____

Signature _____

Name _____
(Please print or type)

Street Address _____
(Please **do not** use P.O. Box)

City, State, Zip _____

My daytime phone number (_____) - _____ - _____

I am a ❏ Builder/Contractor   ❏ Homeowner   ❏ Renter

I ❏ have   ❏ have not selected my general contractor.

Thank you for your order!

9

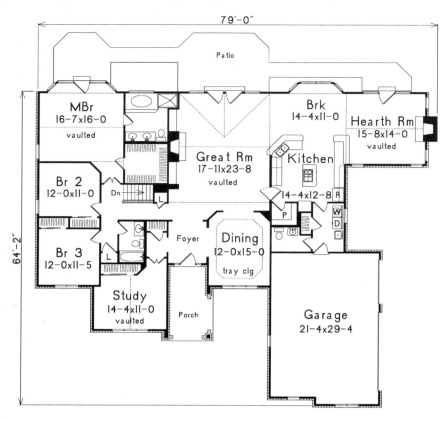

79'-0"

Patio

MBr
16-7x16-0
vaulted

Brk
14-4x11-0

Hearth Rm
15-8x14-0
vaulted

Great Rm
17-11x23-8
vaulted

Kitchen

14-4x12-8

Br 2
12-0x11-0

Dn

L

64-2"

Foyer

Dining
12-0x15-0
tray clg

P

W D

R

Br 3
12-0x11-5

L

Study
14-4x11-0
vaulted

Porch

Garage
21-4x29-4

PLAN DATA

Total Living Area: 2,723
Bedrooms: 3
Baths: 2 1/2
Garage: 3-car
Foundation Type:
  Basement
Features:
  1 1/2 story window
  wall in great room

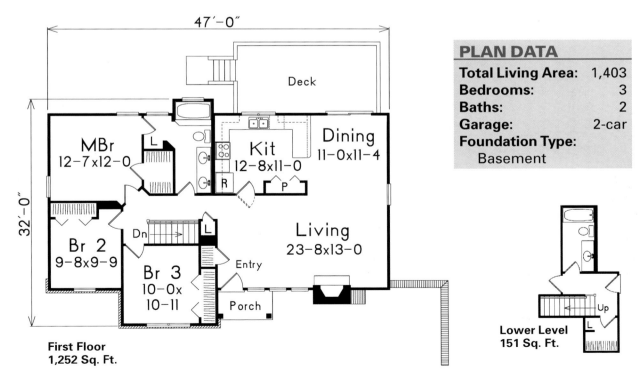

47'-0"

Deck

32'-0"

MBr
12-7x12-0

Kit
12-8x11-0

Dining
11-0x11-4

R

P

L

Dn

Living
23-8x13-0

Br 2
9-8x9-9

Br 3
10-0x
10-11

Entry

Porch

First Floor
1,252 Sq. Ft.

PLAN DATA

Total Living Area: 1,403
Bedrooms: 3
Baths: 2
Garage: 2-car
Foundation Type:
Basement

Up

L

Lower Level
151 Sq. Ft.

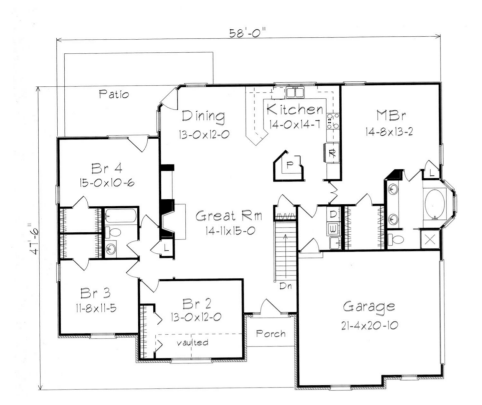

58'-0"

Patio

Dining
13-0x12-0

Kitchen
14-0x14-7

MBr
14-8x13-2

Br 4
15-0x10-6

47'-6"

Great Rm
14-11x15-0

Br 3
11-8x11-5

Br 2
13-0x12-0

vaulted

Porch

Dn

Garage
21-4x20-10

PLAN DATA

Total Living Area:	1,882
Bedrooms:	4
Baths:	2
Garage:	2-car
Foundation Type:	
Basement	

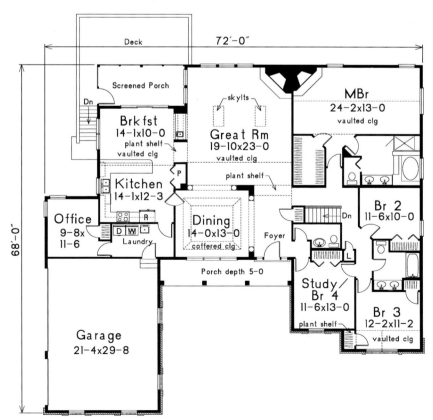

Deck | **72'-0"**

Screened Porch

Dn

Brkfst
14-1x10-0
plant shelf
vaulted clg

skylts

Great Rm
19-10x23-0
vaulted clg

MBr
24-2x13-0
vaulted clg

Kitchen
14-1x12-3

P

plant shelf

Office
9-8x
11-6

D W R

Laundry

Dining
14-0x13-0
coffered clg

Foyer

Dn

Br 2
11-6x10-0

68'-0"

Porch depth 5-0

L

Study/
Br 4
11-6x13-0
plant shelf

Br 3
12-2x11-2
vaulted clg

Garage
21-4x29-8

PLAN DATA

Total Living Area: 2,758
Bedrooms: 4
Baths: 2 1/2
Garage: 3-car
Foundation Type:
Basement

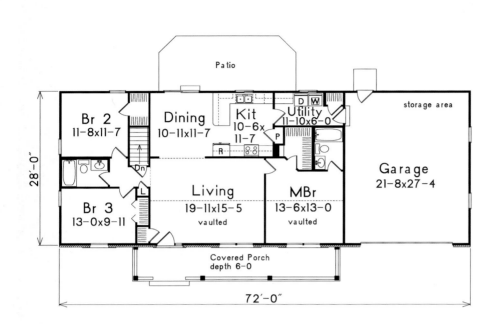

PLAN DATA

Total Living Area: 1,400
Bedrooms: 3
Baths: 2
Garage: 2-car
Foundation Types:
  Basement standard
  Crawl space
Features:
  Garage with storage

Patio

Br 2
11-8x11-7

Dining
10-11x11-7

Kit
10-6x
11-7

Utility
11-10x6-0

storage area

28'-0"

Dn

Br 3
13-0x9-11

Living
19-11x15-5
vaulted

MBr
13-6x13-0
vaulted

Garage
21-8x27-4

Covered Porch
depth 6-0

72'-0"

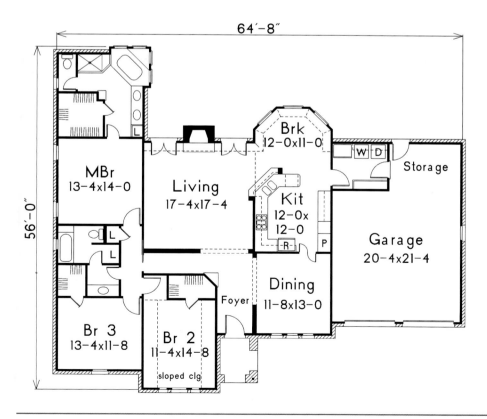

64'-8"

56'-0"

MBr
13-4x14-0

Living
17-4x17-4

Brk
12-0x11-0

Kit
12-0x
12-0

W D

Storage

Garage
20-4x21-4

Dining
11-8x13-0

Foyer

P

R

L

L

L

Br 3
13-4x11-8

Br 2
11-4x14-8

sloped clg

PLAN DATA

Total Living Area: 1,994
Bedrooms: 3
Baths: 2
Garage: 2-car
Foundation Type:
  Slab
Features:
  - 9' ceiling standard
  - 10' ceiling in dining
    room

61'-0"

Br 3
11-0x12-0

Study
10-8x
12-0

Patio

Garage
22-10x20-1

51'-0"

Great Room
20-1x19-5

vaulted clg

Br 2
11-0x10-0

plant shelf

D W

R

P

Dn

Kit/Dining
20-0x18-11

MBr
17-4x14-0
vaulted clg

Entry

Porch

Porch depth 6-0

PLAN DATA

Total Living Area:	2,029
Bedrooms:	4
Baths:	2
Garage:	2-car
Foundation Type:	
Basement	

PLAN DATA

Total Living Area: 1,708
Bedrooms: 3
Baths: 2
Garage: 2-car
Foundation Types:
  Basement standard
  Crawl space

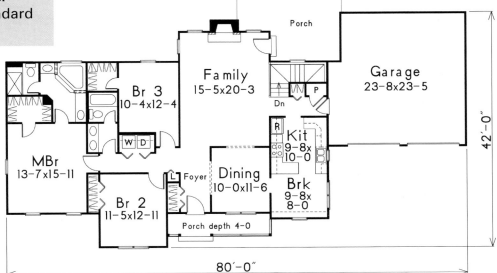

Rear View

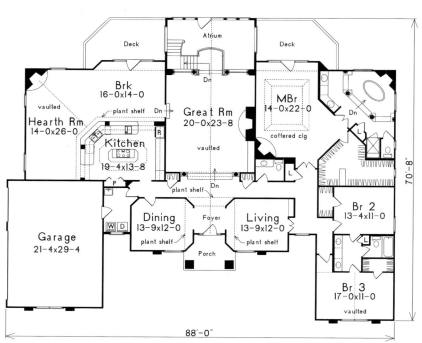

PLAN DATA

Total Living Area: 3,814
Bedrooms: 3
Baths: 2 1/2
Garage: 3-car
Foundation Type:
 Walk-out basement
Features:
 248 square feet in
 lower level atrium

Deck

Atrium

Deck

Brk
16-0x14-0

vaulted

plant shelf

Dn

Great Rm
20-0x23-8

MBr
14-0x22-0

coffered clg

Hearth Rm
14-0x26-0

Kitchen
19-4x13-8

vaulted

Dn

plant shelf

Dn

Br 2
13-4x11-0

Garage
21-4x29-4

W D

Dining
13-9x12-0

plant shelf

Foyer

Living
13-9x12-0

plant shelf

Porch

Br 3
17-0x11-0

vaulted

70'-8"

88'-0"

PLAN DATA

Total Living Area: 2,327
Bedrooms: 3
Baths: 2
Garage: 3-car
Foundation Types:
  Basement
  Crawl space
  Slab
Please specify when ordering

Width: 78'-0"
Depth: 66'-0"

MASTER 13/6 x 16/4

LIVING RM 13/4 x 15/10

FAMILY RM 19/0 x 15/6

PATIO

NOOK 12/8 x 10/6

BDRM-2 12/8 x 10/6

FOYER

DINING 12/0 x 12/6

KITCHEN 17/2 x 8/6

BDRM-3 11/0 x 14/2

UTIL.

GARAGE 33/0 x 21/8

PLAN DATA

Total Living Area: 2,591
Bedrooms: 4
Baths: 3
Garage: 3-car
Foundation Type:
  Slab

SITTING AREA

COVERED PATIO

FAMILY ROOM 15X17 VAULTED CLG. 8" TO 12"

BDRM.#2 12X14 9" CLG.

MSTR. BDRM. 14X20 PULLMAN CLG. 9" TO 11"

COVERED PATIO

BRKFT. 11X11

FORMAL LIVING 12X15 10" CLG.

KIT. 12X13

UTIL.

HALL 9" CLG.

BDRM.#3 11X12 9" CLG.

MSTR. BATH 9" CLG.

HALL 9" CLG.

PANTRY

GALLERY 10" CLG.

BDRM.#4 11X11 9" CLG.

WALK-IN CLOSET

FORMAL DINING 10X12 10" CLG.

ENTRY 10" CLG.

STUDY 11X12 9" CLG.

PORCH

THREE CAR GARAGE 21X32 8" CLG.

70' - 4"

65' - 0"

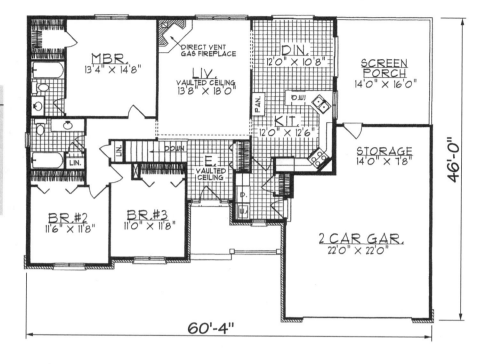

PLAN DATA

Total Living Area: 1,540
Bedrooms: 3
Baths: 2
Garage: 2-car
Foundation Type:
  Basement

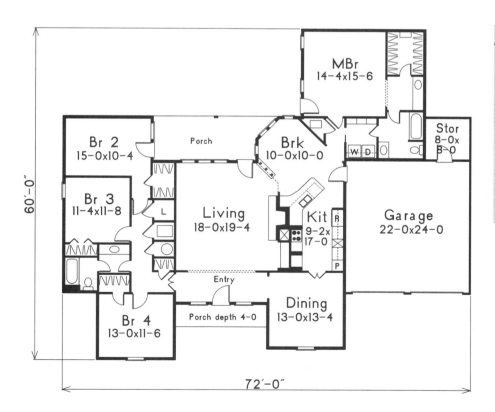

PLAN DATA

Total Living Area: 2,252
Bedrooms: 4
Baths: 2
Garage: 2-car
Foundation Types:
Slab standard
Basement
Crawl space
Features:
2" x 6" exterior walls

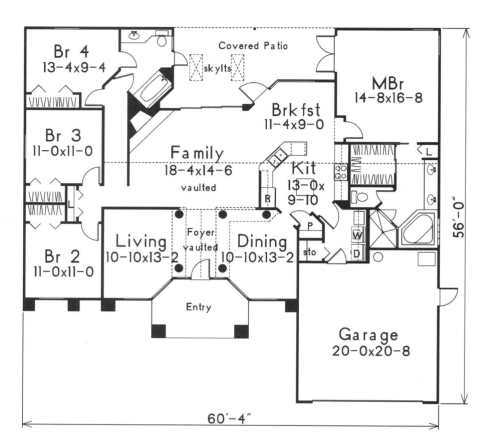

PLAN DATA

Total Living Area: 2,056
Bedrooms: 4
Baths: 2
Garage: 2-car
Foundation Types:
   Slab standard
   Crawl space

Br 4
13-4x9-4

Covered Patio

skylts

MBr
14-8x16-8

Br 3
11-0x11-0

Brkfst
11-4x9-0

Family
18-4x14-6
vaulted

Kit
13-0x
9-10

Living
10-10x13-2

Foyer
vaulted

Dining
10-10x13-2

Br 2
11-0x11-0

sto

Entry

Garage
20-0x20-8

56'-0"

60'-4"

R. BRADSHAW

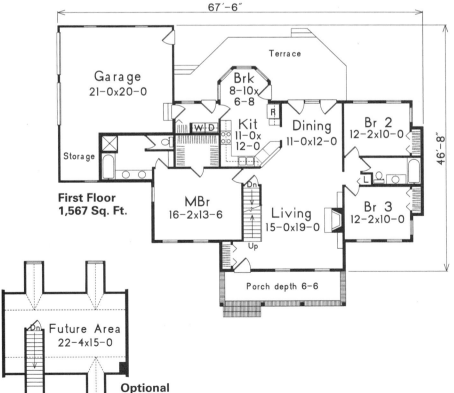

67'-6"

46'-8"

Garage
21-0x20-0

Storage

**First Floor
1,567 Sq. Ft.**

Terrace

Brk
8-10x
6-8

W D

Kit
11-0x
12-0

R

Dining
11-0x12-0

Br 2
12-2x10-0

MBr
16-2x13-6

Dn

Living
15-0x19-0

Br 3
12-2x10-0

Up

Porch depth 6-6

Dn

Future Area
22-4x15-0

**Optional
Second Floor
338 Sq. Ft.**

PLAN DATA

Total Living Area:	1,567
Bedrooms:	3
Baths:	2
Garage:	2-car

Foundation Types:
  Basement standard
  Slab
Features:
  2" x 6" exterior walls

PLAN #562-0105

PLAN DATA

Total Living Area: 1,360
Bedrooms: 3
Baths: 2
Garage: 2-car
Foundation Type:
  Basement

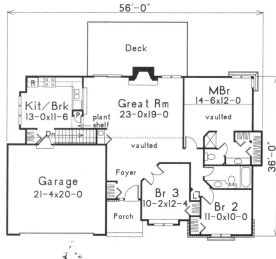

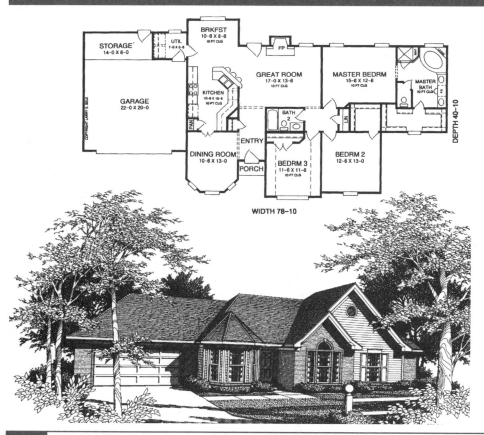

PLAN #562-LBD-17-7A

PLAN DATA

Total Living Area: 1,742
Bedrooms: 3
Baths: 2
Garage: 2-car
Foundation Types:
  Slab
  Crawl space
Please specify when ordering
Features:
  Storage in garage

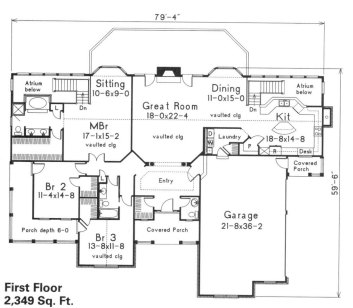

First Floor
2,349 Sq. Ft.

First floor plan labels:
- Atrium below
- Sitting 10-6x9-0
- Dining 11-0x15-0
- Atrium below
- Great Room 18-0x22-4 vaulted clg
- Kit 18-8x14-8
- MBr 17-1x15-2 vaulted clg
- vaulted clg
- Laundry
- Covered Porch
- Entry
- Br 2 11-4x14-8
- Porch depth 6-0
- Covered Porch
- Garage 21-8x36-2
- Br 3 13-8x11-8 vaulted clg
- 79'-4"
- 59'-6"

PLAN DATA

Total Living Area: 3,199
Bedrooms: 3
Baths: 2 1/2
Garage: 3-car
Foundation Type:
  Walk-out basement
Features:
  Double atriums

Lower Level
850 Sq. Ft.

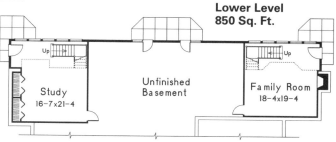

Lower level plan labels:
- Up
- Study 16-7x21-4
- Unfinished Basement
- Family Room 18-4x19-4
- Up

Rear View

← 68'-0" →

← 70'-8" →

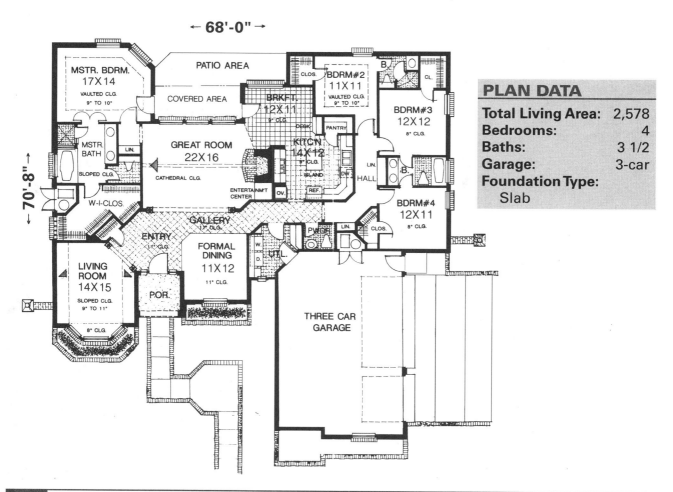

MSTR. BDRM.
17X14
VAULTED CLG.
9" TO 10"

PATIO AREA

BDRM#2
11X11
VAULTED CLG.
9" TO 10"

B

CLOS.

CL.

COVERED AREA

BRKFT.
12X11
9" CLG.

BDRM#3
12X12
8" CLG.

MSTR.
BATH

LIN.

GREAT ROOM
22X16

DESK

PANTRY

SLOPED CLG.

CATHEDRAL CLG.

KITC'N
14X12
9" CLG.

LIN.

B

ISLAND

DW

HALL

ENTERTAINM'T
CENTER

OV.

REF.

W-I-CLOS.

GALLERY
11" CLG.

BDRM#4
12X11
8" CLG.

ENTRY
11" CLG.

FORMAL
DINING
11X12
11" CLG.

PWD.

LIN.

CLOS.

LIVING
ROOM
14X15
SLOPED CLG.
9" TO 11"

POR.

W
D

UTL.

8" CLG.

THREE CAR
GARAGE

PLAN DATA

Total Living Area: 2,578
Bedrooms: 4
Baths: 3 1/2
Garage: 3-car
Foundation Type:
  Slab

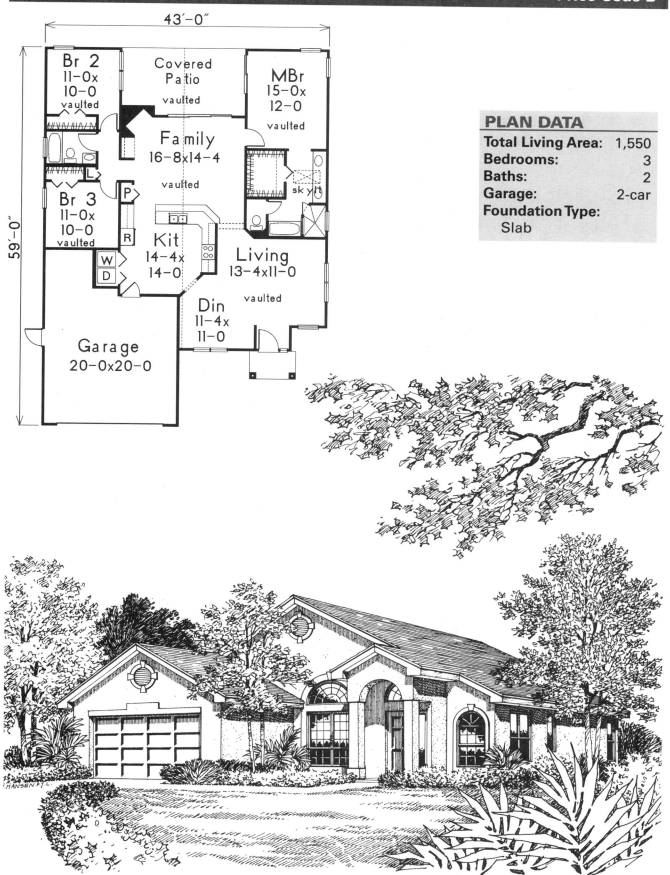

43'-0"

59'-0"

Br 2
11-0x
10-0
vaulted

Covered
Patio
vaulted

MBr
15-0x
12-0
vaulted

Family
16-8x14-4
vaulted

sky lt

Br 3
11-0x
10-0
vaulted

P

R

Kit
14-4x
14-0

W

D

Living
13-4x11-0
vaulted

Din
11-4x
11-0

Garage
20-0x20-0

PLAN DATA

Total Living Area: 1,550
Bedrooms: 3
Baths: 2
Garage: 2-car
Foundation Type:
Slab

PLAN DATA

Total Living Area: 1,689
Bedrooms: 3
Baths: 2
Garage: 2-car
Foundation Types:
   Basement standard
   Slab
   Crawl space

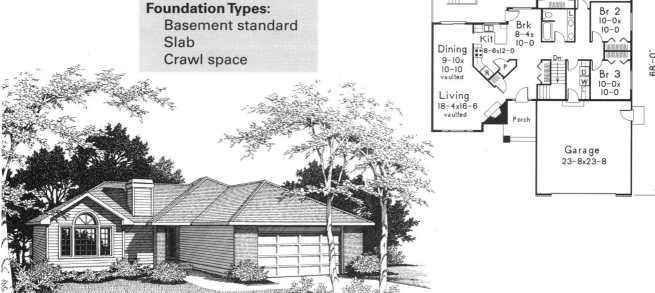

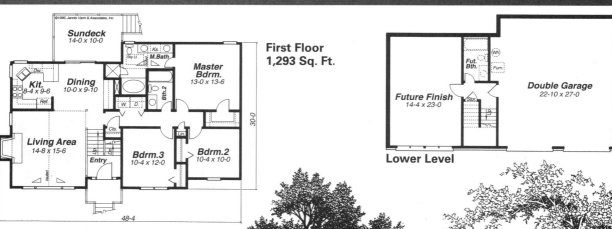

First Floor 1,293 Sq. Ft.

Lower Level

PLAN DATA

Total Living Area: 1,293
Bedrooms: 3
Baths: 2
Garage: 2-car
Foundation Type:
   Basement
Features:
   Drive-under garage

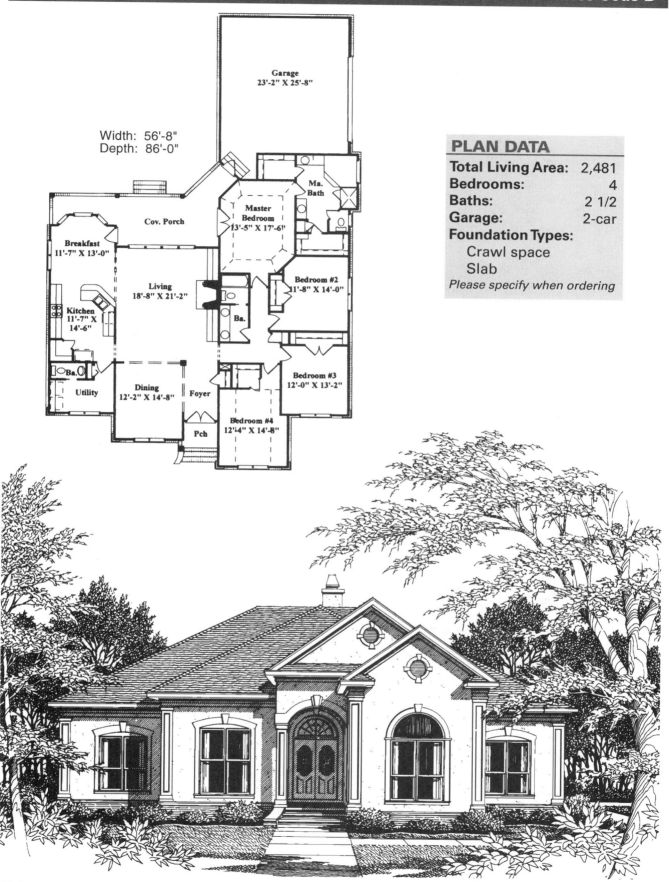

Width: 56'-8"
Depth: 86'-0"

Garage
23'-2" X 25'-8"

Cov. Porch

Ma.
Bath

Master
Bedroom
13'-5" X 17'-6"

Breakfast
11'-7" X 13'-0"

Living
18'-8" X 21'-2"

Bedroom #2
11'-8" X 14'-0"

Kitchen
11'-7" X
14'-6"

Ba.

Ba.

Utility

Dining
12'-2" X 14'-8"

Foyer

Bedroom #3
12'-0" X 13'-2"

Pch

Bedroom #4
12'-4" X 14'-8"

PLAN DATA

Total Living Area: 2,481
Bedrooms: 4
Baths: 2 1/2
Garage: 2-car
Foundation Types:
  Crawl space
  Slab
Please specify when ordering

PLAN #562-0584

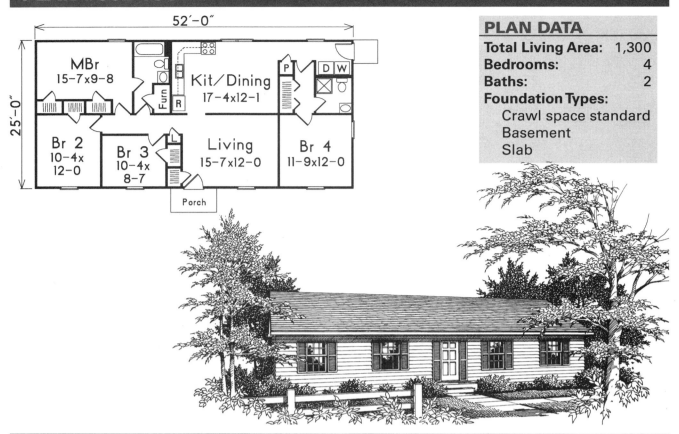

52'-0"

25'-0"

MBr
15-7x9-8

Kit/Dining
17-4x12-1

Furn

R

P

D W

Br 2
10-4x
12-0

Br 3
10-4x
8-7

Living
15-7x12-0

Br 4
11-9x12-0

Porch

PLAN DATA
Total Living Area: 1,300
Bedrooms: 4
Baths: 2
Foundation Types:
   Crawl space standard
   Basement
   Slab

PLAN #562-0506

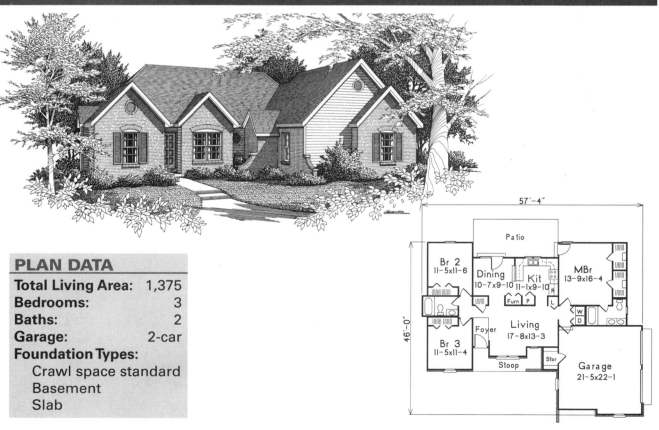

PLAN DATA
Total Living Area: 1,375
Bedrooms: 3
Baths: 2
Garage: 2-car
Foundation Types:
   Crawl space standard
   Basement
   Slab

57'-4"

46'-0"

Patio

Br 2
11-5x11-6

Dining
10-7x9-10

Kit
11-1x9-10

MBr
13-9x16-4

Furn P

L

W
D

Br 3
11-5x11-4

Foyer

Living
17-8x13-3

Stoop

Stor

Garage
21-5x22-1

PLAN DATA

Total Living Area: 792
Bedrooms: 2
Bath: 1
Foundation Types:
    Crawl space standard
    Slab

PLAN DATA

Total Living Area: 1,266
Bedrooms: 3
Baths: 2
Garage: 2-car
Foundation Types:
    Crawl space standard
    Slab
Features:
    2" x 6" exterior walls

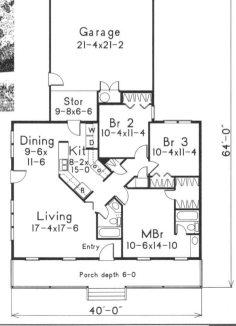

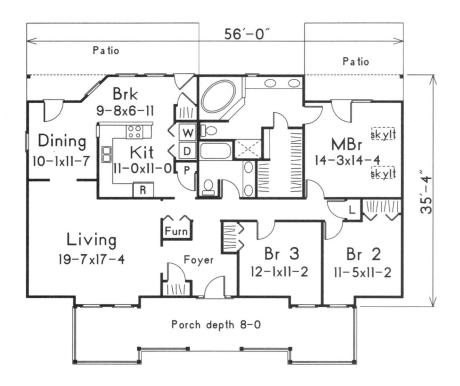

PLAN DATA

Total Living Area:	1,832
Bedrooms:	3
Baths:	2
Garage:	2-car
Foundation Types:	
Crawl space standard	
Basement	
Slab	

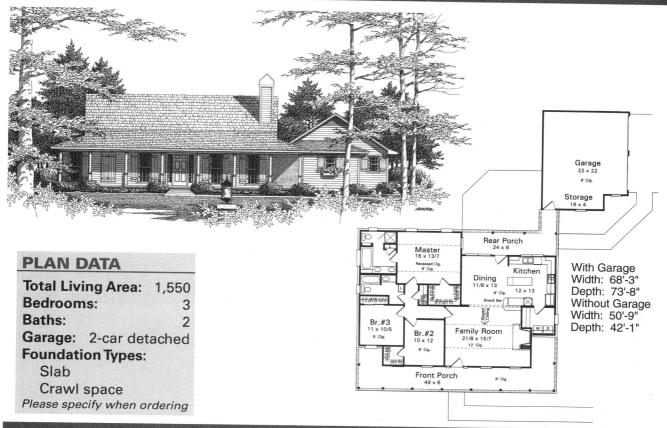

PLAN DATA

Total Living Area: 1,550
Bedrooms: 3
Baths: 2
Garage: 2-car detached
Foundation Types:
  Slab
  Crawl space
Please specify when ordering

With Garage
Width: 68'-3"
Depth: 73'-8"
Without Garage
Width: 50'-9"
Depth: 42'-1"

PLAN #562-JV-1985-A

Price Code C

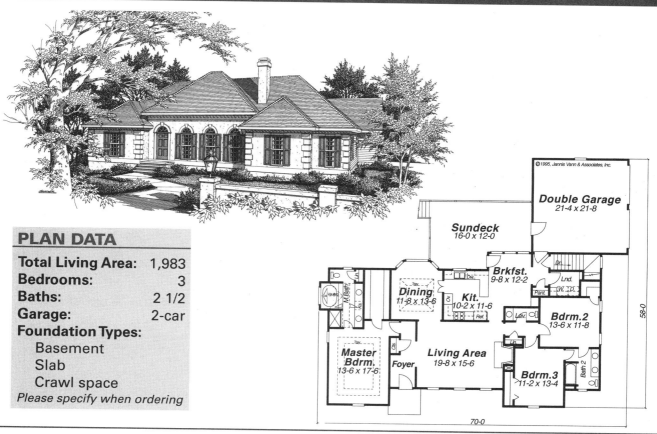

PLAN DATA

Total Living Area: 1,983
Bedrooms: 3
Baths: 2 1/2
Garage: 2-car
Foundation Types:
  Basement
  Slab
  Crawl space
Please specify when ordering

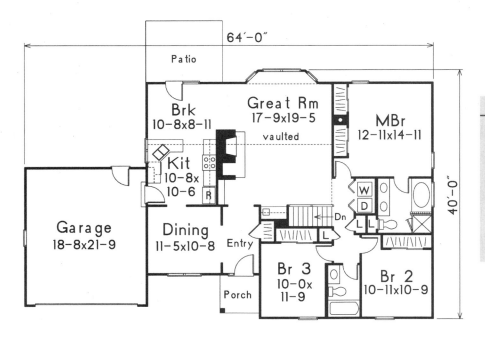

64'-0"

Patio

Brk
10-8x8-11

Great Rm
17-9x19-5
vaulted

MBr
12-11x14-11

Kit
10-8x
10-6

40'-0"

Garage
18-8x21-9

Dining
11-5x10-8

Entry

W
D

Dn

L
L

Br 3
10-0x
11-9

Br 2
10-11x10-9

Porch

PLAN DATA

Total Living Area: 1,605
Bedrooms: 3
Baths: 2
Garage: 2-car
Foundation Types:
 Basement standard
 Slab
 Crawl space

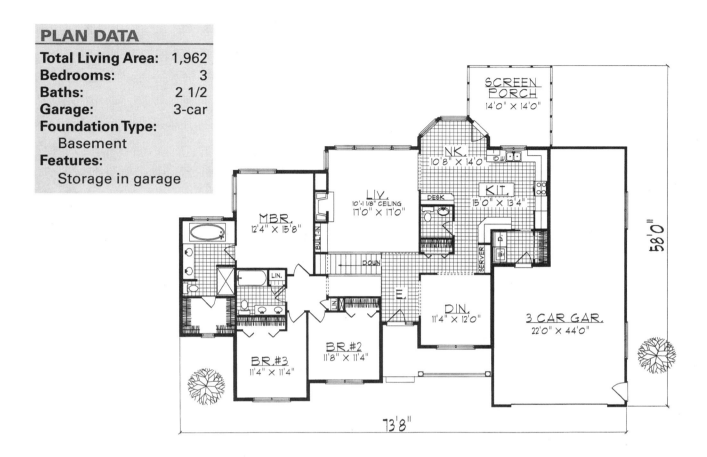

PLAN DATA

Total Living Area: 1,962
Bedrooms: 3
Baths: 2 1/2
Garage: 3-car
Foundation Type:
   Basement
Features:
   Storage in garage

SCREEN PORCH
14'0" X 14'0"

NK.
10'8" X 14'0"

KIT.
15'0" X 13'4"

LIV.
10'-1 1/8" CEILING
17'0" X 17'0"

DESK

MBR.
12'4" X 15'8"

BUILT-IN

DOWN

SERVER

LIN.

DIN.
11'4" X 12'0"

3 CAR GAR.
22'0" X 44'0"

BR.#2
11'8" X 11'4"

BR.#3
11'4" X 11'4"

58'0"

73'8"

PLAN DATA

Total Living Area:	1,869
Bedrooms:	3
Baths:	2
Garage:	2-car

Foundation Types:
 Basement
 Crawl space
 Slab
Please specify when ordering

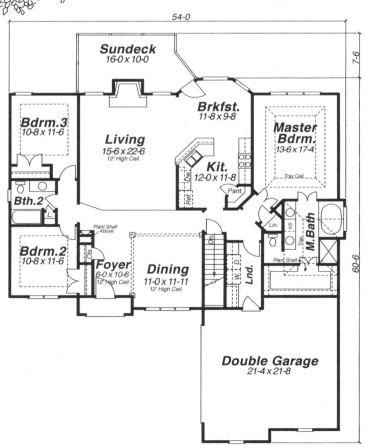

PLAN DATA

Total Living Area: 2,991
Bedrooms: 3
Baths: 2 1/2
Garage: 3-car
Foundation Type:
  Basement

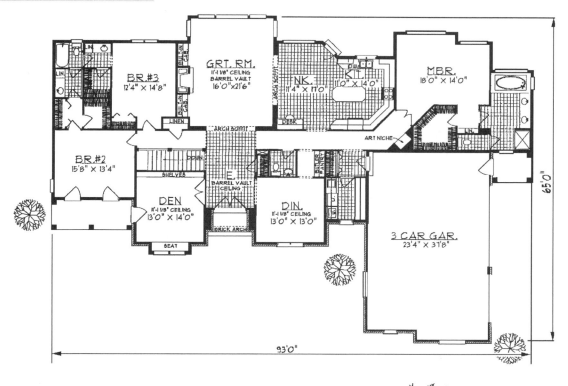

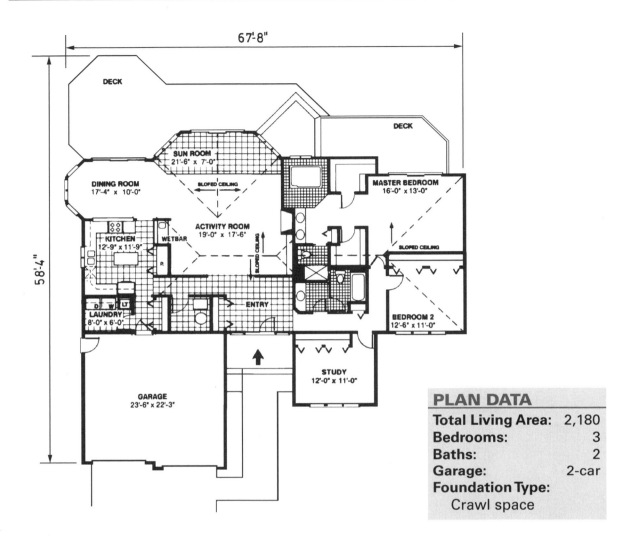

67'-8"

58'-4"

DECK

DECK

SUN ROOM
21'-6" x 7'-0"
SLOPED CEILING

DINING ROOM
17'-4" x 10'-0"

MASTER BEDROOM
16'-0" x 13'-0"

ACTIVITY ROOM
19'-0" x 17'-6"
SLOPED CEILING

SLOPED CEILING

KITCHEN
12'-9" x 11'-9"

WETBAR

LAUNDRY
8'-0" x 6'-0"

D W LT

ENTRY

BEDROOM 2
12'-6" x 11'-0"

GARAGE
23'-6" x 22'-3"

STUDY
12'-0" x 11'-0"

PLAN DATA

Total Living Area:	2,180
Bedrooms:	3
Baths:	2
Garage:	2-car
Foundation Type:	
Crawl space	

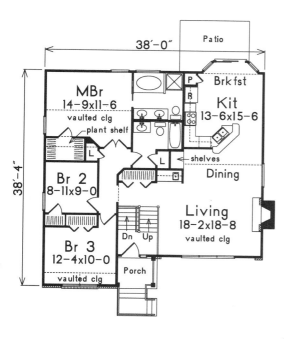

PLAN DATA

Total Living Area: 1,340
Bedrooms: 3
Baths: 2
Garage: 2-car
Foundation Type:
  Basement
Features:
  Drive-under garage
  with storage area

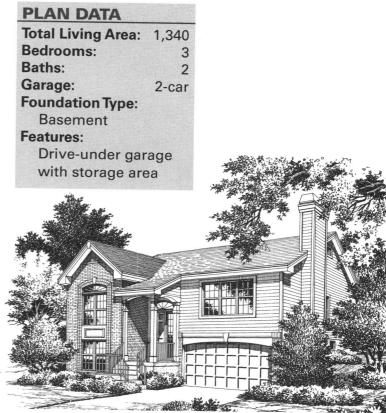

PLAN DATA

Total Living Area: 1,341
Bedrooms: 3
Baths: 2
Garage: 2-car
Foundation Types:
  Slab
  Basement
Please specify when ordering

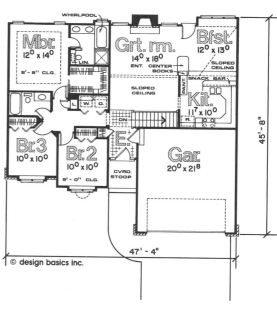

© design basics inc.

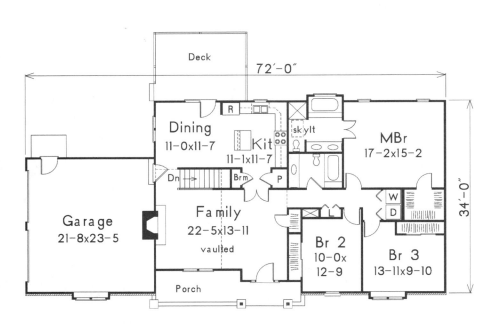

Deck

72'-0"

Dining
11-0x11-7

R

Kit
11-1x11-7

skylt

MBr
17-2x15-2

Dn →

Brm

P

Family
22-5x13-11
vaulted

L

W
D

Garage
21-8x23-5

Br 2
10-0x
12-9

Br 3
13-11x9-10

34'-0"

Porch

PLAN DATA
Total Living Area: 1,643
Bedrooms: 3
Baths: 2
Garage: 2-car
Foundation Types:
 Basement standard
 Slab
 Crawl space

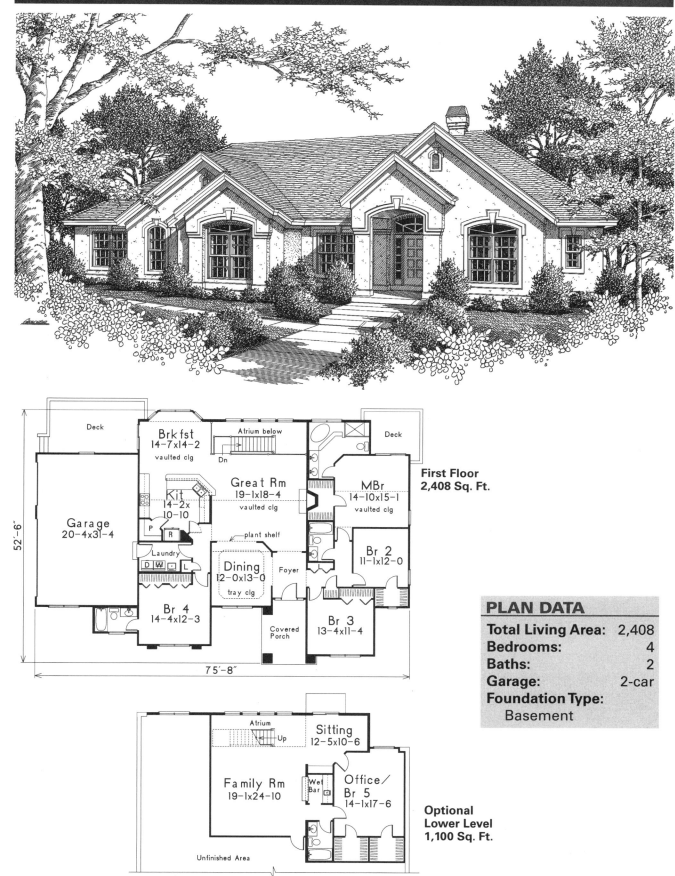

Deck

Brk fst
14-7x14-2
vaulted clg

Atrium below
Dn

Great Rm
19-1x18-4
vaulted clg

MBr
14-10x15-1
vaulted clg

Deck

**First Floor
2,408 Sq. Ft.**

Kit
14-2x
10-10

P

R

plant shelf

Garage
20-4x31-4

Laundry
D W L

Dining
12-0x13-0
tray clg

Foyer

Br 2
11-1x12-0

52'-6"

Br 4
14-4x12-3

Covered Porch

Br 3
13-4x11-4

75'-8"

Atrium
Up

Sitting
12-5x10-6

Family Rm
19-1x24-10

Wet Bar

**Office/
Br 5**
14-1x17-6

**Optional
Lower Level
1,100 Sq. Ft.**

Unfinished Area

PLAN DATA

Total Living Area:	2,408
Bedrooms:	4
Baths:	2
Garage:	2-car
Foundation Type: Basement	

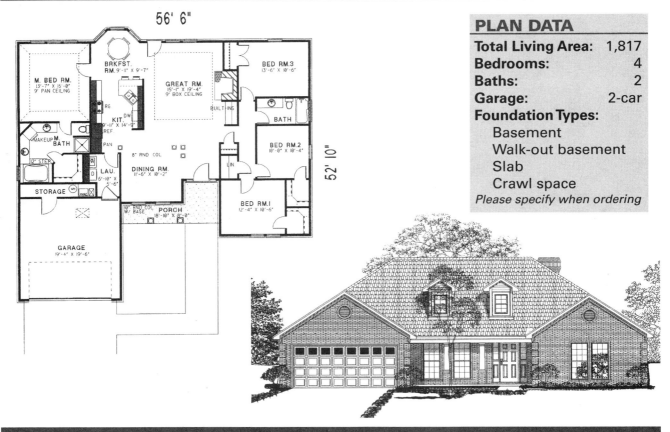

56' 6"

BRKFST. RM. 9'-11" X 9'-7"

M. BED RM. 13'-7" X 15'-0" 9' PAN CEILING

GREAT RM. 15'-1" X 19'-4" 9' BOX CEILING

BED RM.3 13'-6" X 10'-6"

BATH

KIT. 9'-11" X 14'-9"

BED RM.2 10'-0" X 10'-6"

MAKEUP M. BATH

DINING RM. 11'-6" X 10'-2"

8" RND COL

12" STEP

LAU. 6'-10" X 5'-6"

STORAGE

PORCH 18'-10" X 8'-0"

BED RM.1 12'-4" X 10'-6"

10" RND COL W/ BASE

GARAGE 19'-4" X 19'-6"

52' 10"

PLAN DATA

Total Living Area: 1,817
Bedrooms: 4
Baths: 2
Garage: 2-car
Foundation Types:
   Basement
   Walk-out basement
   Slab
   Crawl space
Please specify when ordering

74'-0"

MBr 12-3x13-6

Kit 8-1x13-6

Dining 18-1x13-6

Garage 23-8x23-5

28'-0"

Br 2 12-3x10-3

Br 3 12-1x10-3

Great Rm 22-1x13-7

Porch 28-0x5-0

PLAN DATA

Total Living Area: 1,400
Bedrooms: 3
Baths: 2
Garage: 2-car
Foundation Types:
   Crawl space standard
   Basement
   Slab

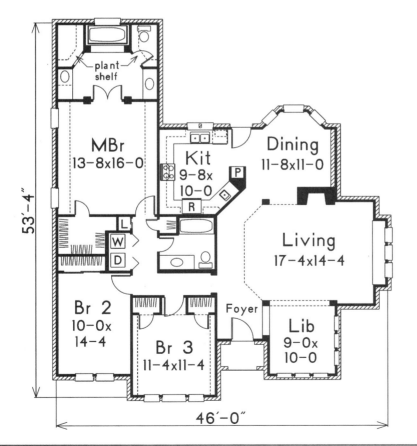

plant shelf

MBr
13-8x16-0

Kit
9-8x
10-0

Dining
11-8x11-0

P

R

L

W

D

Living
17-4x14-4

Br 2
10-0x
14-4

Br 3
11-4x11-4

Foyer

Lib
9-0x
10-0

53'-4"

46'-0"

PLAN DATA

Total Living Area: 1,824
Bedrooms: 3
Baths: 2
Garage: 2-car detached
Foundation Type:
   Slab
Features:
   10' ceiling in living
   room

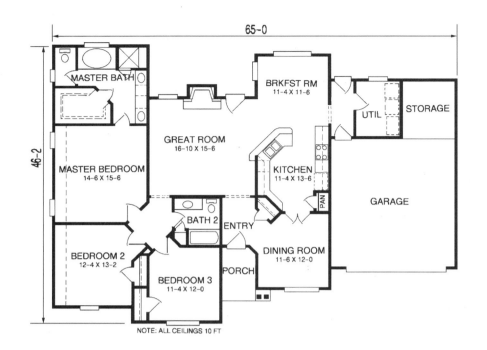

65-0

46-2

MASTER BATH

BRKFST RM
11-4 X 11-6

UTIL

STORAGE

GREAT ROOM
16-10 X 15-6

MASTER BEDROOM
14-6 X 15-6

KITCHEN
11-4 X 13-6

GARAGE

PAN

BATH 2

ENTRY

BEDROOM 2
12-4 X 13-2

DINING ROOM
11-6 X 12-0

PORCH

BEDROOM 3
11-4 X 12-0

NOTE: ALL CEILINGS 10 FT

PLAN DATA

Total Living Area: 1,862
Bedrooms: 3
Baths: 2
Garage: 2-car
Foundation Types:
Crawl space
Slab
Please specify when ordering
Features:
- 10' ceilings
- Storage in garage

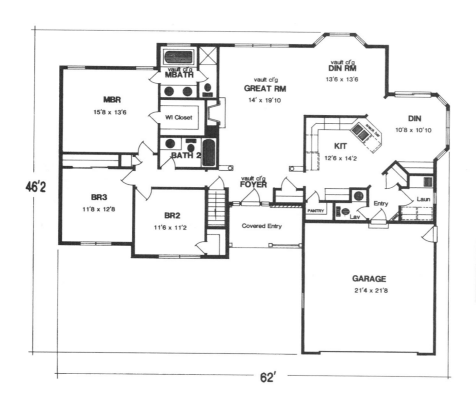

46'2

62'

MBR
15'8 x 13'6

vault cl'g
MBATH

Wl Closet

BATH 2

vault cl'g
GREAT RM
14' x 19'10

vault cl'g
DIN RM
13'6 x 13'6

DIN
10'8 x 10'10

KIT
12'6 x 14'2

snack bar

vault cl'g
FOYER

BR3
11'8 x 12'8

BR2
11'6 x 11'2

Covered Entry

PANTRY

Entry

Laun

Lav

GARAGE
21'4 x 21'8

PLAN DATA

Total Living Area:	1,875
Bedrooms:	3
Baths:	2 1/2
Garage:	2-car
Foundation Type:	
Basement	

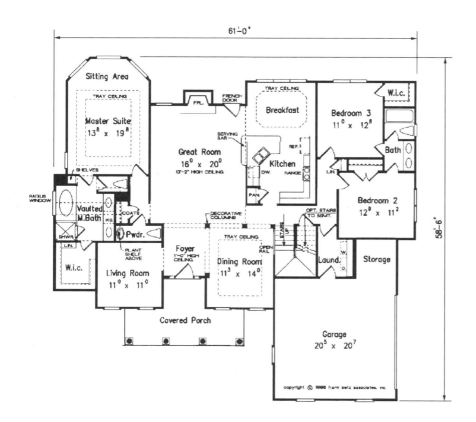

Sitting Area

TRAY CEILING

Master Suite
13⁸ x 19⁸

SHELVES

RADIUS WINDOW

Vaulted M.Bath

K.B.

COATS

SHWR

Pwdr.

LIN.

PLANT SHELF ABOVE

W.i.c.

Living Room
11⁰ x 11⁰

Foyer
11'-0" CEILING

FPL.

FRENCH DOOR

TRAY CEILING

Breakfast

SERVING BAR

Kitchen

REF.

DW   RANGE

PAN.

DECORATIVE COLUMNS

Great Room
16⁰ x 20⁰
13'-2" HIGH CEILING

Dining Room
11³ x 14⁰

TRAY CEILING

W.i.c.

Bedroom 3
11⁰ x 12⁸

Bath

LIN.

Bedroom 2
12⁹ x 11²

OPT. STAIRS TO BSMT.

STAIRS

OPEN RAIL

Laund.
W. D.

Storage

58'-6"

Covered Porch

Garage
20⁵ x 20⁷

copyright © 1996 frank betz associates. inc.

61'-0"

PLAN DATA

Total Living Area:	2,072
Bedrooms:	3
Baths:	2 1/2
Garage:	2-car
Foundation Types:	
Basement	
Walk-out basement	
Crawl space	

Please specify when ordering

PLAN DATA

Total Living Area:	1,725
Bedrooms:	3
Baths:	2
Garage:	2-car

Foundation Types:
  Slab
  Crawl space
Please specify when ordering

COPYRIGHT LARRY E. BELK

GARAGE

UTIL
REAR ENTRY
PORCH

BEDRM 2
11-0 X 12-6
9 FT CLG

BEDRM 3
11-0 X 10-0
9 FT CLG

GREAT RM
17-0 X 17-0
11 FT CLG

BRKFST RM
10-4 X 10-0
11 FT VAULTED CLG

BATH 2

ARCH   ARCH

KITCHEN
8-6 X 17-0
9 FT CLG

MASTER BATH
9 FT CLG

DINING RM
12-0 X 12-8
11 FT CLG

FOYER
11 FT CLG

PANTRY   DESK

MASTER BEDRM
13-0 X 14-8
9 FT CLG

SEAT

PORCH

DEPTH 72-8

WIDTH 56-4

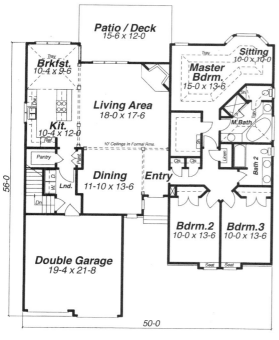

Patio / Deck
15-6 x 12-0

Brkfst.
10-4 x 9-6

Sitting
10-0 x 10-0

Master Bdrm.
15-0 x 13-6

Living Area
18-0 x 17-6

Kit.
10-4 x 12-0

Ref.

Pantry

M.Bath

10' Ceilings In Formal Rms.

Dining
11-10 x 13-6

Entry

Linen

Bath 2

Lnd.

Dn

Bdrm.2
10-0 x 13-6

Bdrm.3
10-0 x 13-6

Seat   Seat

Double Garage
19-4 x 21-8

56-0

50-0

PLAN DATA

Total Living Area:	1,840
Bedrooms:	3
Baths:	2 1/2
Garage:	2-car

Foundation Types:
  Walk-out basement
  Slab
  Crawl space
Please specify when ordering

PLAN DATA

Total Living Area:	1,562
Bedrooms:	3
Baths:	2
Garage:	2-car
Foundation Type:	
Basement	
Features:	
Varied ceiling heights	

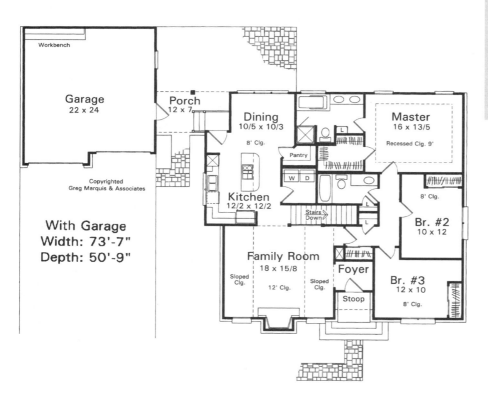

Workbench

Garage
22 x 24

Porch
12 x 7

Dining
10/5 x 10/3

8' Clg.

Master
16 x 13/5

Recessed Clg. 9'

Pantry

W   D

Copyrighted
Greg Marquis & Associates

Kitchen
12/2 x 12/2

8' Clg.

Br. #2
10 x 12

With Garage
Width: 73'-7"
Depth: 50'-9"

Stairs
Down

Family Room
18 x 15/8

Foyer

Br. #3
12 x 10

Sloped
Clg.

12' Clg.

Sloped
Clg.

Stoop

8' Clg.

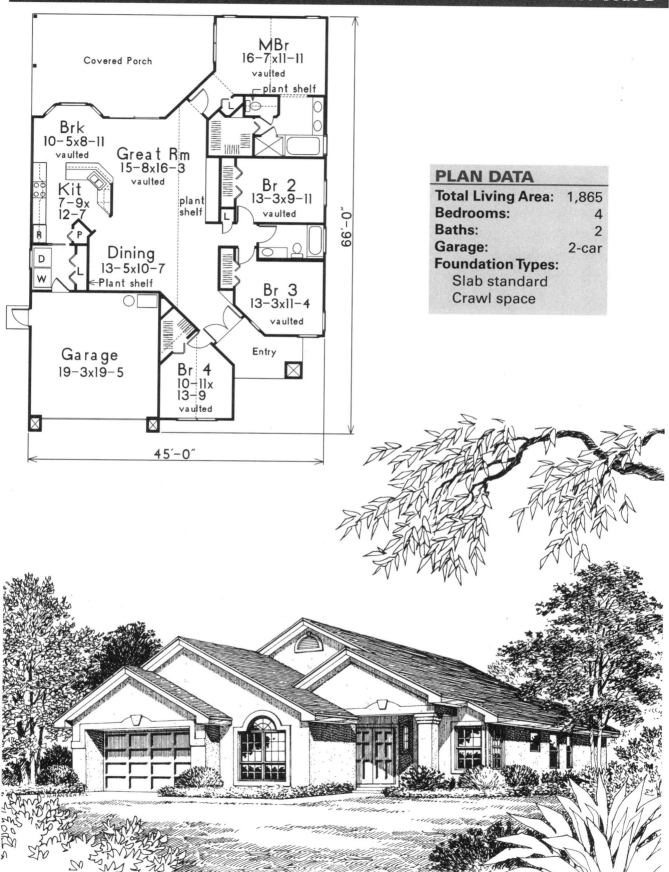

Covered Porch

MBr
16-7x11-11
vaulted

plant shelf

Brk
10-5x8-11
vaulted

Great Rm
15-8x16-3
vaulted

Kit
7-9x
12-7

Br 2
13-3x9-11
vaulted

plant shelf

Dining
13-5x10-7

Plant shelf

Br 3
13-3x11-4
vaulted

Garage
19-3x19-5

Br 4
10-11x
13-9
vaulted

Entry

66'-0"

45'-0"

PLAN DATA

Total Living Area:	1,865
Bedrooms:	4
Baths:	2
Garage:	2-car
Foundation Types:	
Slab standard	
Crawl space	

68'-2"

62'-8"

Br 2
14-6×11-0

Patio

Brk

Family
18-4×14-8

MBr
14-4×17-4
vaulted

Living
17-0×18-8

Kitchen
13-8×12-6

Br 3
11-0×11-6

Foyer

Dining
11-8×13-4

Garage
20-0×20-2

Br 4
11-6×13-0
coffered

Porch

PLAN DATA
Total Living Area: 2,517
Bedrooms: 4
Baths: 2 1/2
Garage: 2-car
Foundation Types:
  Slab standard
  Crawl space
Features:
  - 2" x 6" exterior walls
  - Varied ceiling heights

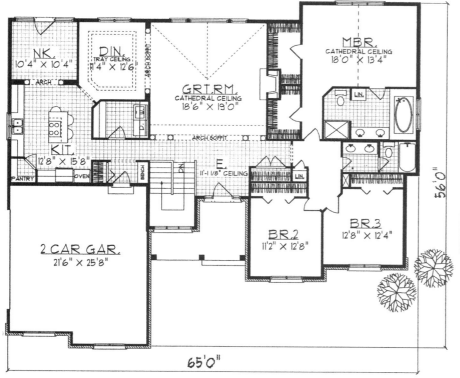

NK.
10'4" X 10'4"

DIN.
TRAY CEILING
11'4" X 12'6"

GRT. RM.
CATHEDRAL CEILING
18'6" X 19'0"

MBR.
CATHEDRAL CEILING
18'0" X 13'4"

ARCH.

LIN.

KIT.
12'8" X 15'8"

PANTRY

OVEN

BENCH

DN.

E.
11'-1 1/8" CEILING

LIN.

2 CAR GAR.
21'6" X 25'8"

BR. 2
11'2" X 12'8"

BR. 3
12'8" X 12'4"

56'0"

65'0"

PLAN DATA

Total Living Area:	2,229
Bedrooms:	3
Baths:	2
Garage:	2-car
Foundation Type:	
Basement	

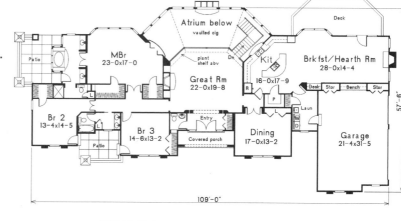

**First Floor
3,050 Sq. Ft.**

PLAN DATA

Total Living Area: 4,826
Bedrooms: 4
Baths: 3 1/2
Garage: 3-car
Foundation Type:
Walk-out basement
Features:
Lawn and garden
workroom

**Lower Level
1,776 Sq. Ft.**

Interior View

PLAN DATA

Total Living Area:	2,874
Bedrooms:	4
Baths:	2 1/2
Garage:	2-car
Foundation Type:	
Basement	

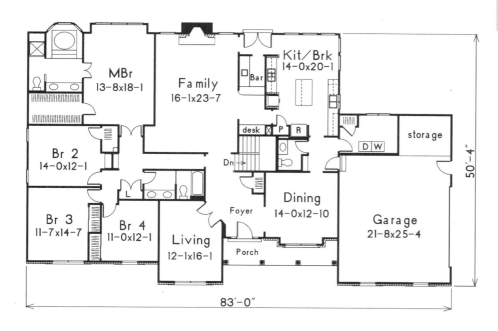

MBr
13-8x18-1

Family
16-1x23-7

Kit/Brk
14-0x20-1

Bar

Br 2
14-0x12-1

desk P R

storage

D W

Dn

Br 3
11-7x14-7

Br 4
11-0x12-1

Living
12-1x16-1

Foyer

Porch

Dining
14-0x12-10

Garage
21-8x25-4

50'-4"

83'-0"

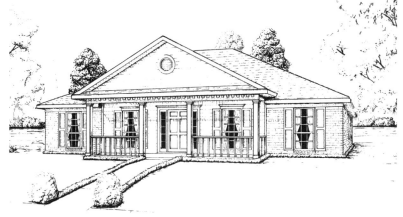

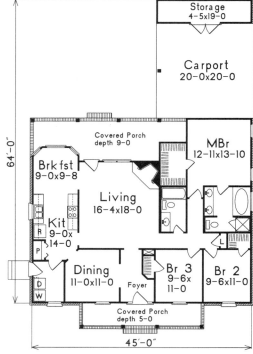

Storage
4–5x19–0

Carport
20–0x20–0

64'–0"

Covered Porch
depth 9–0

MBr
12–11x13–10

Brk fst
9–0x9–8

Living
16–4x18–0

Kit
9–0x
14–0

R

P

Dining
11–0x11–0

Foyer

Br 3
9–6x
11–0

Br 2
9–6x11–0

L

D
W

Covered Porch
depth 5–0

45'–0"

PLAN DATA

Total Living Area: 1,556
Bedrooms: 3
Baths: 2
Garage: 2-car carport
Foundation Type:
  Slab

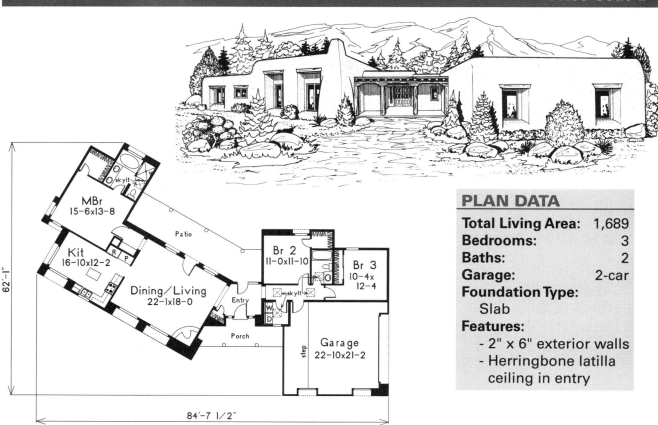

62'–1"

MBr
15–6x13–8

skylt

Patio

Kit
16–10x12–2

R P

Dining/Living
22–1x18–0

Entry

Porch

Br 2
11–0x11–10

Br 3
10–4x
12–4

skylt

W
D

step

Garage
22–10x21–2

84'–7 1/2"

PLAN DATA

Total Living Area: 1,689
Bedrooms: 3
Baths: 2
Garage: 2-car
Foundation Type:
  Slab
Features:
  - 2" x 6" exterior walls
  - Herringbone latilla
    ceiling in entry

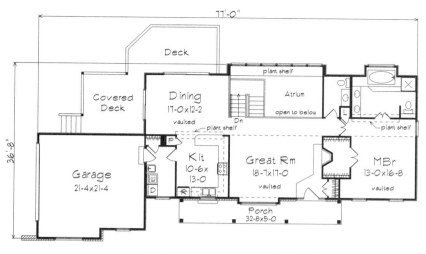

First Floor
1,297 Sq. Ft.

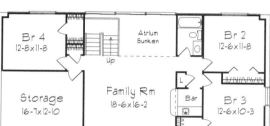

Lower Level
1,234 Sq. Ft.

PLAN DATA

Total Living Area:	2,531
Bedrooms:	4
Baths:	2 1/2
Garage:	2-car
Foundation Type:	
Walk-out basement	

Rear View

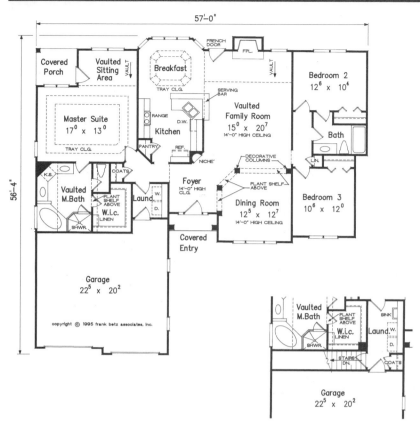

57'-0"

56'-4"

Covered Porch

Vaulted Sitting Area

Breakfast
TRAY CLG.

FRENCH DOOR

FPL.

VAULT

VAULT

SERVING BAR

Bedroom 2
12⁶ x 10⁴

Master Suite
17⁰ x 13⁰
TRAY CLG.

RANGE
D.W.
Kitchen

Vaulted Family Room
15⁰ x 20⁷
14'-0" HIGH CEILING

Bath

PANTRY

REF.

NICHE'

DECORATIVE COLUMNS

LIN.

K.S.

COATS

Vaulted M.Bath

PLANT SHELF ABOVE

Laund.

W.
D.

Foyer
14'-0" HIGH CLG.

PLANT SHELF ABOVE

W.i.c.

LINEN

SHWR.

Dining Room
12⁵ x 12⁷
14'-0" HIGH CEILING

Bedroom 3
10⁶ x 12⁰

Covered Entry

Garage
22⁵ x 20²

copyright © 1995 frank betz associates, inc.

PLAN DATA

Total Living Area:	1,779
Bedrooms:	3
Baths:	2
Garage:	2-car

Foundation Types:
　Basement
　Crawl space
Please specify when ordering

Vaulted M.Bath

PLANT SHELF ABOVE

SINK

W.i.c.

LINEN

Laund.

W.
D.

SHWR.

STAIRS DN.

COATS

Garage
22⁵ x 20²

OPT. BASEMENT STAIR LOCATION

PLAN DATA

Total Living Area: 1,734
Bedrooms: 3
Baths: 2
Garage: 2-car
Foundation Type:
  Crawl space
Features:
  Sunken floor in great
  room

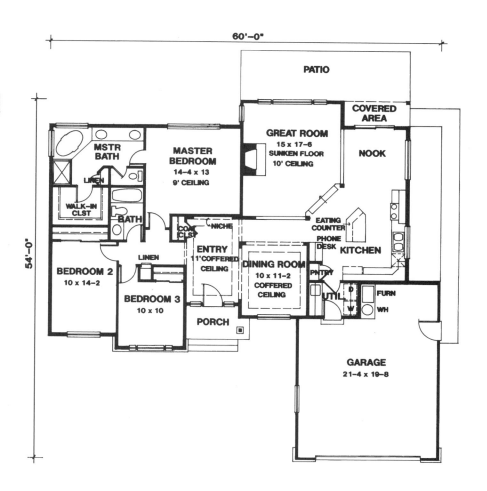

PLAN DATA

Total Living Area: 1,675
Bedrooms: 3
Baths: 2
Garage: 2-car
Foundation Types:
  Crawl space
  Slab
Please specify when ordering
Features:
  Alternate design
  included is 100% ADA
  compliant

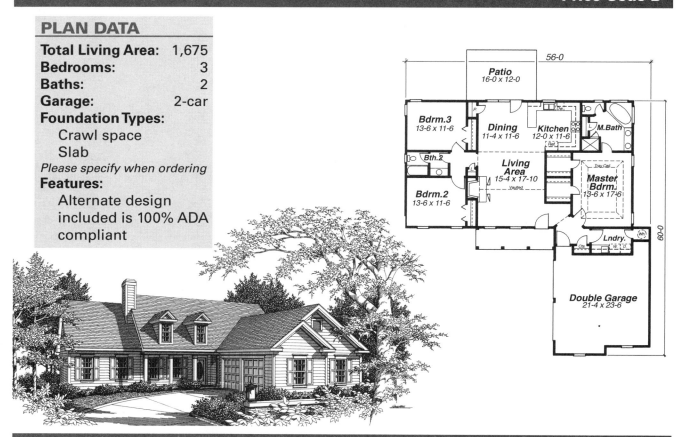

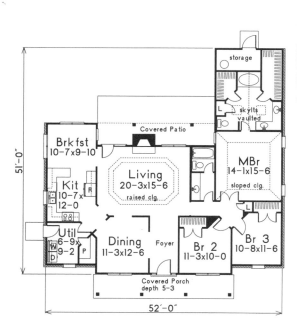

PLAN DATA

Total Living Area: 1,844
Bedrooms: 3
Baths: 2
Foundation Type:
  Slab

PLAN DATA

Total Living Area: 1,436
Bedrooms: 3
Baths: 2
Garage: 2-car
Foundation Type:
 Basement

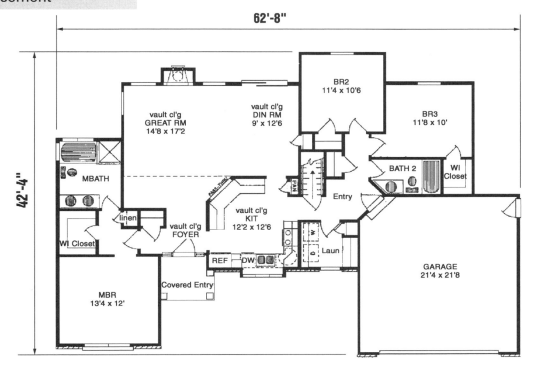

62'-8"

42'-4"

vault cl'g
GREAT RM
14'8 x 17'2

vault cl'g
DIN RM
9' x 12'6

BR2
11'4 x 10'6

BR3
11'8 x 10'

MBATH

BATH 2

WI
Closet

linen

vault cl'g
FOYER

vault cl'g
KIT
12'2 x 12'6

PAN

Entry

WI Closet

REF DW

Laun

MBR
13'4 x 12'

Covered Entry

GARAGE
21'4 x 21'8

M.MAXON

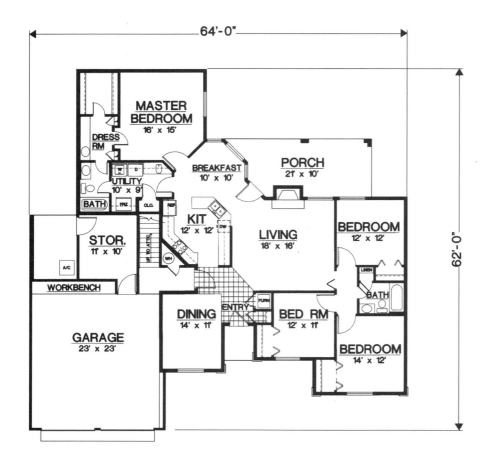

64'-0"

MASTER BEDROOM
16' x 15'

DRESS RM

UTILITY
10' x 9'

BATH

BREAKFAST
10' x 10'

PORCH
21' x 10'

KIT
12' x 12'

LIVING
18' x 16'

BEDROOM
12' x 12'

STOR.
11' x 10'

A/C

WORKBENCH

WH

LINEN

BATH

GARAGE
23' x 23'

DINING
14' x 11'

ENTRY

FURN

BED RM
12' x 11'

BEDROOM
14' x 12'

62'-0"

PLAN DATA

Total Living Area:	1,828
Bedrooms:	4
Baths:	2
Garage:	2-car

Foundation Types:
Slab
Crawl space
Basement
Please specify when ordering

Features:
2" x 6" exterior walls

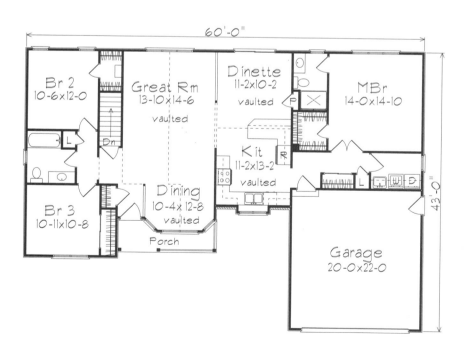

60'-0"

Br 2
10-6x12-0

Great Rm
13-10x14-6
vaulted

Dinette
11-2x10-2
vaulted

MBr
14-0x14-10

Dn

Kit
11-2x13-2
vaulted

Dining
10-4x12-8
vaulted

Br 3
10-11x10-8

Porch

43'-0"

Garage
20-0x22-0

PLAN DATA

Total Living Area:	1,546
Bedrooms:	3
Baths:	2
Garage:	2-car
Foundation Type:	
Basement	

PLAN DATA

Total Living Area:	1,834
Bedrooms:	4
Baths:	2
Garage:	2-car
Foundation Type:	
Slab	

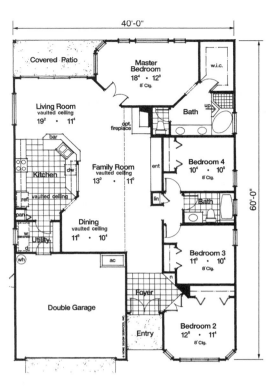

PLAN #562-N087

Price Code AAA

PLAN DATA

Total Living Area:	784
Bedrooms:	3
Bath:	1
Foundation Type:	
Pier	

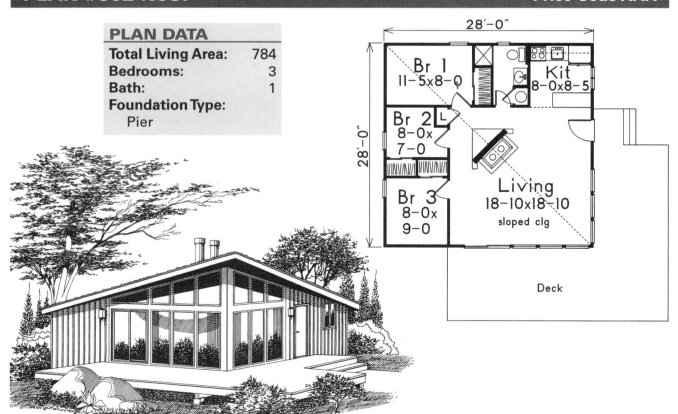

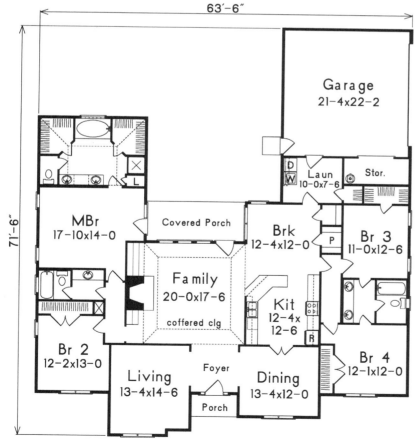

63'-6"

71'-6"

Garage
21-4x22-2

MBr
17-10x14-0

Covered Porch

Laun
10-0x7-6

D
W

Stor.

Brk
12-4x12-0

Br 3
11-0x12-6

P

Family
20-0x17-6

coffered clg

Kit
12-4x
12-6

R

Br 2
12-2x13-0

Living
13-4x14-6

Foyer

Dining
13-4x12-0

Br 4
12-1x12-0

Porch

PLAN DATA

Total Living Area:	2,558
Bedrooms:	4
Baths:	3
Garage:	2-car
Foundation Types:	
Slab standard	
Crawl space	
Features:	
9' ceilings	

Code D

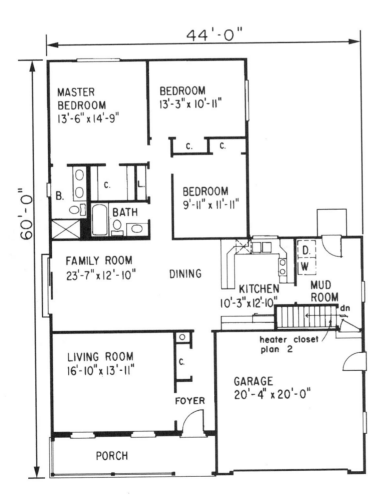

44'-0"

MASTER
BEDROOM
13'-6" x 14'-9"

BEDROOM
13'-3" x 10'-11"

c.   c.

60'-0"

B.   c.   L.

BEDROOM
9'-11" x 11'-11"

BATH

FAMILY ROOM
23'-7" x 12'-10"

DINING

D
W

KITCHEN
10'-3" x 12'-10"

MUD
ROOM

dn

heater closet
plan 2

LIVING ROOM
16'-10" x 13'-11"

c.

GARAGE
20'-4" x 20'-0"

FOYER

PORCH

PLAN DATA

Total Living Area:	1,668
Bedrooms:	3
Baths:	2
Garage:	2-car

Foundation Types:
  Plan #562-1216-1
  Partial basement/
  crawl space
  Plan #562-1216-2
  Crawl space & slab

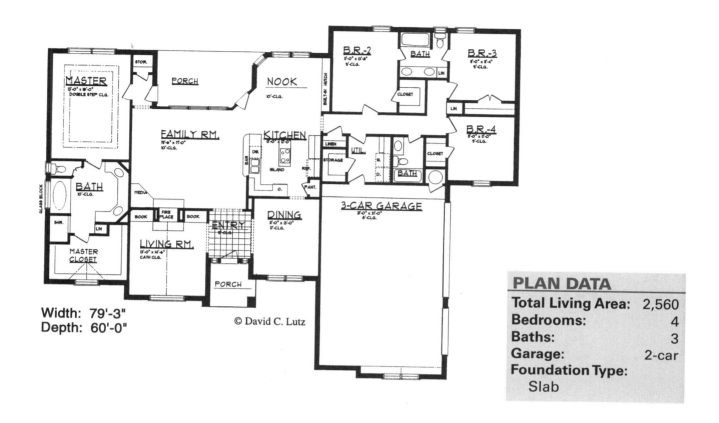

Width: 79'-3"
Depth: 60'-0"

© David C. Lutz

PLAN DATA

Total Living Area:	2,560
Bedrooms:	4
Baths:	3
Garage:	2-car
Foundation Type:	
Slab	

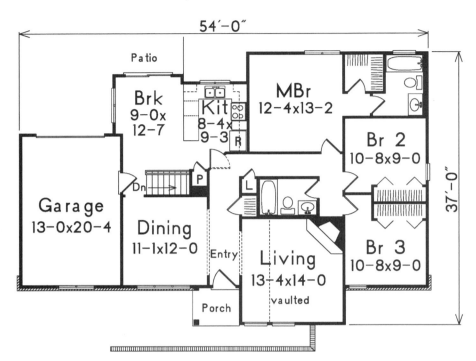

54'-0"

Patio

Brk
9-0x
12-7

Kit
8-4x
9-3

MBr
12-4x13-2

Br 2
10-8x9-0

37'-0"

Garage
13-0x20-4

Dn

P

L

Dining
11-1x12-0

Entry

Living
13-4x14-0
vaulted

Br 3
10-8x9-0

Porch

PLAN DATA

Total Living Area:	1,321
Bedrooms:	3
Baths:	2
Garage:	1-car
Foundation Type:	
Basement	

PLAN #562-0276

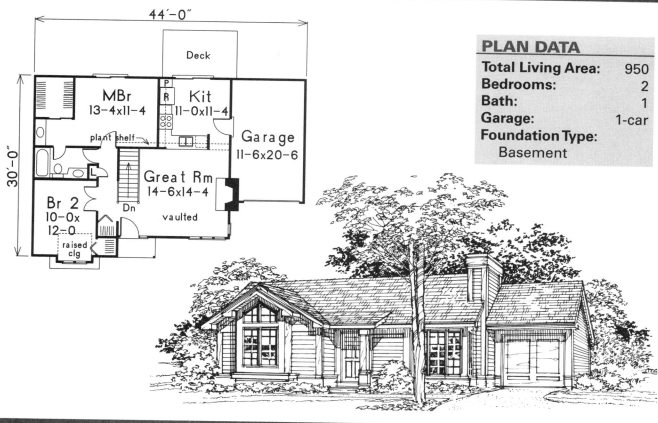

44'-0"

Deck

MBr
13-4x11-4

Kit
11-0x11-4

plant shelf

Garage
11-6x20-6

Great Rm
14-6x14-4

Dn

vaulted

Br 2
10-0x
12-0

raised
clg

30'-0"

PLAN DATA

Total Living Area:	950
Bedrooms:	2
Bath:	1
Garage:	1-car
Foundation Type:	
Basement	

PLAN #562-1227-1 & 2

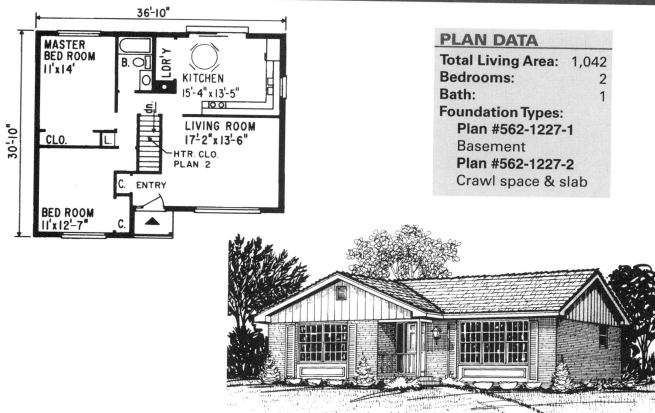

36'-10"

MASTER
BED ROOM
11'x14'

B.

LDR'Y

KITCHEN
15'-4" x 13'-5"

CLO.

L.

LIVING ROOM
17'-2" x 13'-6"

HTR. CLO.
PLAN 2

C. ENTRY

BED ROOM
11'x12'-7"

C.

30'-10"

PLAN DATA

Total Living Area:	1,042
Bedrooms:	2
Bath:	1
Foundation Types:	
Plan #562-1227-1	
Basement	
Plan #562-1227-2	
Crawl space & slab	

Width: 66'-5"
Depth: 60'-0"

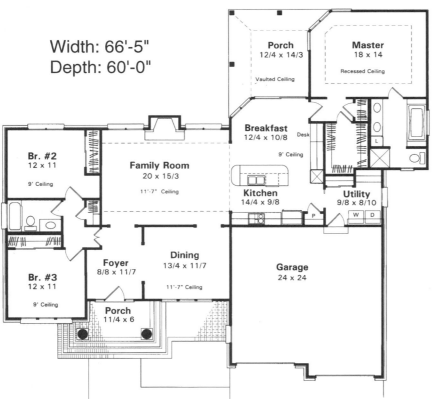

PLAN DATA

Total Living Area:	1,849
Bedrooms:	3
Baths:	2
Garage:	2-car
Foundation Types:	
Crawl space	
Slab	
Please specify when ordering	

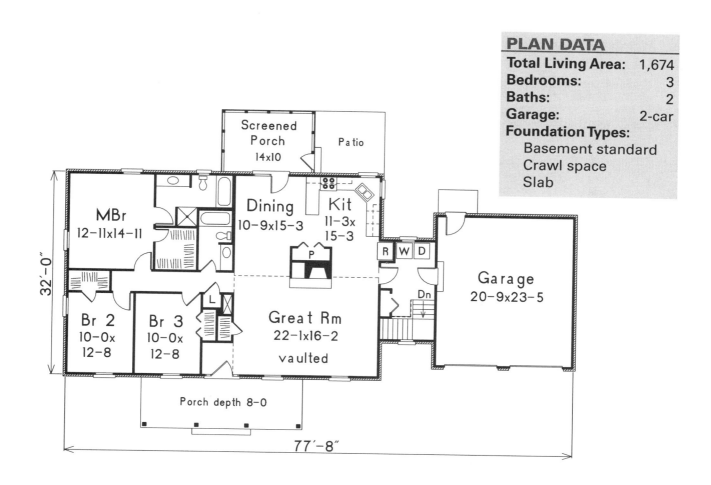

PLAN DATA

Total Living Area: 1,674
Bedrooms: 3
Baths: 2
Garage: 2-car
Foundation Types:
  Basement standard
  Crawl space
  Slab

Screened Porch 14x10

Patio

MBr 12-11x14-11

Dining 10-9x15-3

Kit 11-3x 15-3

R W D

Garage 20-9x23-5

Dn

P

Great Rm 22-1x16-2 vaulted

Br 2 10-0x 12-8

Br 3 10-0x 12-8

L

32'-0"

Porch depth 8-0

77'-8"

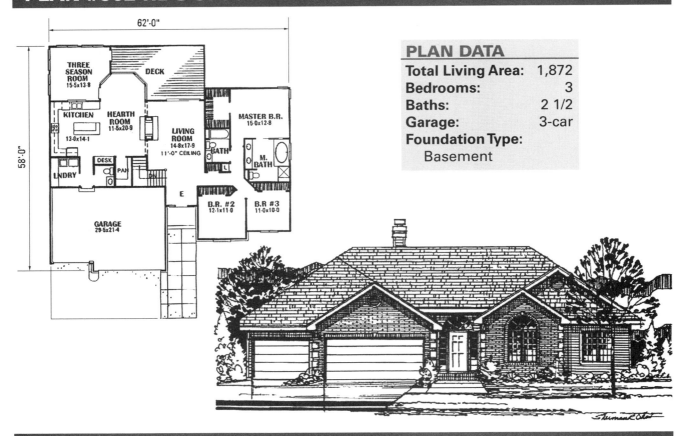

62'-0"

58'-0"

THREE SEASON ROOM
15-5x13-8

DECK

KITCHEN
13-0x14-1

HEARTH ROOM
11-5x20-9

LIVING ROOM
14-8x17-9
11'-0" CEILING

MASTER B.R.
15-0x12-8

BATH

M. BATH

DESK

PAN

LNDRY

E

B.R. #2
12-1x11-0

B.R #3
11-0x10-0

GARAGE
29-5x21-4

PLAN DATA

Total Living Area: 1,872
Bedrooms: 3
Baths: 2 1/2
Garage: 3-car
Foundation Type:
  Basement

PLAN DATA

Total Living Area: 1,871
Bedrooms: 3
Baths: 2
Garage: 2-car
Foundation Types:
  Basement
  Crawl space
Please specify when ordering

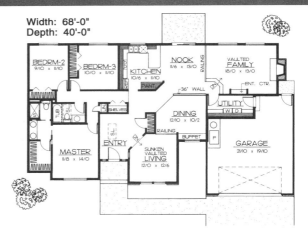

Width: 68'-0"
Depth: 40'-0"

BEDRM-2
9/10 x 11/10

BEDRM-3
10/0 x 11/10

KITCHEN
10/6 x 11/0

NOOK
11/6 x 13/0

VAULTED FAMILY
18/0 x 13/0

ENT. CTR.

PANT

36" WALL

RAILING

UTILITY
W D

SHELVES

DINING
12/10 x 10/2

BUFFET

GARAGE
21/10 x 19/10

MASTER
11/8 x 14/0

ENTRY

SUNKEN VAULTED LIVING
12/0 x 12/6

RAILING

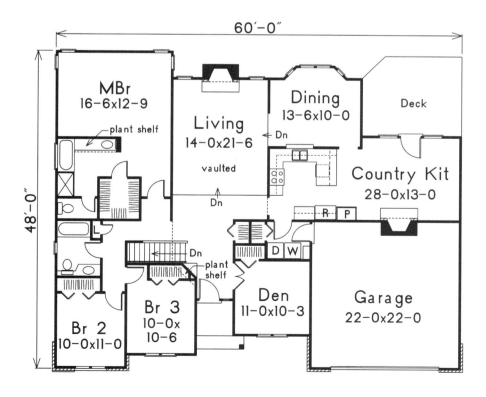

60'-0"

48'-0"

MBr
16-6x12-9

plant shelf

Living
14-0x21-6

vaulted

Dn

Dn

Dining
13-6x10-0

Deck

Country Kit
28-0x13-0

R P

D W

plant shelf

Br 3
10-0x
10-6

Den
11-0x10-3

Garage
22-0x22-0

Br 2
10-0x11-0

Dn

plant shelf

PLAN DATA

Total Living Area:	1,993
Bedrooms:	3
Baths:	2
Garage:	2-car
Foundation Type:	
Basement	

PLAN DATA

Total Living Area: 1,550
Bedrooms: 3
Baths: 2
Garage: 2-car
Foundation Types:
Plan #562-1118-1
Basement
Plan #562-1118-2
Crawl space & slab

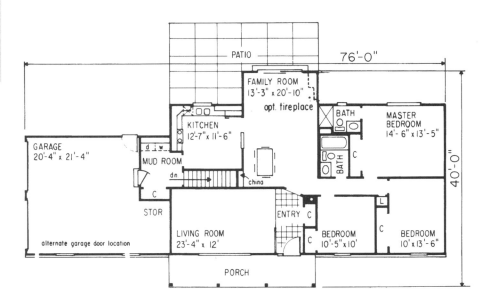

PLAN DATA

Total Living Area: 1,802
Bedrooms: 3
Baths: 2
Garage: 2-car
Foundation Type:
  Basement
Features:
  Storage in garage

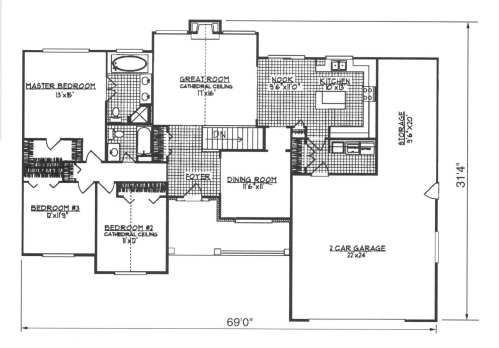

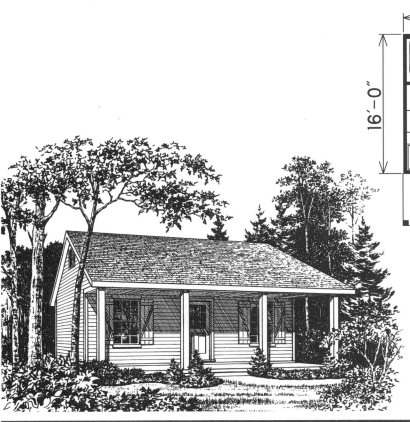

26'-0"

16'-0"

Sitting/ Sleeping
12-9x15-4

Kit/Din
11-4x9-10

Covered Porch depth 6-0

PLAN DATA

Total Living Area: 416
Bedrooms:
Sitting/Sleeping area
Bath: 1
Foundation Type:
Slab

PLAN DATA

Total Living Area: 1,135
Bedrooms: 3
Baths: 2
Garage: 2-car
Foundation Types:
Basement standard
Crawl space
Features:
2" x 6" exterior walls

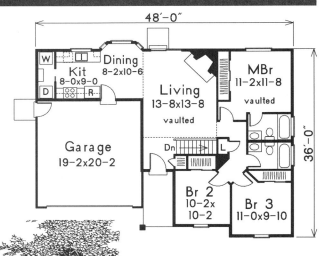

48'-0"

36'-0"

W

Kit
8-0x9-0

D R

Dining
8-2x10-6

Living
13-8x13-8
vaulted

MBr
11-2x11-8
vaulted

Garage
19-2x20-2

Dn L

Br 2
10-2x 10-2

Br 3
11-0x9-10

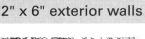

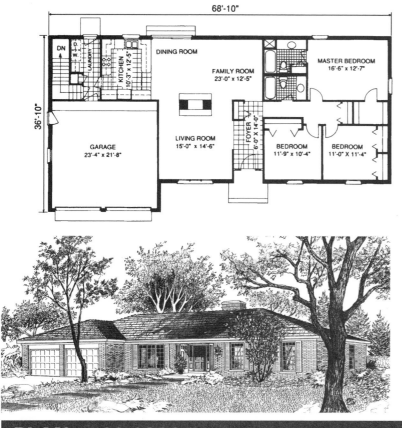

68'-10"

36'-10"

DN

D. W.

LAUNDRY

KITCHEN
10'-3" x 12'-5"

DINING ROOM

FAMILY ROOM
23'-0" x 12'-5"

MASTER BEDROOM
16'-6" x 12'-7"

GARAGE
23'-4" x 21'-8"

LIVING ROOM
15'-0" x 14'-6"

FOYER
6'-0" x 14'-0"

BEDROOM
11'-9" x 10'-4"

BEDROOM
11'-0" X 11'-4"

PLAN DATA

Total Living Area:	1,723
Bedrooms:	3
Baths:	2
Garage:	2-car

Foundation Types:
   Plan #562-1286-1
   Basement
   Plan #562-1286-2
   Crawl space & slab
Features:
   2" x 6" exterior walls

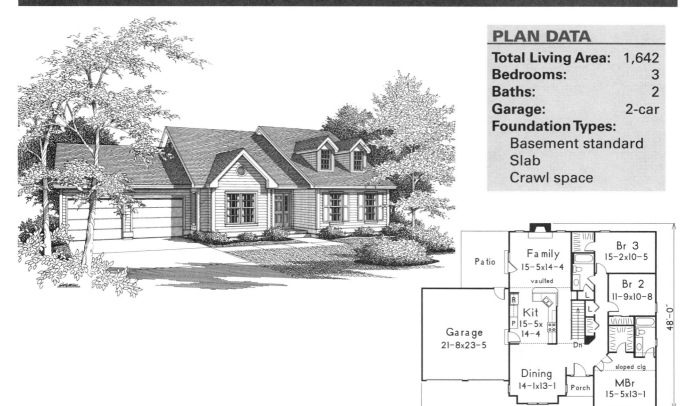

PLAN DATA

Total Living Area:	1,642
Bedrooms:	3
Baths:	2
Garage:	2-car

Foundation Types:
   Basement standard
   Slab
   Crawl space

Patio

Family
15-5x14-4
vaulted

Br 3
15-2x10-5

Br 2
11-9x10-8

Kit
15-5x
14-4

Garage
21-8x23-5

Dn

sloped clg

Dining
14-1x13-1

Porch

MBr
15-5x13-1

48'-0"

59'-4"

PLAN #562-0294

PLAN DATA

Total Living Area: 1,655
Bedrooms: 3
Baths: 2
Garage: 2-car
Foundation Type:
  Crawl space
Features:
- 9' ceiling in master bedroom
- 10' ceiling in family room

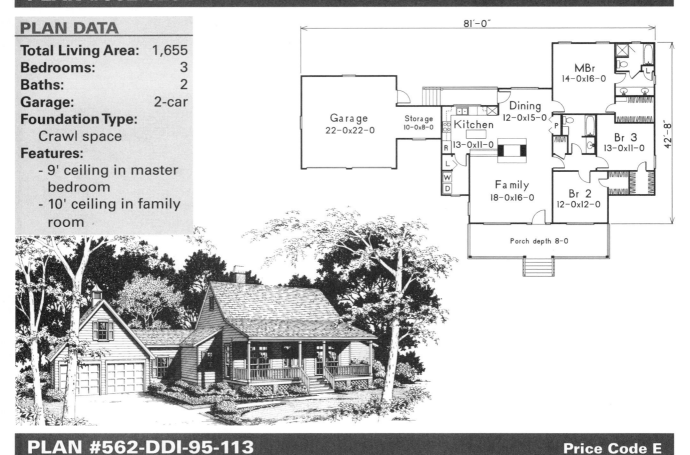

PLAN #562-DDI-95-113

PLAN DATA

Total Living Area: 2,710
Bedrooms: 3
Baths: 2 1/2
Garage: 2-car
Foundation Types:
  Basement
  Crawl space
  Slab
Please specify when ordering
Features:
  Varied ceiling heights

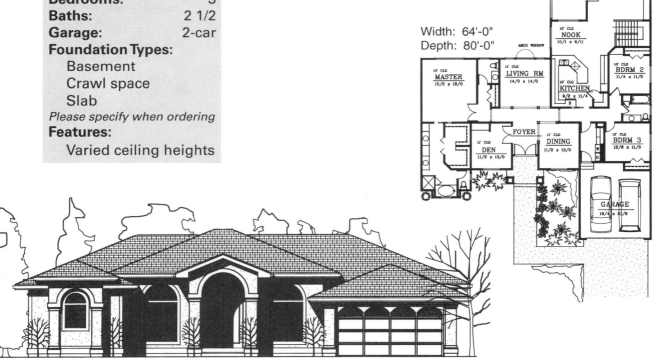

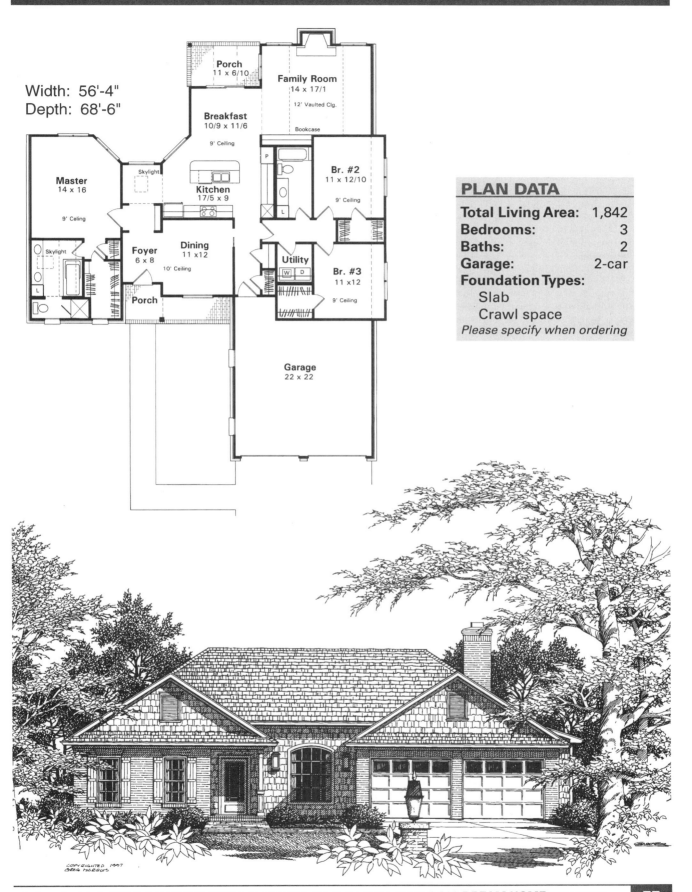

Width: 56'-4"
Depth: 68'-6"

Porch
11 x 6/10

Family Room
14 x 17/1

12' Vaulted Clg.

Bookcase

Breakfast
10/9 x 11/6

9' Ceiling

Master
14 x 16

Skylight

9' Ceiling

Kitchen
17/5 x 9

P

Br. #2
11 x 12/10

9' Ceiling

L

Skylight

Foyer
6 x 8

Dining
11 x 12

10' Ceiling

Utility
W D

Br. #3
11 x 12

9' Ceiling

Porch

Garage
22 x 22

PLAN DATA

Total Living Area:	1,842
Bedrooms:	3
Baths:	2
Garage:	2-car
Foundation Types:	
Slab	
Crawl space	

Please specify when ordering

COPYRIGHTED 1997
GREG MARQUIS

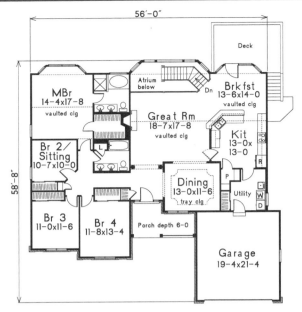

56'-0"

Deck

MBr
14-4x17-8
vaulted clg

Atrium
below

Dn

Brkfst
13-6x14-0
vaulted clg

Great Rm
18-7x17-8
vaulted clg

Kit
13-0x
13-0

Br 2/
Sitting
10-7x10-0

L

R

Dining
13-0x11-6
tray clg

P

Utility

W
D

Br 3
11-0x11-6

Br 4
11-8x13-4

Porch depth 6-0

Garage
19-4x21-4

58'-8"

**First Floor
2,218 Sq. Ft.**

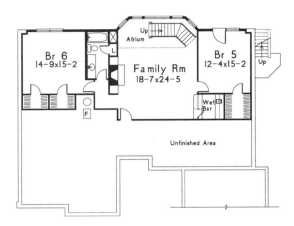

Up

Atrium

Br 6
14-9x15-2

L

Family Rm
18-7x24-5

Br 5
12-4x15-2

Up

F

Wet
Bar

Unfinished Area

**Optional
Lower Level
1,217 Sq. Ft.**

PLAN DATA

Total Living Area:	2,218
Bedrooms:	4
Baths:	2
Garage:	2-car
Foundation Type:	
Walk-out basement	

Rear View

PLAN #562-LBD-10-1B

Price Code AA

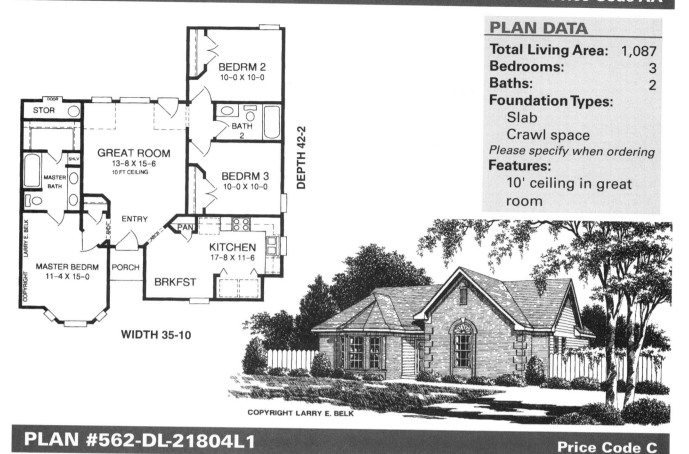

BEDRM 2
10-0 X 10-0

DOOR
STOR

BATH 2

GREAT ROOM
13-8 X 15-6
10 FT CEILING

DEPTH 42-2

SHLV

MASTER BATH

BEDRM 3
10-0 X 10-0

ENTRY

PAN

COPYRIGHT LARRY E. BELK

MASTER BEDRM
11-4 X 15-0

PORCH

KITCHEN
17-8 X 11-6

BRKFST

WIDTH 35-10

COPYRIGHT LARRY E. BELK

PLAN DATA

Total Living Area: 1,087
Bedrooms: 3
Baths: 2
Foundation Types:
  Slab
  Crawl space
Please specify when ordering
Features:
  10' ceiling in great room

PLAN #562-DL-21804L1

Price Code C

PLAN DATA

Total Living Area: 2,180
Bedrooms: 4
Baths: 2
Garage: 2-car
Foundation Type:
  Slab
Features:
  10' ceiling in family room

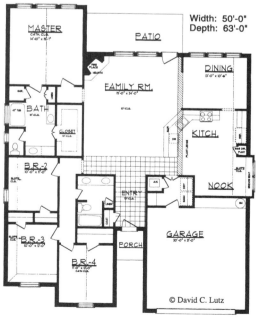

MASTER
CATH. CLG.
14'-0" x 15'-1"

PATIO

Width: 50'-0"
Depth: 63'-0"

FIRE PLACE HEARTH

DINING
13'-0" x 10'-6"

FAMILY RM.
17'-0" x 24'-0"
10' CLG.

BATH

KITCH.

CLOSET

B.R.-2
10'-0" x 11'-0"

ENTRY

NOOK

B.R.-3
10'-0" x 10'-0"

B.R.-4
11'-0" x 11'-0"
CATH. CLG.

PORCH

GARAGE
20'-0" x 21'-0"

© David C. Lutz

PLAN DATA

Total Living Area: 2,322
Bedrooms: 3
Baths: 2 1/2
Garage: 2-car
Foundation Types:
  Basement
  Crawl space
  Slab
Please specify when ordering

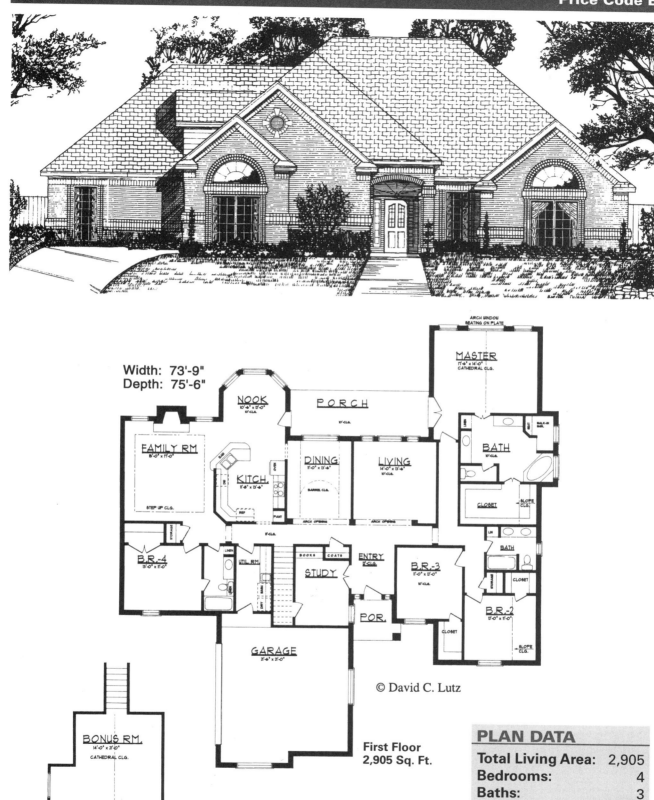

Width: 73'-9"
Depth: 75'-6"

ARCH WINDOW
SEATING ON PLATE

MASTER
17'-6" x 14'-0"
CATHEDRAL CLG.

NOOK
10'-6" x 12'-0"
10' CLG.

PORCH
10' CLG.

BATH
10' CLG.

WALK-IN
CLOS.

FAMILY RM
19'-0" x 17'-0"

KITCH.
11'-6" x 13'-6"

DINING
11'-0" x 13'-6"

LIVING
14'-0" x 13'-6"
10' CLG.

STEP UP CLG.

BARREL CLG.

CLOSET

SLOPE CLG.

ARCH OPENING

ARCH OPENING

11' CLG.

STORAGE

BATH

B.R.-4
13'-0" x 12'-0"

LINEN

UTIL. RM

BOOKS COATS

STUDY

ENTRY
11' CLG.

B.R.-3
11'-0" x 12'-0"
10' CLG.

CLOSET

STORAGE

B.R.-2
11'-0" x 11'-0"

POR.

© David C. Lutz

GARAGE
21'-6" x 21'-0"

CLOSET

SLOPE CLG.

First Floor
2,905 Sq. Ft.

BONUS RM.
14'-0" x 21'-0"
CATHEDRAL CLG.

Optional
Second Floor
340 Sq. Ft.

PLAN DATA

Total Living Area:	2,905
Bedrooms:	4
Baths:	3
Garage:	2-car
Foundation Type: Slab	

PLAN #562-JA-90199

PLAN DATA

Total Living Area:	1,801
Bedrooms:	3
Baths:	2 1/2
Garage:	3-car
Foundation Type:	
Basement	

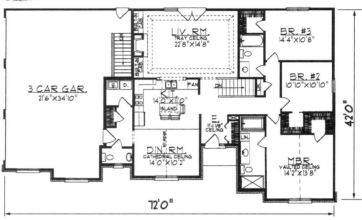

3 CAR GAR.
21'6"X34'10"

LIV. RM.
TRAY CEILING
22'8"X14'8"

BR. #3
14'4"X10'8"

BR. #2
10'10"X10'10"

KIT
14'0"X11'0"
ISLAND

D.IN. RM.
CATHEDRAL CEILING
14'0"X10'2"

11'-1 1/8"
CEILING

M.B.R.
VAULTED CEILING
14'2"X13'8"

42'0"

72'0"

PLAN #562-1285-1 & 2

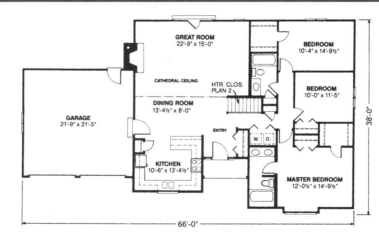

GREAT ROOM
22'-9" x 15'-0"

BEDROOM
10'-4" x 14'-9½"

CATHEDRAL CEILING

HTR. CLOS.
PLAN 2

BEDROOM
10'-0" x 11'-5"

GARAGE
21'-9" x 21'-5"

DINING ROOM
13'-4½" x 8'-0"

ENTRY

W. D.

38'-0"

KITCHEN
10'-6" x 13'-4½"

MASTER BEDROOM
12'-0½" x 14'-9½"

66'-0"

PLAN DATA

Total Living Area:	1,540
Bedrooms:	3
Baths:	2
Garage:	2-car
Foundation Types:	
Plan #562-1285-1	
Basement	
Plan #562-1285-2	
Crawl space	

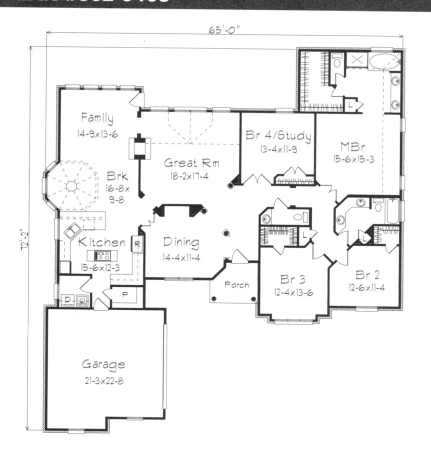

65'-0"

72'-2"

Family
14-9x13-6

Brk
16-8x
9-8

Great Rm
18-2x17-4

Br 4/Study
13-4x11-9

MBr
15-6x15-3

Kitchen
15-6x12-3

Dining
14-4x11-4

R

P

Porch

Br 3
12-4x13-6

Br 2
12-6x11-4

Garage
21-3x22-8

PLAN DATA

Total Living Area: 2,598
Bedrooms: 4
Baths: 2 1/2
Garage: 2-car
Foundation Types:
 Slab standard
 Crawl space
Features:
 Varied ceiling heights

PLAN DATA

Total Living Area:	1,853
Bedrooms:	3
Baths:	3
Garage:	2-car
Foundation Type:	
Basement	

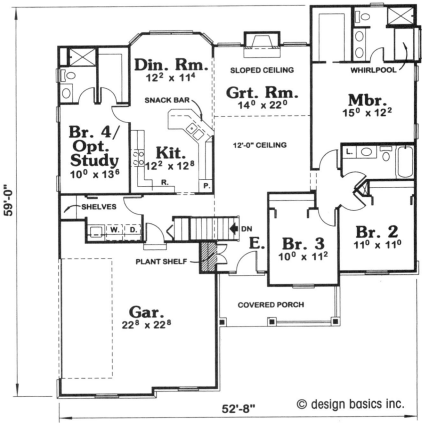

59'-0"

Din. Rm.
12^2 x 11^4

SLOPED CEILING

WHIRLPOOL

SNACK BAR

Grt. Rm.
14^0 x 22^0

Mbr.
15^0 x 12^2

Br. 4/ Opt. Study
10^0 x 13^6

Kit.
12^2 x 12^8

12'-0" CEILING

R.

P.

L.

SHELVES

W. D.

DN

E.

Br. 3
10^0 x 11^2

Br. 2
11^0 x 11^0

PLANT SHELF

Gar.
22^8 x 22^8

COVERED PORCH

© design basics inc.

52'-8"

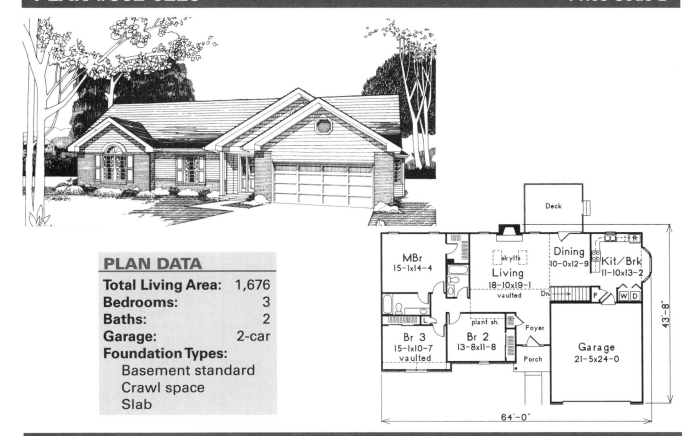

PLAN DATA

Total Living Area: 1,676
Bedrooms: 3
Baths: 2
Garage: 2-car
Foundation Types:
  Basement standard
  Crawl space
  Slab

Deck

MBr
15-1x14-4

sky lts

Living
18-10x19-1
vaulted

Dining
10-0x12-9

Kit/Brk
11-10x13-2

Dn

W D
P

L

plant sh.

Foyer

Br 3
15-1x10-7
vaulted

Br 2
13-8x11-8

Garage
21-5x24-0

Porch

43'-8"

64'-0"

20'-0"
50'-0"
PATIO
OPT'L FIREPLACE

STORAGE

KITCHEN
12' x 11'-7"

FAMILY
ROOM
15' x 15'

BATH

MASTER
BED ROOM
13'-6" x 13'-6"

LAUNDRY & HTR.
CLO. PLAN-2

B.

C.

dn

LIVING ROOM
25'-6" x 12'

ENTRY

CLO.

L.

GARAGE
19'-8" x 23'-4"

C.

BED ROOM
10'-7" x 10'

C.

BED ROOM
10' x 11'

28'-5"

PLAN DATA

Total Living Area: 1,408
Bedrooms: 3
Baths: 2
Garage: 2-car
Foundation Types:
  Plan #562-N286-1
  Basement
  Plan #562-N286-2
  Crawl space & slab

Width: 76'-0"
Depth: 58'-0"

tray ci'g
DIN
11' x 13'

MBR
15'6 X 13'6

DIN RM
11'8 x 13'6

FAMILY RM
15'6 x 13'6

KIT
12' X 15'8

MBATH

WI Closet

REF

PANTRY

BR CL

Laun

BR2
11' X 12'
Plus Bay

LINEN

BATH 2

Lav

Entry

W   D

BR3
11'4 X 12'

FOYER

LIV RM
13' X 15

GARAGE
21'8 X 21'8

STORAGE
6 X 13'4

Barrel Vault
Covered Entry

FLAT
CL'G

FLAT
CL'G

PLAN DATA

Total Living Area:	2,278
Bedrooms:	3
Baths:	2 1/2
Garage:	2-car
Foundation Type:	
Basement	

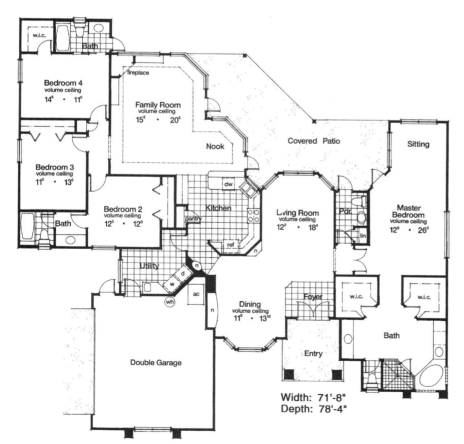

w.i.c.

Bath

Bedroom 4
volume ceiling
14⁸ • 11⁰

fireplace

Family Room
volume ceiling
15⁸ • 20⁶

Bedroom 3
volume ceiling
11⁰ • 13⁰

Nook

Covered Patio

Sitting

Bath

dw

Kitchen

Bedroom 2
volume ceiling
12⁰ • 12⁰

pantry

Bath

ref

Living Room
volume ceiling
12⁰ • 18⁴

Pdr.

lin

Master Bedroom
volume ceiling
12⁸ • 26⁰

Utility

d

w

wh

ac

Dining
volume ceiling
11⁸ • 13¹⁰

Foyer

w.i.c.

w.i.c.

Double Garage

Entry

Bath

Width: 71'-8"
Depth: 78'-4"

PLAN DATA

Total Living Area:	2,636
Bedrooms:	4
Baths:	4
Garage:	2-car
Foundation Type:	
Slab	

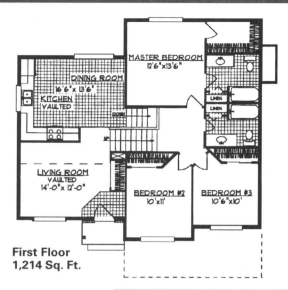

First Floor
1,214 Sq. Ft.

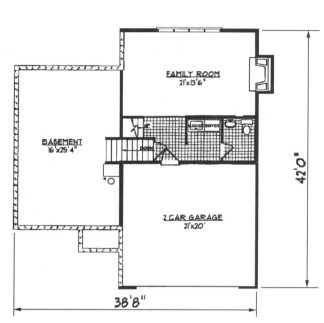

Lower Level
449 Sq. Ft.

PLAN DATA

Total Living Area:	1,663
Bedrooms:	3
Baths:	2 1/2
Garage:	2-car
Foundation Type:	
Basement	
Features:	
Drive-under garage	

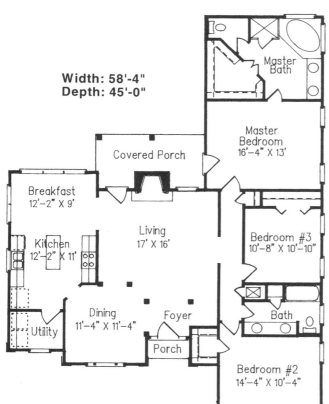

Width: 58'-4"
Depth: 45'-0"

Master Bath

Master Bedroom
16'-4" X 13'

Covered Porch

Breakfast
12'-2" X 9'

Kitchen
12'-2" X 11'

Living
17' X 16'

Bedroom #3
10'-8" X 10'-10"

Dining
11'-4" X 11'-4"

Foyer

Bath

Utility

Porch

Bedroom #2
14'-4" X 10'-4"

PLAN DATA

Total Living Area: 1,704
Bedrooms: 3
Baths: 2
Garage: 2-car
Foundation Type:
  Slab

PLAN DATA

Total Living Area: 1,868
Bedrooms: 3
Baths: 2 1/2
Garage: 2-car
Foundation Types:
  Slab standard
  Crawl space
Features:
  - 2" x 6" exterior walls
  - 12' ceiling in living
    room

Stor
10-6x5-4

Stor
10-6x5-4

Garage
21-4x22-0

Patio

sloped clg

Br 2
11-6x12-4

skylight

skylight

D
W

Living
19-10x15-6

Kit
11-0x
12-0

MBr
17-8x13-4

R

P

coffered clg

Entry

Dining
12-2x11-6

vaulted

Br 3
11-6x13-4

vaulted

Porch depth 4-0

Eating
11-0x9-6

vaulted

64'-0"

62'-0"

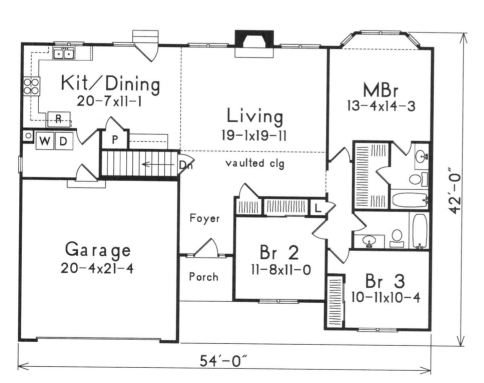

PLAN DATA

Total Living Area:	1,558
Bedrooms:	3
Baths:	2
Garage:	2-car
Foundation Type:	
Basement	

PLAN #562-1117

PLAN DATA

Total Living Area: 1,440
Bedrooms: 3
Baths: 2
Garage: 2-car
Foundation Types:
  Basement
  Crawl space
  Slab
Please specify when ordering

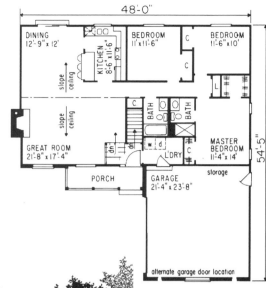

PLAN #562-JFD-10-1692-1

PLAN DATA

Total Living Area: 1,692
Bedrooms: 3
Baths: 2 1/2
Garage: 2-car
Foundation Type:
  Basement

PLAN DATA

Total Living Area: 1,285
Bedrooms: 3
Baths: 2
Foundation Types:
  Crawl space standard
  Basement
  Slab

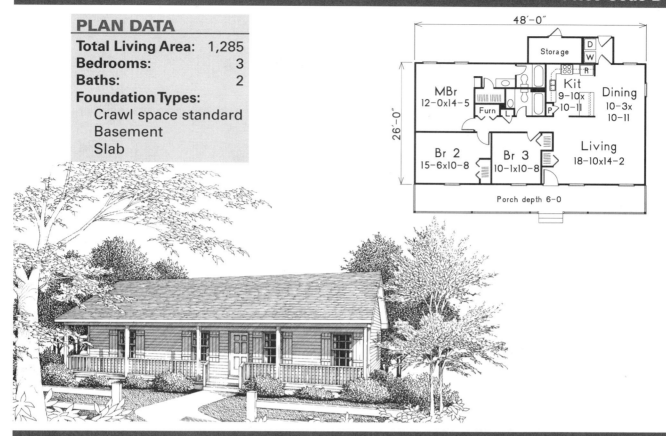

PLAN #562-0297

Price Code A

PLAN DATA

Total Living Area: 1,320
Bedrooms: 3
Baths: 2
Foundation Type:
  Crawl space

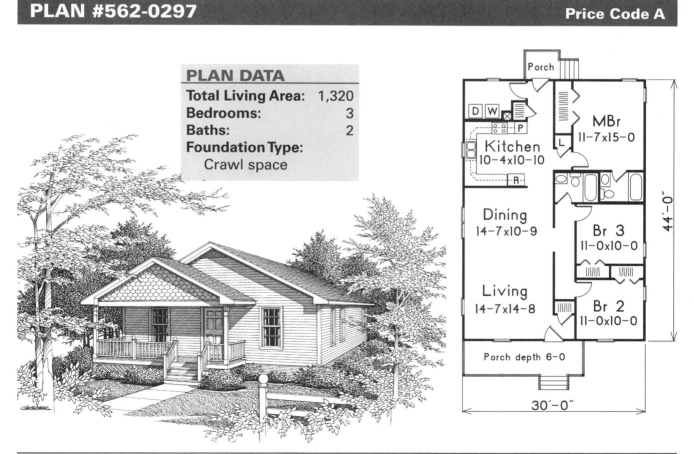

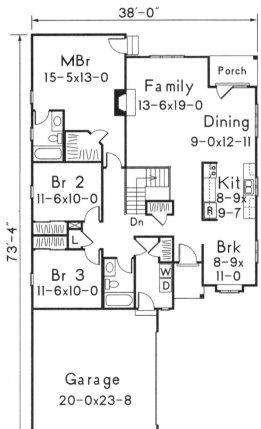

38'-0"

73'-4"

MBr
15-5x13-0

Family
13-6x19-0

Porch

Dining
9-0x12-11

Br 2
11-6x10-0

Kit
8-9x
9-7

R

Dn

L

Br 3
11-6x10-0

W
D

Brk
8-9x
11-0

Garage
20-0x23-8

PLAN DATA

Total Living Area: 1,624
Bedrooms: 3
Baths: 2
Garage: 2-car
Foundation Types:
  Basement standard
  Crawl space
  Slab

PLAN DATA

Total Living Area: 1,575
Bedrooms: 3
Baths: 2
Garage: 2-car
Foundation Types:
  Slab
  Crawl space
Please specify when ordering

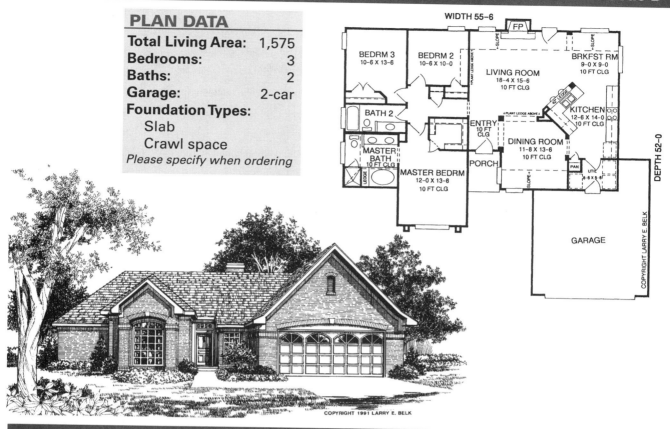

COPYRIGHT LARRY E. BELK

WIDTH 55–6

FP

BEDRM 3
10–6 X 13–6

BEDRM 2
10–6 X 10–0

LIVING ROOM
18–4 X 15–6
10 FT CLG

BRKFST RM
9–0 X 9–0
10 FT CLG

BATH 2

KITCHEN
12–6 X 14–0
10 FT CLG

ENTRY
10 FT
CLG

MASTER
BATH
10 FT CLG

DINING ROOM
11–8 X 13–6
10 FT CLG

PORCH

PAN

UTIL

MASTER BEDRM
12–0 X 13–6
10 FT CLG

DEPTH 52–0

GARAGE

COPYRIGHT 1991 LARRY E. BELK

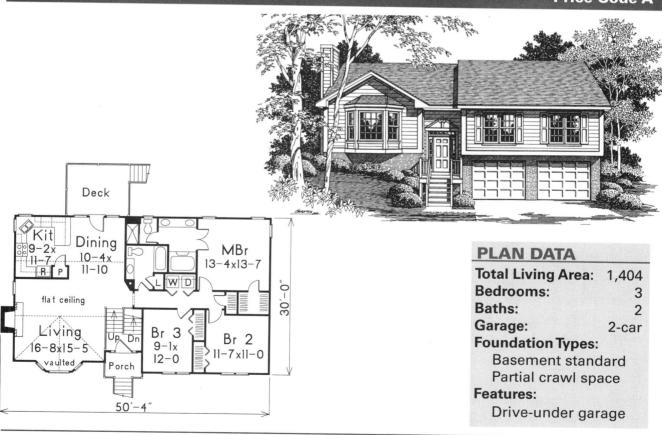

Deck

Kit
9–2x
11–7

Dining
10–4x
11–10

MBr
13–4x13–7

R P

L W D

flat ceiling

Living
16–8x15–5

Up Dn

Br 3
9–1x
12–0

Br 2
11–7x11–0

Porch

vaulted

30'–0"

50'–4"

PLAN DATA

Total Living Area: 1,404
Bedrooms: 3
Baths: 2
Garage: 2-car
Foundation Types:
  Basement standard
  Partial crawl space
Features:
  Drive-under garage

© design basics inc.

56' - 0"

55' - 4"

Br. 2
11⁰ x 11⁰

Br. 3
11⁰ x 11⁰

SHELVES

Gar.
23⁴ x 22⁴

Kit.
12¹⁰ x 12⁰

Bfst.
11⁴ x 11⁴

Grt. rm.
15⁰ x 20⁰
10'- 0" CEILING

DN

LIN.

W.

D.

Din.
11⁰ x 14⁰
10'- 0" CLG.

E.

Mbr.
14⁰ x 15⁰
10'- 0" CLG.

WHIRLPOOL

COVERED PORCH

PLAN DATA

Total Living Area: 1,806
Bedrooms: 3
Baths: 2
Garage: 2-car
Foundation Types:
  Slab
  Basement
Please specify when ordering
Features:
  10' ceilings in great
  room, dining room
  and master bedroom

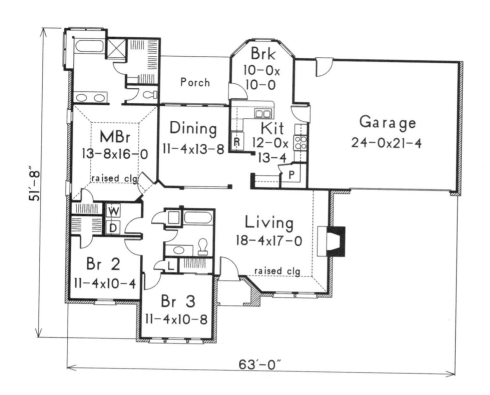

Brk
10-0x
10-0

Porch

Garage
24-0x21-4

MBr
13-8x16-0

Dining
11-4x13-8

Kit
12-0x
13-4

R

P

raised clg

W
D

Living
18-4x17-0

Br 2
11-4x10-4

L

Br 3
11-4x10-8

raised clg

51'-8"

63'-0"

PLAN DATA

Total Living Area:	1,707
Bedrooms:	3
Baths:	2
Garage:	2-car
Foundation Type: Slab	

PLAN DATA

Total Living Area:	1,880
Bedrooms:	3
Baths:	2
Garage:	2-car
Foundation Type:	
Slab	
Features:	
Varied ceiling heights	

Width: 59'-0"
Depth: 58'-1"

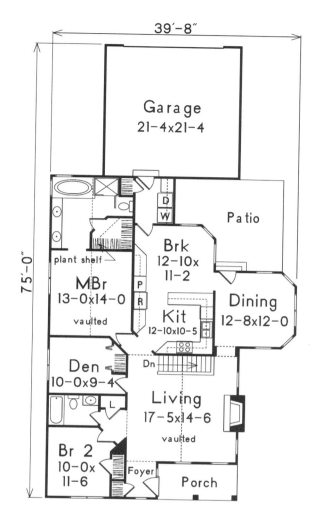

39'-8"

75'-0"

Garage
21-4x21-4

Patio

Brk
12-10x
11-2

plant shelf

MBr
13-0x14-0
vaulted

P
R

Dining
12-8x12-0

Kit
12-10x10-5

Den
10-0x9-4

Dn

Living
17-5x14-6
vaulted

Br 2
10-0x
11-6

Foyer

Porch

PLAN DATA

Total Living Area:	1,558
Bedrooms:	2
Baths:	2
Garage:	2-car
Foundation Type:	
Basement	

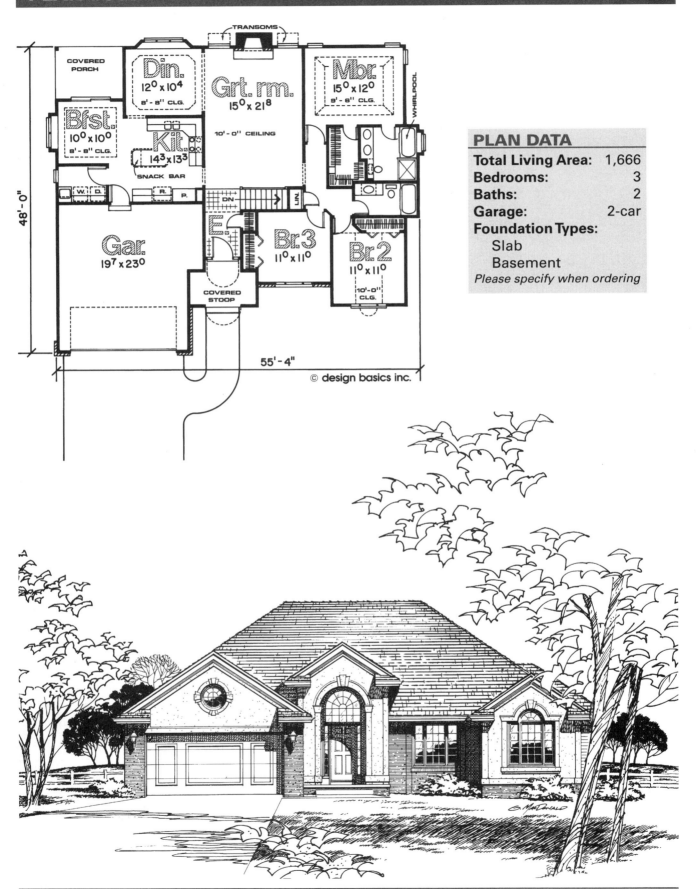

TRANSOMS

COVERED PORCH

Din.
12⁰ x 10⁴
8' - 8" CLG.

Grt. rm.
15⁰ x 21⁸
10' - 0" CEILING

Mbr.
15⁰ x 12⁰
9' - 6" CLG.

WHIRLPOOL

Bfst.
10⁰ x 10⁰
8' - 8" CLG.

Kit.
14³ x 13³

SNACK BAR

W. D.   R.   P.

DN   LIN.

Gar.
19⁷ x 23⁰

Br.3
11⁰ x 11⁰

Br.2
11⁰ x 11⁰
10' - 0" CLG.

COVERED STOOP

48' - 0"

55' - 4"

© design basics inc.

PLAN DATA

Total Living Area:	1,666
Bedrooms:	3
Baths:	2
Garage:	2-car

Foundation Types:
Slab
Basement
Please specify when ordering

G. McDonald

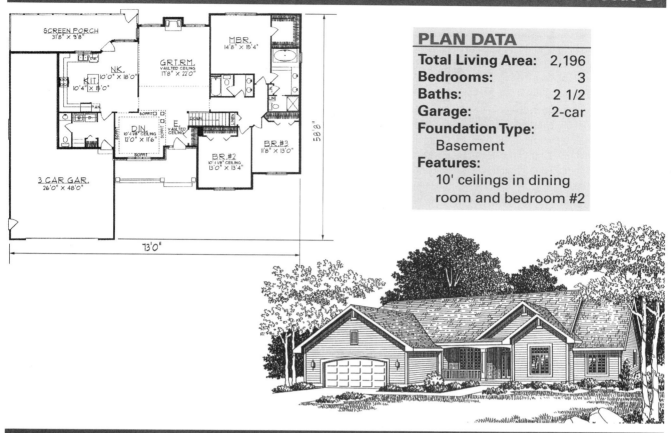

SCREEN PORCH
31'8" X 9'8"

G.R.T.RM.
VAULTED CEILING
17'8" X 22'0"

M.B.R.
14'8" X 15'4"

NK.
10'0" X 18'0"

KIT.
10'4" X 15'0"

DIN.
10'4 1/8" CEILING
12'0" X 11'6"

B.R.#2
10'4 1/8" CEILING
13'0" X 13'4"

B.R.#3
11'8" X 13'0"

3 CAR GAR.
26'0" X 48'0"

73'0"

58'8"

PLAN DATA

Total Living Area: 2,196
Bedrooms: 3
Baths: 2 1/2
Garage: 2-car
Foundation Type:
  Basement
Features:
  10' ceilings in dining
  room and bedroom #2

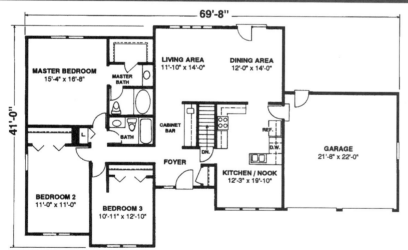

69'-8"

41'-0"

MASTER BEDROOM
15'-4" x 16'-8"

MASTER
BATH

L

BATH

CABINET
BAR

DN.

FOYER

LIVING AREA
11'-10" x 14'-0"

DINING AREA
12'-0" x 14'-0"

REF.

D.W.

KITCHEN / NOOK
12'-3" x 19'-10"

GARAGE
21'-8" x 22'-0"

BEDROOM 2
11'-0" x 11'-0"

BEDROOM 3
10'-11" x 12'-10"

PLAN DATA

Total Living Area: 1,704
Bedrooms: 3
Baths: 2
Garage: 2-car
Foundation Type:
  Basement

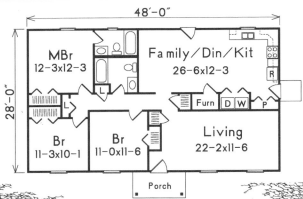

48'-0"

28'-0"

MBr
12-3x12-3

Family/Din/Kit
26-6x12-3

Furn | D | W | P

Living
22-2x11-6

Br
11-3x10-1

Br
11-0x11-6

Porch

PLAN DATA

Total Living Area:	1,344
Bedrooms:	3
Baths:	2
Foundation Types:	
Crawl space standard	
Basement	
Slab	

PLAN DATA

Total Living Area:	1,368
Bedrooms:	3
Baths:	2
Garage:	2-car
Foundation Type:	
Basement	

48'-0"

49'-4"

MBr
14-0x12-6
vaulted

Br 2
12-0x10-0

Br 3
11-0x9-0

Patio

Kitchen/Brk
19-0x10-8

Dining

Garage
21-4x19-4

Great Rm
19-0x18-0
vaulted

Dn

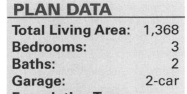

PLAN #562-DBI-5003

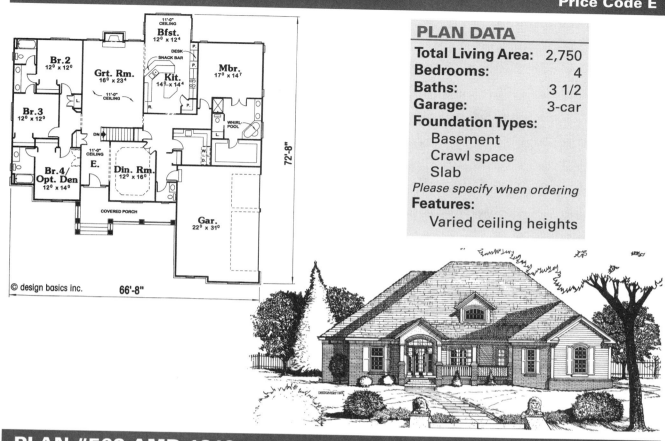

PLAN DATA

Total Living Area: 2,750
Bedrooms: 4
Baths: 3 1/2
Garage: 3-car
Foundation Types:
  Basement
  Crawl space
  Slab
Please specify when ordering
Features:
  Varied ceiling heights

PLAN #562-AMD-1219

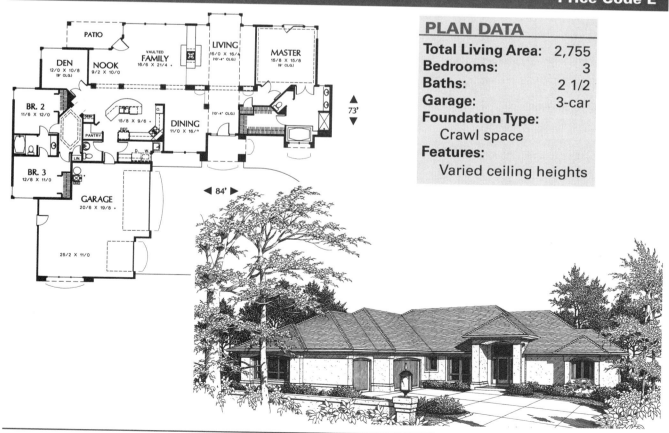

PLAN DATA

Total Living Area: 2,755
Bedrooms: 3
Baths: 2 1/2
Garage: 3-car
Foundation Type:
  Crawl space
Features:
  Varied ceiling heights

PLAN DATA

Total Living Area: 1,856
Bedrooms: 3
Baths: 2
Garage: 2-car
Foundation Types:
  Slab standard
  Crawl space
Features:
  - 2" x 6" exterior walls
  - 12' ceiling in living
    room

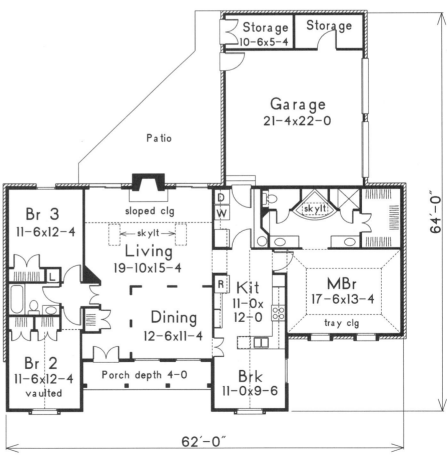

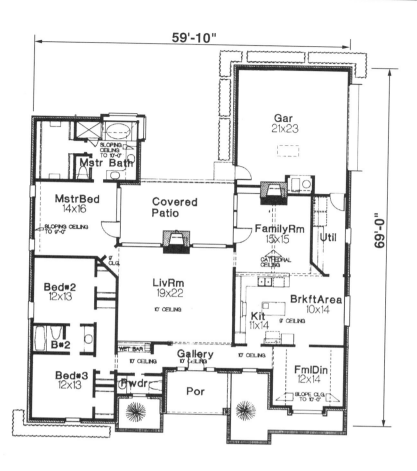

59'-10"

69'-0"

Gar
21x23

Mstr Bath

SLOPING CEILING TO 10'-0"

MstrBed
14x16

SLOPING CEILING TO 9'-0"

Covered
Patio

FamilyRm
15x15

Util

9' CLG

CATHEDRAL CEILING

Bed#2
12x13

LivRm
19x22

10' CEILING

Kit
11x14

BrkftArea
10x14

9' CEILING

B#2

WET BAR

Gallery

10' CEILING

10' CEILING

10' CEILING

FmlDin
12x14

Bed#3
12x13

Pwdr

Por

SLOPE CLG TO 10'-0"

PLAN DATA

Total Living Area: 2,470
Bedrooms: 3
Baths: 2 1/2
Garage: 2-car
Foundation Types:
 Crawl space
 Slab
Please specify when ordering
Features:
 Varied ceiling heights

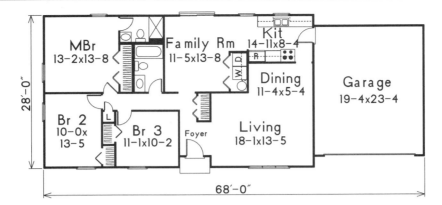

MBr
13-2x13-8

Family Rm
11-5x13-8

Kit
14-11x8-4

Garage
19-4x23-4

Dining
11-4x5-4

W.D.

R

Br 2
10-0x
13-5

Br 3
11-1x10-2

Foyer

Living
18-1x13-5

28'-0"

68'-0"

PLAN DATA

Total Living Area:	1,343
Bedrooms:	3
Baths:	2
Garage:	2-car
Foundation Types:	
Crawl space standard	
Basement	

48'-0"

MASTER BEDROOM
12'-6" x 10'-10"

MASTER BATH

DINING AREA
13'-10" x 10'-0"

D.W.

REF.

KITCHEN
10'-4" x 10'-10"

BATH 1

L

DN.

W. D.

OPTIONAL GARAGE
21'-8" x 23'-3"

BEDROOM #2
10'-1" x 12'-1"

BEDROOM #3
10'-1" x 12'-1"

GREAT ROOM
21'-7" x 14'-7"

30'-0"

4'-0"

OPTIONAL PORCH

PLAN DATA

Total Living Area:	1,364
Bedrooms:	3
Baths:	2
Foundation Type:	
Basement	
Features:	
Optional 2-car garage and covered porch	

PLAN #562-N131

PLAN DATA

Total Living Area:	733
Bedrooms:	2
Bath:	1
Foundation Type:	
Pier	

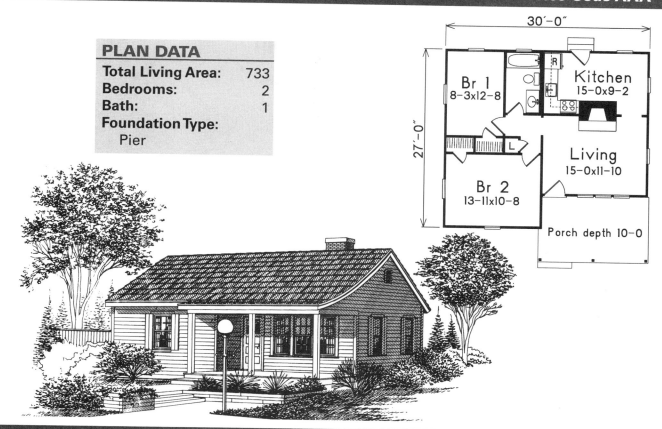

30′-0″

27′-0″

Br 1
8-3x12-8

Kitchen
15-0x9-2

Br 2
13-11x10-8

Living
15-0x11-10

Porch depth 10-0

PLAN #562-0505

44′-0″

26′-0″

MBr
12-10x12-2

Dining/Kit
18-7x11-2

Furn

Br 2
12-3x10-7

Br 3
10-10x
10-7

Living
17-4x11-11

Porch

PLAN DATA

Total Living Area:	1,104
Bedrooms:	3
Baths:	2
Foundation Types:	
Crawl space standard	
Basement	
Slab	

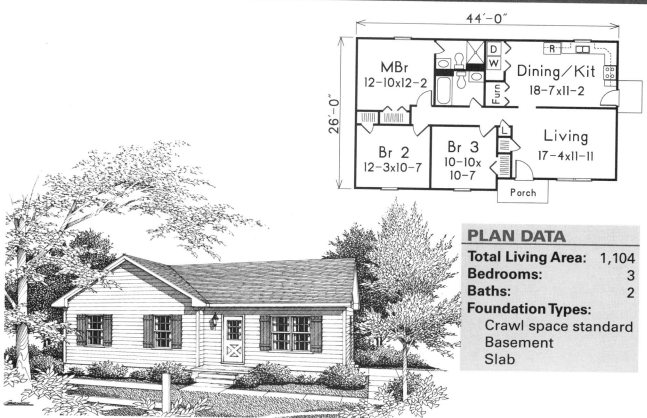

PLAN DATA

Total Living Area: 1,735
Bedrooms: 3
Baths: 2
Garage: 2-car
Foundation Type:
  Basement
Features:
  Varied ceiling heights

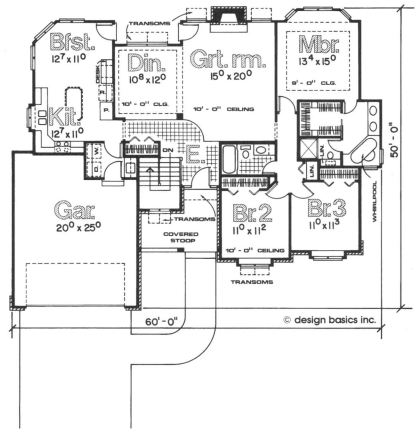

Bfst.
12⁷ x 11⁰

Din.
10⁸ x 12⁰
10' - 0" CLG.

Grt. rm.
15⁰ x 20⁰
10' - 0" CEILING

Mbr.
13⁴ x 15⁰
9' - 0" CLG.

Kit.
12⁷ x 11⁰

TRANSOMS

Gar.
20⁰ x 25⁰

Br. 2
11⁰ x 11²
10' - 0" CEILING

Br. 3
11⁰ x 11³

COVERED STOOP

TRANSOMS

WHIRLPOOL

50' - 0"

60' - 0"

© design basics inc.

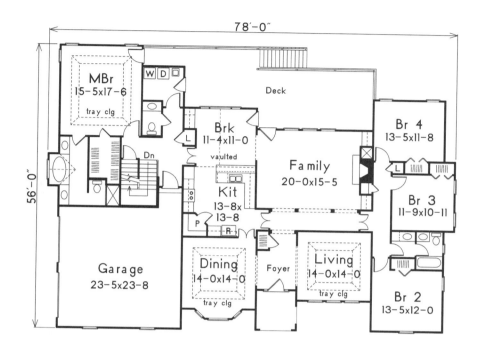

78'-0"

56'-0"

MBr
15-5x17-6
tray clg

W D

Deck

Br 4
13-5x11-8

Dn

Brk
11-4x11-0
vaulted

Family
20-0x15-5

L

Br 3
11-9x10-11

Kit
13-8x
13-8

P

R

Foyer

Living
14-0x14-0
tray clg

Garage
23-5x23-8

Dining
14-0x14-0
tray clg

Br 2
13-5x12-0

PLAN DATA

Total Living Area: 2,718
Bedrooms: 4
Baths: 2 1/2
Garage: 2-car
Foundation Type:
Basement
Features:
- 12' ceiling in family room
- 9' ceiling in kitchen

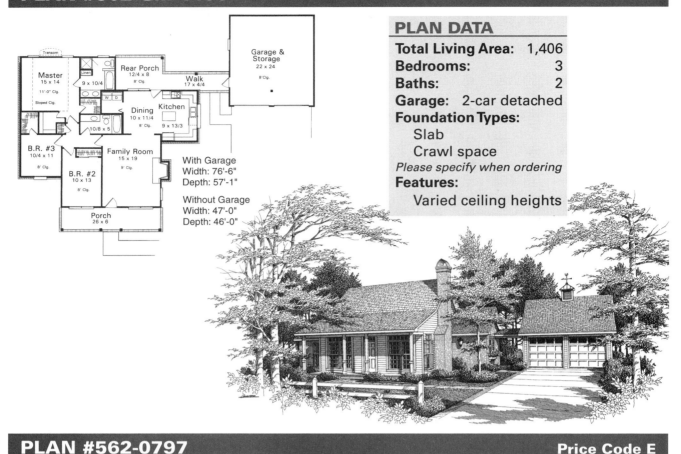

Master 15 x 14
11'-0" Clg.
Sloped Clg.

Transom

Rear Porch 12/4 x 8
8' Clg.

Linen

Walk 17 x 4/4

Garage & Storage 22 x 24
8' Clg.

9 x 10/4

B.R. #3 10/4 x 11
8' Clg.

Dining 10 x 11/4
8' Clg.

Kitchen 9 x 13/3

10/8 x 5

Family Room 15 x 19
9' Clg.

B.R. #2 10 x 13
8' Clg.

Porch 26 x 6

With Garage
Width: 76'-6"
Depth: 57'-1"

Without Garage
Width: 47'-0"
Depth: 46'-0"

PLAN DATA

Total Living Area: 1,406
Bedrooms: 3
Baths: 2
Garage: 2-car detached
Foundation Types:
  Slab
  Crawl space
Please specify when ordering
Features:
  Varied ceiling heights

PLAN DATA

Total Living Area: 2,651
Bedrooms: 3
Baths: 2
Garage: 2-car
Foundation Types:
  Basement
  Crawl space
  Slab
Please specify when ordering
Features:
  Varied ceiling heights

Width 76'-0"
Depth 57'-0"

PATIO 24'-0"x12'-0"

FAMILY ROOM 19'-8"x21'-1" (VAULTED)

MSTR BEDROOM 15'-0"x17'-1" (10' TRAY CLG)

MSTR BATH

LNDRY

BREAKFAST 11'-7"x17'-1"

KITCHEN 11'-0"x17'-1"

W.I.C.

PANTRY

FRIG

W.I.C.

LINEN

BEDROOM #2 11'-10"x15'-8"

HALL BATH

BEDROOM #3 13'-11"x16'8"
(10' CLG)

RAISED CLG

FOYER (10' CLG)

DINING ROOM 13'-11"x16'8" (10' CLG)

GARAGE 20'-0"x22'-0"

W.I.C. **W.I.C.**

COVERED PORCH 38'-0"x8'-0"

PLAN DATA

Total Living Area: 2,255
Bedrooms: 3
Baths: 2
Garage: 2-car
Foundation Type:
Crawl space
Features:
Sunken living room
with 12' ceiling

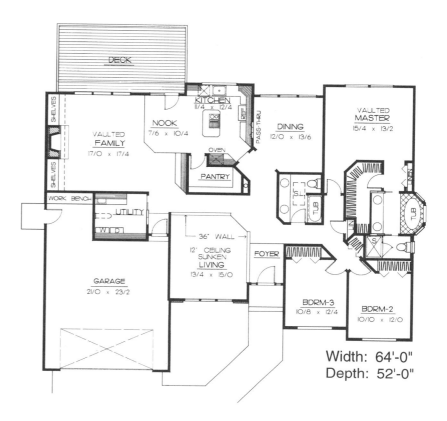

DECK

KITCHEN
11/4 x 12/4

VAULTED
MASTER
15/4 x 13/2

NOOK
7/6 x 10/4

DINING
12/0 x 13/6

VAULTED
FAMILY
17/0 x 17/4

OVEN

PANTRY

WORK BENCH

UTILITY

36" WALL
12' CEILING
SUNKEN
LIVING
13/4 x 15/0

FOYER

GARAGE
21/0 x 23/2

BDRM-3
10/8 x 12/4

BDRM-2
10/10 x 12/0

Width: 64'-0"
Depth: 52'-0"

PLAN DATA

Total Living Area: 1,407
Bedrooms: 3
Baths: 2
Garage: 2-car
Foundation Type:
  Basement
Features:
  Drive-under garage

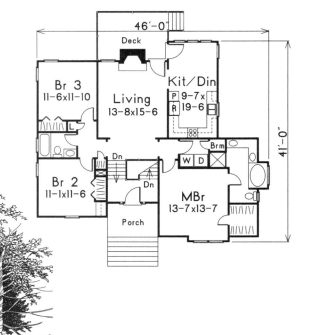

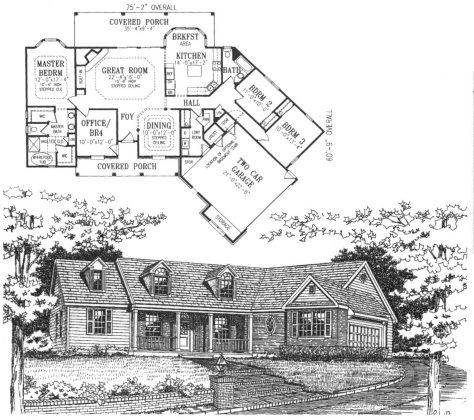

PLAN DATA

Total Living Area: 1,897
Bedrooms: 3
Baths: 2
Garage: 2-car
Foundation Types:
  Basement
  Crawl space
  Slab
Please specify when ordering

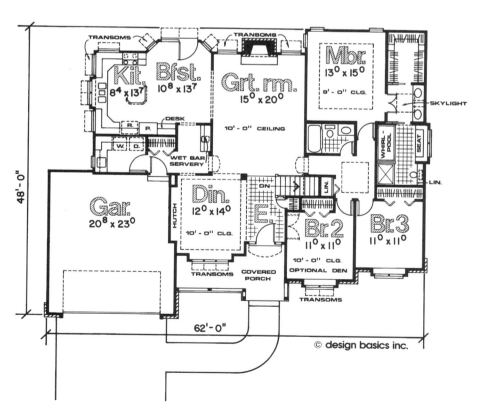

PLAN DATA

Total Living Area:	1,850
Bedrooms:	3
Baths:	2
Garage:	2-car
Foundation Type:	
Basement	
Features:	
Varied ceiling heights	

PLAN DATA

Total Living Area: 1,665
Bedrooms: 3
Baths: 2
Garage: 2-car
Foundation Type:
Slab
Features:
Varied ceiling heights

Width: 50'-0"
Depth: 55'-0"

Width: 77'-0"
Depth: 41'-8"

PLAN DATA

Total Living Area: 2,228
Bedrooms: 3
Baths: 2
Garage: 2-car
Foundation Type:
Basement

56'-0"

Deck

MBr
16-0x16-0
vaulted

Living
15-0x17-4
vaulted

Din
11-4x12-0

Deck

Covered
Porch

63'-0"

plant shelf

Kit
11-8x
12-6

Brk
9-6x10-0

Foyer

Den/Br 3
12-0x11-0

Dn

W   D

Br 2
12-0x12-0

Garage
21-4x21-8

PLAN DATA

Total Living Area:	1,958
Bedrooms:	3
Baths:	2
Garage:	2-car
Foundation Type:	
Basement	

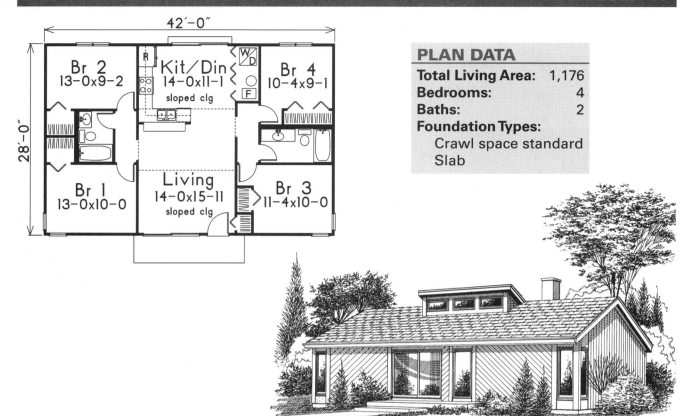

42'-0"

28'-0"

Br 2
13-0x9-2

Kit/Din
14-0x11-1
sloped clg

Br 4
10-4x9-1

W/D

F

Br 1
13-0x10-0

Living
14-0x15-11
sloped clg

Br 3
11-4x10-0

PLAN DATA

Total Living Area: 1,176
Bedrooms: 4
Baths: 2
Foundation Types:
Crawl space standard
Slab

PLAN DATA

Total Living Area: 2,221
Bedrooms: 4
Baths: 3
Garage: 2-car
Foundation Type:
Slab
Features:
Varied ceiling heights

Bedroom 3
12⁴ • 10⁰
10' Ceiling

Bath

Covered Patio
volume ceiling

Master Bedroom
15⁴ • 14⁰
10' Ceiling

w.i.c.

Breakfast
volume ceiling

Bedroom 2
12⁴ • 11⁰
10' Ceiling

fireplace

Family Room
volume ceiling
16⁰ • 16⁰

desk

w.i.c.

Bath
10' Ceiling

Kitchen
volume ceiling

Utility

ac

Bath

Bedroom 4
12⁴ • 11⁰
10' Ceiling

Living Room
volume ceiling
12⁰ • 11⁰

Foyer

Dining
volume ceiling
12⁰ • 11⁰

Double Garage

Entry

Width: 65'-0"
Depth: 50'-0"

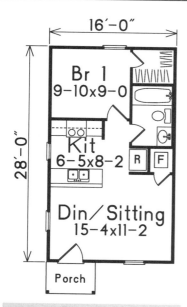

16'-0"

28'-0"

Br 1
9-10x9-0

Kit
6-5x8-2   R F

Din/Sitting
15-4x11-2

Porch

PLAN DATA

Total Living Area:	448
Bedroom:	1
Bath:	1
Foundation Type:	
Slab	

PLAN DATA

Total Living Area:	1,092
Bedrooms:	3
Baths:	1 1/2
Garage:	1-car
Foundation Type:	
Basement	

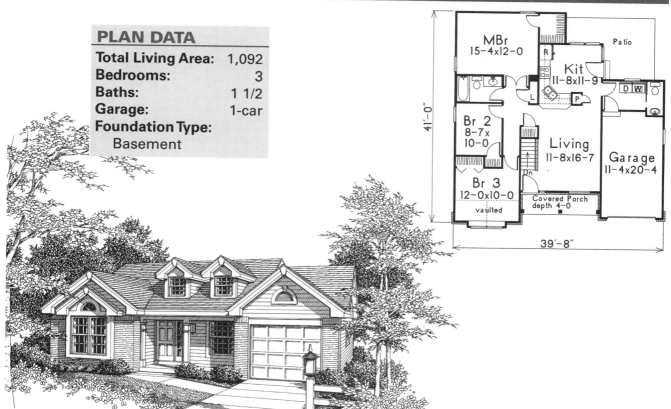

MBr
15-4x12-0

Patio

Kit
11-8x11-9

41'-0"

Br 2
8-7x
10-0

Living
11-8x16-7

Garage
11-4x20-4

Br 3
12-0x10-0
vaulted

Covered Porch
depth 4-0

39'-8"

PLAN DATA

Total Living Area:	1,769
Bedrooms:	3
Baths:	2
Garage:	2-car
Foundation Type:	
Basement	
Features:	
Drive-under garage	

Sundeck
16-0 x 14-0

Dining
12-6 x 11-6

Kit.
9-0 x 11-4

Brkfst.
9-8 x 13-6

Bdrm. 3
13-6 x 11-0

M.Bath

Master Bdrm.
13-6 x 17-2

Foyer
5-8 x 11-6

Living Area
19-8 x 15-6

Bdrm. 2
13-6 x 11-8

28-0

© 1985, Jannis Vann & Associates, Inc.

Porch

62-0

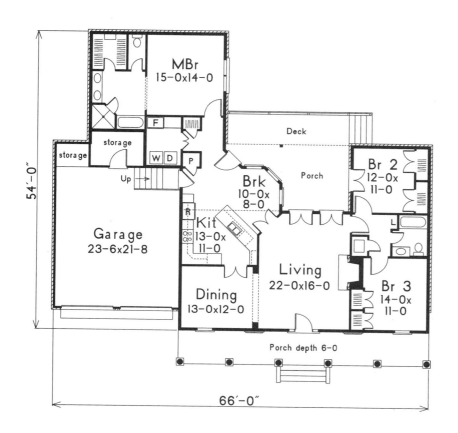

54'-0"

66'-0"

MBr
15-0x14-0

storage

storage

F

W D P

Up

Deck

Porch

Brk
10-0x8-0

Br 2
12-0x11-0

Garage
23-6x21-8

Kit
13-0x11-0

Living
22-0x16-0

L

Dining
13-0x12-0

Br 3
14-0x11-0

Porch depth 6-0

PLAN DATA

Total Living Area: 1,800
Bedrooms: 3
Baths: 2
Garage: 2-car
Foundation Types:
  Crawl space standard
  Slab
Features:
  2" x 6" exterior walls

PLAN DATA

Total Living Area: 1,800
Bedrooms: 3
Baths: 2 1/2
Garage: 2-car
Foundation Types:
　Plan #562-1267-1
　Basement
　Plan #562-1267-2
　Slab

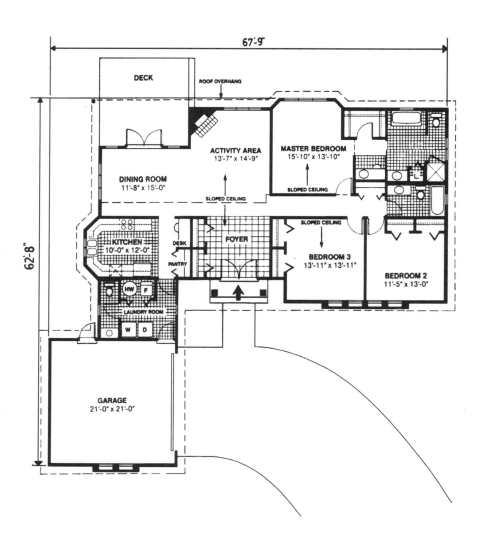

DECK

ROOF OVERHANG

ACTIVITY AREA
13'-7" x 14'-9"

MASTER BEDROOM
15'-10" x 13'-10"

SLOPED CEILING

DINING ROOM
11'-8" x 15'-0"

SLOPED CEILING

SLOPED CEILING

KITCHEN
10'-0" x 12'-0"

DESK

FOYER

PANTRY

BEDROOM 3
13'-11" x 13'-11"

BEDROOM 2
11'-5" x 13'-0"

HW F

LAUNDRY ROOM

W D

GARAGE
21'-0" x 21'-0"

67'-9"

62'-8"

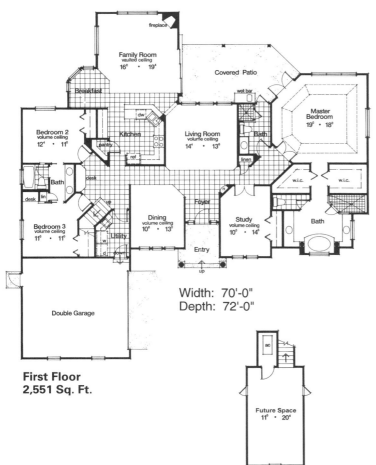

First Floor
2,551 Sq. Ft.

Width: 70'-0"
Depth: 72'-0"

Optional
Second Floor
287 Sq. Ft.

PLAN DATA

Total Living Area:	2,551
Bedrooms:	3
Baths:	3
Garage:	2-car
Foundation Type:	
Slab	

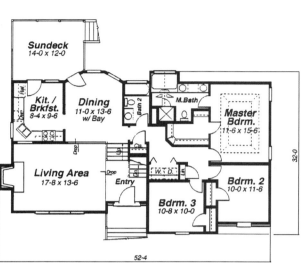

PLAN DATA

Total Living Area: 1,389
Bedrooms: 3
Baths: 2
Garage: 2-car
Foundation Type:
  Basement
Features:
  Drive- under garage

Sundeck
14-0 x 12-0

Kit. /
Brkfst.
8-4 x 9-6

Dining
11-0 x 13-6
w/ Bay

Bath 2

M.Bath

Master
Bdrm.
11-6 x 15-6

Living Area
17-8 x 13-6

Entry

W.T.D.

Bdrm. 3
10-8 x 10-0

Bdrm. 2
10-0 x 11-6

32-0

52-4

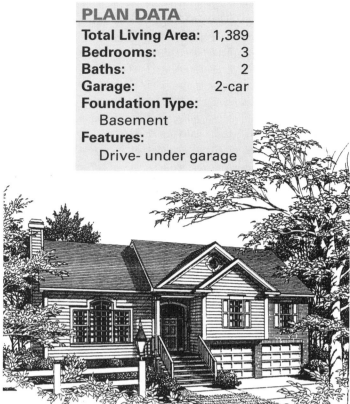

PLAN DATA

Total Living Area: 1,042
Bedrooms: 3
Bath: 1
Foundation Type:
  Basement

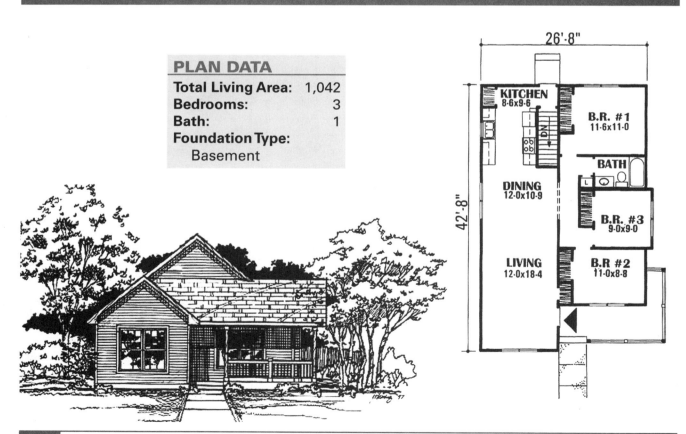

26'-8"

KITCHEN
8-6x9-6

B.R. #1
11-6x11-0

BATH

DINING
12-0x10-9

B.R. #3
9-0x9-0

LIVING
12-0x18-4

B.R #2
11-0x8-8

42'-8"

PLAN DATA

Total Living Area: 2,911
Bedrooms: 4
Baths: 3 1/2
Garage: 3-car
Foundation Types:
  Basement
  Slab
Please specify when ordering
Features:
  Varied ceiling heights

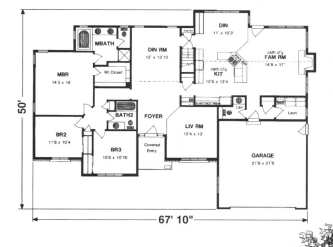

PLAN DATA

Total Living Area: 2,096
Bedrooms: 3
Baths: 2 1/2
Garage: 2-car
Foundation Type:
  Basement

PLAN DATA

Total Living Area: 2,042
Bedrooms: 3
Baths: 2 1/2
Garage: 2-car
Foundation Type:
  Basement
Features:
  10' ceilings in family
  and living rooms

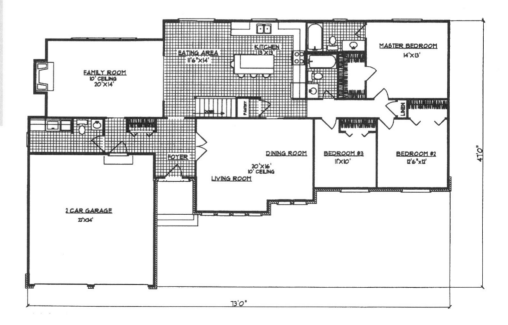

PLAN DATA

Total Living Area: 1,890
Bedrooms: 3
Baths: 2
Garage: 2-car
Foundation Type:
  Crawl space
Features:
  Storage in garage

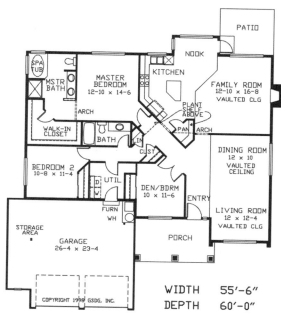

WIDTH 55'-6"
DEPTH 60'-0"

COPYRIGHT 1998 GSDG, INC.

PLAN #562-CHP-1432-A-142

Price Code A

PLAN DATA

Total Living Area: 1,405
Bedrooms: 3
Baths: 2
Foundation Type:
  Slab

Width: 42'
Depth: 51'

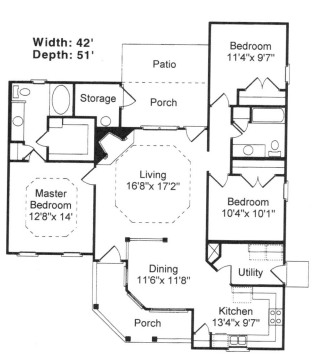

PLAN DATA

Total Living Area: 1,687
Bedrooms: 3
Baths: 2
Garage: 2-car
Foundation Types:
  Slab
  Crawl space
  Walk-out basement
  Basement
Please specify when ordering

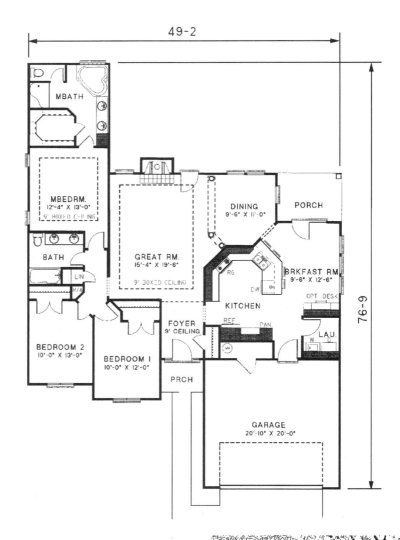

PLAN #562-0315

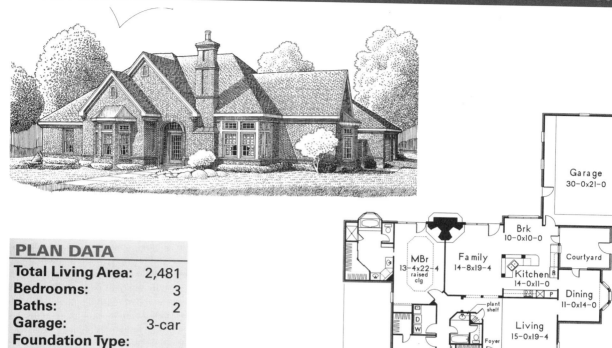

PLAN DATA

Total Living Area:	2,481
Bedrooms:	3
Baths:	2
Garage:	3-car
Foundation Type:	
Slab	

Garage
30-0x21-0

Brk
10-0x10-0

MBr
13-4x22-4
raised
clg

Family
14-8x19-4

Courtyard

Kitchen
14-0x11-0

Dining
11-0x14-0

plant
shelf

Living
15-0x19-4

Foyer

Br 3
11-4x13-0

Br 2
12-0x11-0

79'-8"

74'-4"

PLAN #562-JV-2033-A

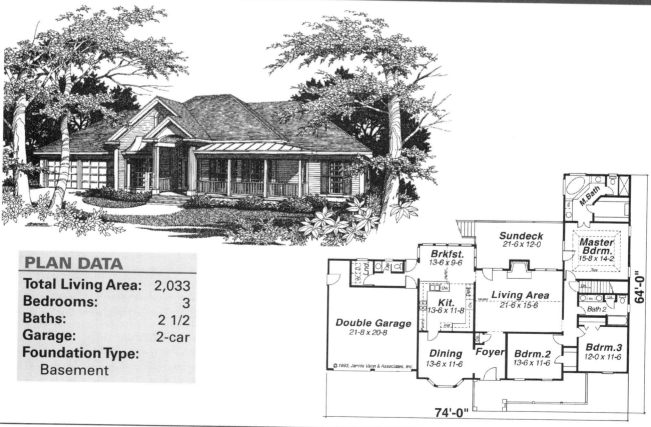

PLAN DATA

Total Living Area:	2,033
Bedrooms:	3
Baths:	2 1/2
Garage:	2-car
Foundation Type:	
Basement	

M.Bath

Sundeck
21-6 x 12-0

Master
Bdrm.
15-8 x 14-2

Brkfst.
13-6 x 9-6

Living Area
21-6 x 15-6

Bath 2

Kit.
13-6 x 11-8

Double Garage
21-8 x 20-8

Dining
13-6 x 11-6

Foyer

Bdrm.2
13-6 x 11-6

Bdrm.3
12-0 x 11-6

© 1993, Jannis Vann & Associates, Inc.

64'-0"

74'-0"

PLAN DATA

Total Living Area: 1,511
Bedrooms: 3
Baths: 2
Garage: 2-car
Foundation Type:
Basement
Features:
- 11' ceiling in great room
- 9' ceiling in dining room

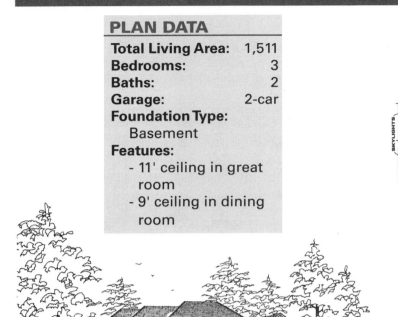

© design basics inc.

First Floor
1,850 Sq. Ft.

PLAN DATA

Total Living Area: 1,896
Bedrooms: 3
Baths: 2 1/2
Garage: 3-car
Foundation Type:
Basement
Features:
Drive-under garage

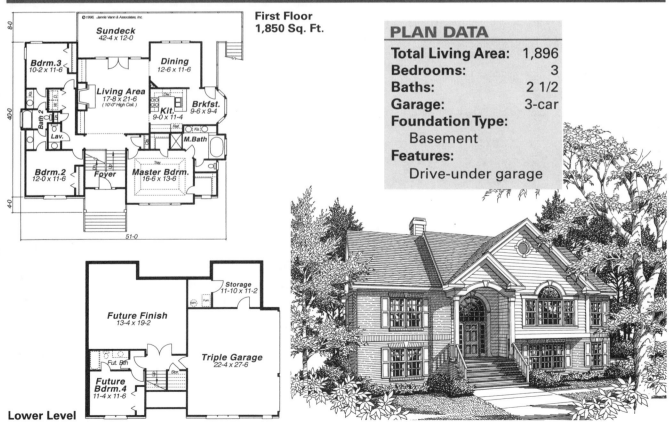

Lower Level

65'-8"

61'-7"

PORCH

M.BATH

BRKFAST
RM.
13'-0" X 12'-0"

M.BED RM.
16'-0" X 13'-0"
10' PAN CEILING

FAMILY RM.
17'-10" X 16'-0"

KITCHEN
13'-0" X 12'-0"

REF.

BED RM. 2
17'-0" X 11'-8"

DW

PAN

LIN

BATH

GALLERY

BATH

8" BOXED
COLUMNS

BED RM. 3
13'-0" X 11'-6"

FRENCH
DOORS

FOYER
10' CEILING

FAMILY
DINING RM.
11'-0" X 13'-6"
11' BOXED
CEILING

LAU.

W

BED RM. 4
11'-0" X 10'-8"

STUDY
11'-6" X 15'-0"

POR.

GARAGE
23'-0" X 22'-0"

PLAN DATA

Total Living Area:	2,439
Bedrooms:	4
Baths:	3
Garage:	2-car
Foundation Types:	

Basement
Crawl space
Walk-out basement
Slab
Please specify when ordering

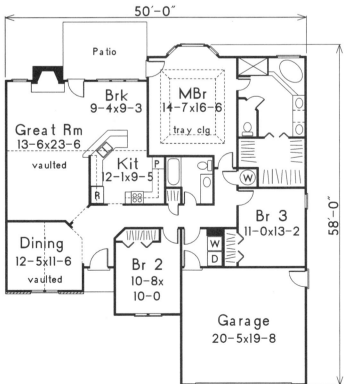

PLAN DATA

Total Living Area:	1,862
Bedrooms:	3
Baths:	2
Garage:	2-car
Foundation Types:	
Slab standard	
Crawl space	

PLAN DATA

Total Living Area:	527
Bedroom:	1
Bath:	1
Foundation Type:	
Crawl space	

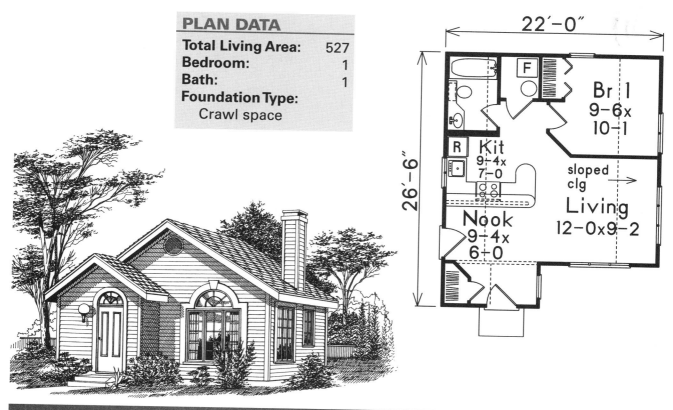

PLAN DATA

Total Living Area:	1,020
Bedrooms:	2
Bath:	1
Foundation Type:	
Slab	

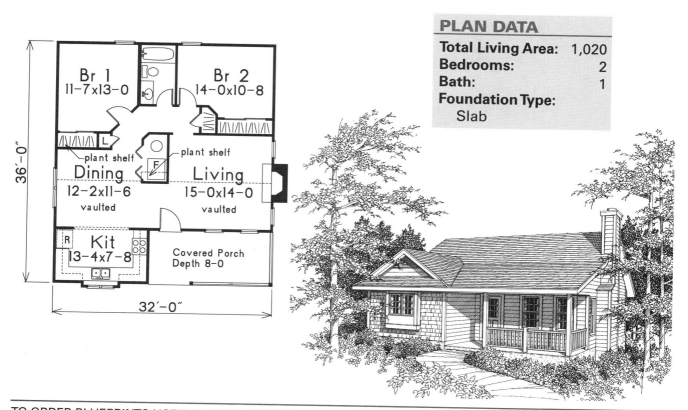

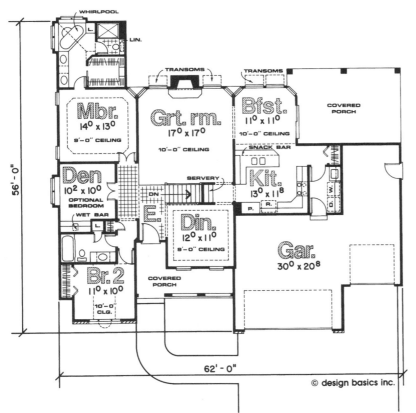

PLAN DATA

Total Living Area: 1,651
Bedrooms: 2
Baths: 2
Garage: 3-car
Foundation Types:
   Slab
   Basement
Please specify when ordering
Features:
   Varied ceiling heights

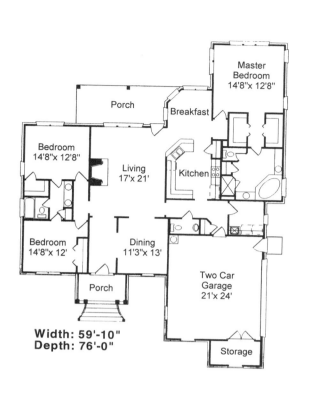

Master
Bedroom
14'8"x 12'8"

Porch

Breakfast

Bedroom
14'8"x 12'8"

Living
17'x 21'

Kitchen

Bedroom
14'8"x 12'

Dining
11'3"x 13'

Two Car
Garage
21'x 24'

Porch

Width: 59'-10"
Depth: 76'-0"

Storage

PLAN DATA

Total Living Area:	2,263
Bedrooms:	3
Baths:	2 1/2
Garage:	2-car
Foundation Types:	
Slab	
Crawl space	

Please specify when ordering

PLAN DATA

Total Living Area:	1,819
Bedrooms:	3
Baths:	2
Garage:	2-car
Foundation Type:	
Basement	
Features:	
9' ceilings	

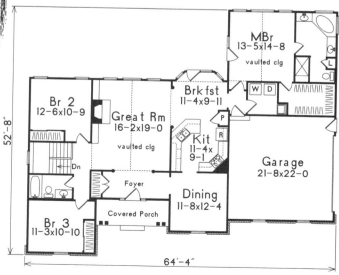

MBr
13-5x14-8
vaulted clg

Br 2
12-6x10-9

Great Rm
16-2x19-0
vaulted clg

Brk fst
11-4x9-11

Kit
11-4x
9-1

Dn

52'-8"

Garage
21-8x22-0

Foyer

Dining
11-8x12-4

Br 3
11-3x10-10

Covered Porch

64'-4"

PLAN #562-0515

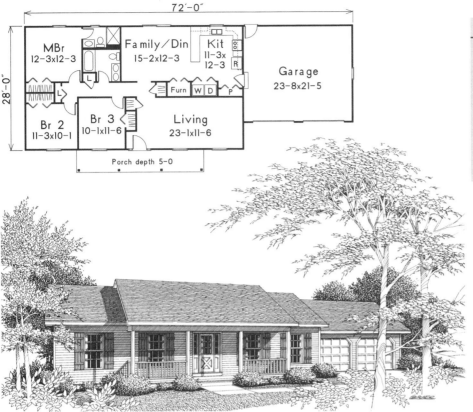

72'-0"

28'-0"

MBr
12-3x12-3

Family/Din
15-2x12-3

Kit
11-3x
12-3

Garage
23-8x21-5

Br 3
10-1x11-6

Living
23-1x11-6

Br 2
11-3x10-1

Furn W D P

R

Porch depth 5-0

PLAN DATA

Total Living Area:	1,344
Bedrooms:	3
Baths:	2
Garage:	2-car
Foundation Types:	

Crawl space standard
Basement
Slab

PLAN #562-0217

PLAN DATA

Total Living Area:	1,360
Bedrooms:	3
Baths:	2
Garage:	2-car
Foundation Types:	

Basement standard
Crawl space
Slab

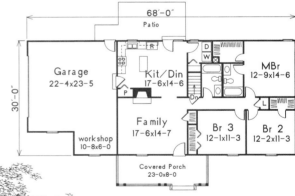

68'-0"

Patio

30'-0"

Garage
22-4x23-5

Kit/Din
17-6x14-6

D
W

MBr
12-9x14-6

Family
17-6x14-7

Br 3
12-1x11-3

Br 2
12-2x11-3

workshop
10-8x6-0

Covered Porch
23-0x8-0

PLAN DATA

Total Living Area: 1,856
Bedrooms: 3
Baths: 2
Garage: 2-car
Foundation Types:
  Basement
  Crawl space
  Slab
Please specify when ordering
Features:
  12' ceilings in foyer,
  and family, living and
  dining rooms

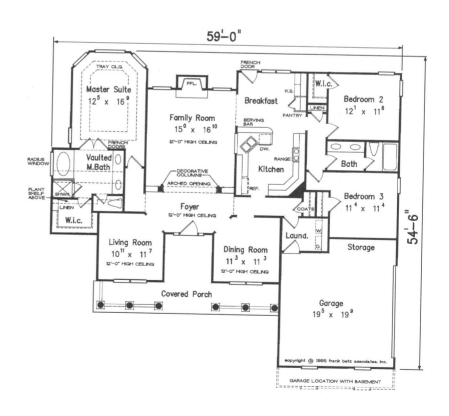

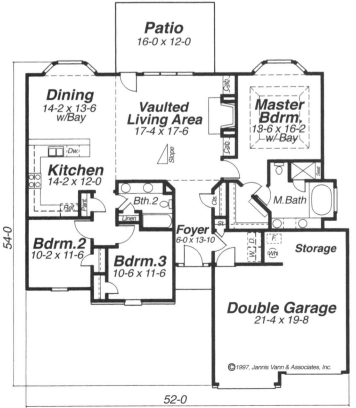

Patio
16-0 x 12-0

Dining
14-2 x 13-6
w/Bay

**Vaulted
Living Area**
17-4 x 17-6

**Master
Bdrm.**
13-6 x 16-2
w/Bay

Kitchen
14-2 x 12-0

Dw.

Slope

Cab.

Cab.

Bth.2

M.Bath

Seat

Ref. *Pant.*

Linen

Cts.

Foyer
6-0 x 13-10

St.

Bdrm.2
10-2 x 11-6

Bdrm.3
10-6 x 11-6

W. D.

F.

WH

Storage

54-0

Double Garage
21-4 x 19-8

© 1997, Jannis Vann & Associates, Inc.

52-0

PLAN DATA

Total Living Area: 1,646
Bedrooms: 3
Baths: 2
Garage: 2-car
Foundation Types:
    Crawl space
    Slab
Please specify when ordering
Features:
    9' ceilings

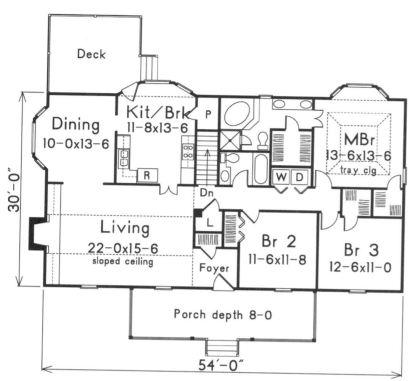

Deck

Dining
10-0x13-6

Kit/Brk
11-8x13-6

P

MBr
13-6x13-6
tray clg

W D

30'-0"

Living
22-0x15-6
sloped ceiling

Dn

L

Br 2
11-6x11-8

Br 3
12-6x11-0

Foyer

Porch depth 8-0

54'-0"

PLAN DATA

Total Living Area:	1,668
Bedrooms:	3
Baths:	2
Garage:	2-car
Foundation Type:	
Basement	
Features:	
Drive-under garage	

PLAN DATA

Total Living Area:	1,630
Bedrooms:	3
Baths:	2
Garage:	2-car
Foundation Type:	
Basement	

PLAN #562-0717

Price Code A

PLAN DATA

Total Living Area:	1,268
Bedrooms:	3
Baths:	2
Garage:	2-car
Foundation Type:	
Basement	

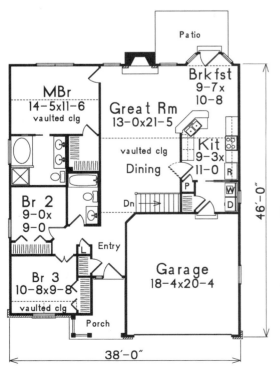

PLAN DATA

Total Living Area:	720
Bedrooms:	2
Bath:	1
Foundation Types:	
Crawl space standard	
Slab	

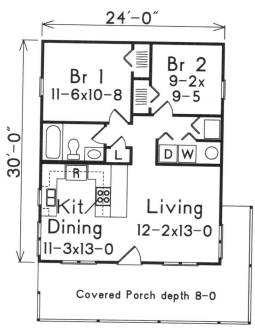

Br 1
11-6x10-8

Br 2
9-2x 9-5

L

D W

R

Kit/Dining
11-3x13-0

Living
12-2x13-0

24'-0"

30'-0"

Covered Porch depth 8-0

44'-0"

60'-8"

BR 2
13/1x10/0

M. BR
12/1x15/4

COVERED DECK

BR 3
9/6x9/7

CLO

BATH

BRKFST
10/0x12/1

KIT
11/6x12/1

DN

LIVING
15/8x13/5

GARAGE
21/5x23/0

COVERED PORCH

PLAN DATA

Total Living Area:	1,231
Bedrooms:	3
Bath:	1
Garage:	2-car
Foundation Type:	
Basement	

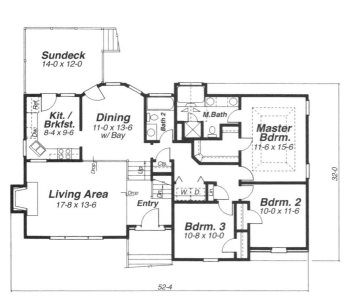

First Floor
1,411 Sq. Ft.

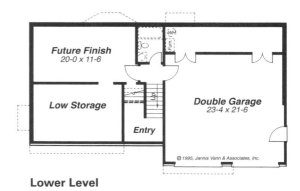

Lower Level

PLAN DATA

Total Living Area:	1,411
Bedrooms:	3
Baths:	2
Garage:	2-car
Foundation Type:	
Basement	
Features:	
Drive-under garage	

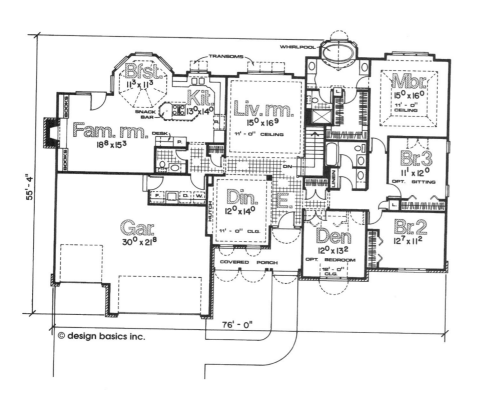

TRANSOMS

WHIRLPOOL

Bfst.
11³ x 11³

Kit.
13⁰ x 14⁰

SNACK BAR

Liv. rm.
15⁰ x 16⁹
11' - 0" CEILING

Mbr.
15⁰ x 16⁰
11' - 0" CEILING

Fam. rm.
18⁸ x 15³

DESK

P

Br. 3
11¹ x 12⁰
OPT. SITTING

DN

LINEN

Din.
12⁰ x 14⁰
11' - 0" CLG.

HUTCH

F.

D.

W.

E.

Den
12⁰ x 13²
OPT. BEDROOM
11' - 0" CLG.

Br. 2
12⁷ x 11²

Gar.
30⁰ x 21⁸

BOOKS

BOOKS

55' - 4"

COVERED PORCH

76' - 0"

© design basics inc.

PLAN DATA

Total Living Area:	2,498
Bedrooms:	3
Baths:	2 1/2
Garage:	3-car
Foundation Type:	
Basement	
Features:	
Varied ceiling heights	

PLAN DATA

Total Living Area:	2,412
Bedrooms:	4
Baths:	2
Garage:	3-car
Foundation Type:	
Walk-out basement	

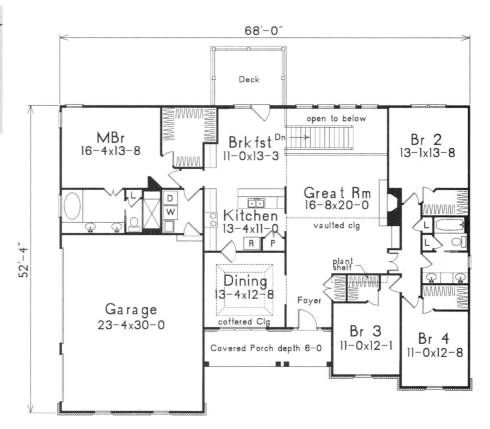

68'-0"

52'-4"

Deck

MBr
16-4x13-8

Brk fst Dn
11-0x13-3

open to below

Br 2
13-1x13-8

L

D
W

Great Rm
16-8x20-0
vaulted clg

Kitchen
13-4x11-0

R P

L

L

plant shelf

Dining
13-4x12-8
coffered Clg

Foyer

Br 3
11-0x12-1

Br 4
11-0x12-8

Garage
23-4x30-0

Covered Porch depth 6-0

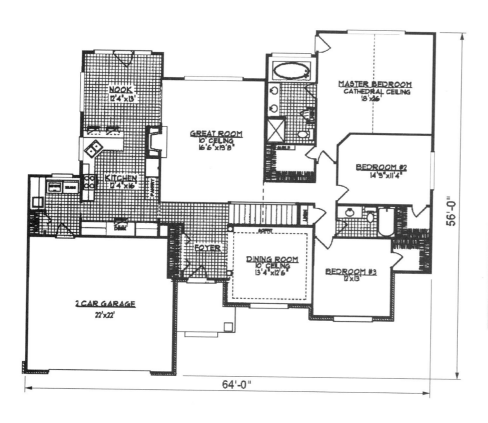

PLAN DATA

Total Living Area:	2,204
Bedrooms:	3
Baths:	2
Garage:	2-car
Foundation Type:	
Basement	
Features:	
Varied ceiling heights	

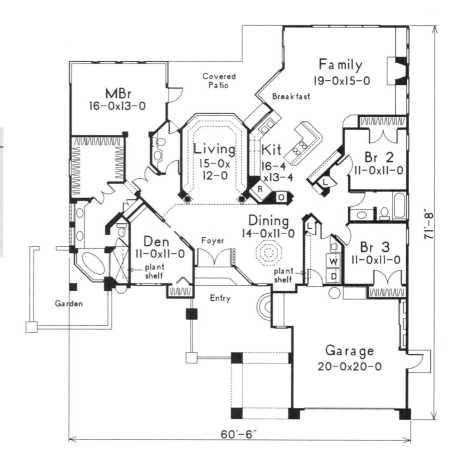

PLAN DATA

Total Living Area: 2,397
Bedrooms: 3
Baths: 2 1/2
Garage: 2-car
Foundation Type:
Slab

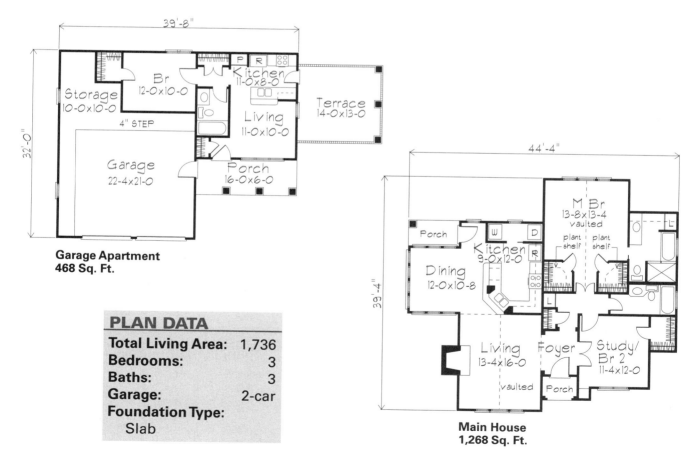

**Garage Apartment
468 Sq. Ft.**

**Main House
1,268 Sq. Ft.**

PLAN DATA

Total Living Area: 1,736
Bedrooms: 3
Baths: 3
Garage: 2-car
Foundation Type:
  Slab

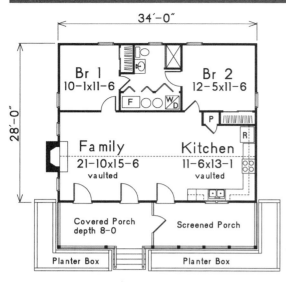

34'-0"

28'-0"

Br 1
10-1x11-6

Br 2
12-5x11-6

F

W
D

P

R

Family
21-10x15-6
vaulted

Kitchen
11-6x13-1
vaulted

Covered Porch
depth 8-0

Screened Porch

Planter Box

Planter Box

PLAN DATA

Total Living Area:	962
Bedrooms:	2
Bath:	1
Foundation Type:	
Crawl space	

PLAN DATA

Total Living Area:	1,263
Bedrooms:	3
Baths:	2
Garage:	2-car
Foundation Types:	
Basement	
Crawl space	
Slab	

Please specify when ordering

Features:
9' ceilings throughout
most of home

42'

MASTER
BEDROOM
12'8" X 13'6"
9' CLG.

PORCH

KITCHEN
9' X 11'6"

DINING
10'6" X 11'6"
9' CLG.

EATING BAR
9' CLG.

PANTRY

OPTIONAL BASEMENT STAIRS

BEDROOM 2
10' X 9'8"
9' CLG.

DN

ARCH

ARCH

ARCH

54'

LIVING ROOM
14'4" X 14'6"

VAULTED CEILING

W
D

BEDROOM 3
10' X 9'8"
9' CLG.

PORCH

GARAGE
21'4" X 19'6"

© W. L. Martin Designs

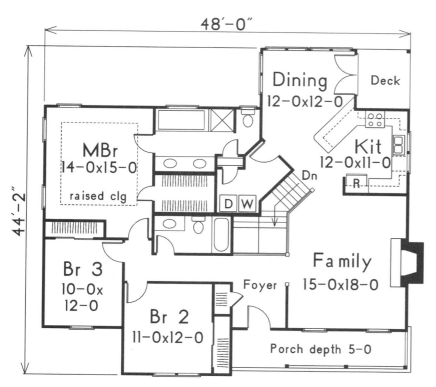

48'-0"

44'-2"

MBr
14-0x15-0
raised clg

Dining
12-0x12-0

Deck

Kit
12-0x11-0

Dn

D W

R

Br 3
10-0x
12-0

Br 2
11-0x12-0

Foyer

Family
15-0x18-0

Porch depth 5-0

PLAN DATA

Total Living Area:	1,631
Bedrooms:	3
Baths:	2
Garage:	2-car
Foundation Type:	
Basement	
Features:	

- 9' ceilings
- Drive-under garage

PLAN DATA

Total Living Area:	1,191
Bedrooms:	3
Baths:	2
Garage:	2-car
Foundation Types:	
Slab	
Crawl space	

Please specify when ordering

Features:
  2" x 6" exterior walls

PLAN #562-JFD-10-1842-2

Price Code C

PLAN DATA

Total Living Area:	1,842
Bedrooms:	3
Baths:	2
Garage:	2-car
Foundation Type:	
Basement	

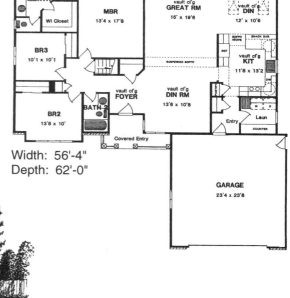

Width: 56'-4"
Depth: 62'-0"

PLAN DATA

Total Living Area: 2,467
Bedrooms: 3
Baths: 3
Garage: 2-car
Foundation Type:
 Slab
Features:
 Varied ceiling heights

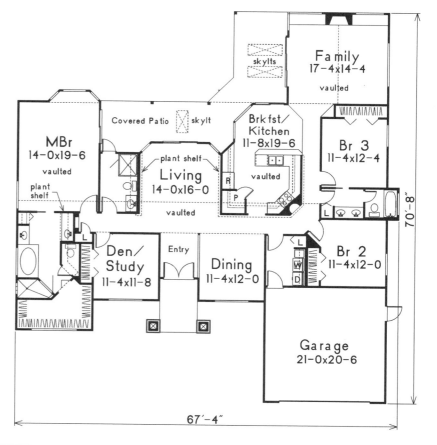

PLAN DATA

Total Living Area:	1,606
Bedrooms:	3
Baths:	2
Garage:	2-car
Foundation Type:	Slab

Width: 50'-0"
Depth: 42'-0"

PLAN #562-0746

Price Code D

PLAN DATA

Total Living Area:	2,516
Bedrooms:	3
Baths:	2 1/2
Garage:	3-car
Foundation Type:	Basement
Features:	12' ceiling in living areas

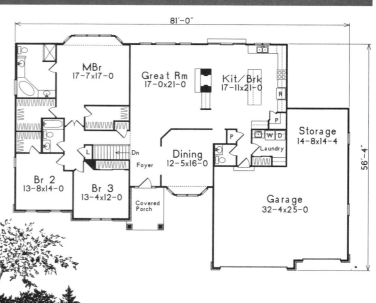

PLAN DATA

Total Living Area: 1,932
Bedrooms: 3
Baths: 2
Garage: 2-car
Foundation Types:
  Plan #562-1275-1
  Basement
  Plan #562-1275-2
  Crawl space & slab

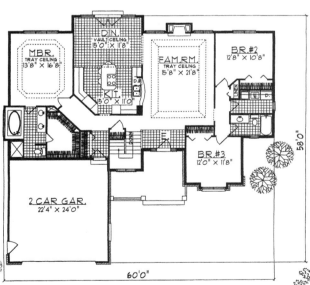

PLAN DATA

Total Living Area: 1,919
Bedrooms: 3
Baths: 2
Garage: 2-car
Foundation Type:
  Basement

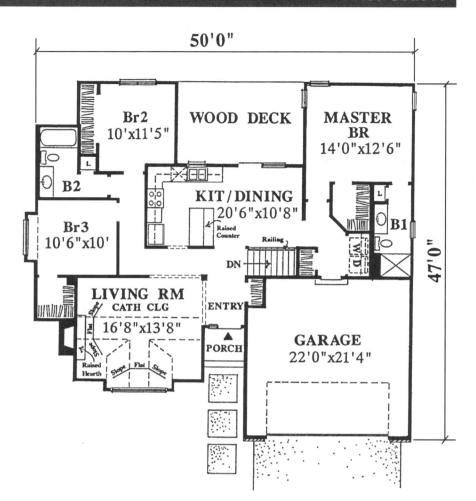

50'0"

47'0"

Br2
10'x11'5"

WOOD DECK

MASTER BR
14'0"x12'6"

B2

KIT/DINING
20'6"x10'8"

Raised Counter

Br3
10'6"x10'

Railing

B1

L

DN

W.D

LIVING RM
CATH CLG
16'8"x13'8"

Slope
Flat
Slope

Raised Hearth

Slope
Flat
Slope

ENTRY

PORCH

GARAGE
22'0"x21'4"

PLAN DATA

Total Living Area:	1,425
Bedrooms:	3
Baths:	2
Garage:	2-car
Foundation Type:	
Basement	

64'-6"

Bedroom 2
12¹ x 11⁶

RADIUS WINDOW

FPL.

RADIUS WINDOW

FRENCH DOOR

PANTRY

Breakfast

DESK

TRAY CEILING

Master Suite
15⁰ x 18⁰

Sitting Room

Family Room
16⁰ x 19⁶
13'-5" HIGH CEILING

PASS THRU

DW.

ISLAND

Kitchen

REF.

PLANT SHELF ABOVE

Bath

LINEN

PLANT SHELF ABOVE

COATS

RANGE

Laund.

FRENCH DOOR

Vaulted M.Bath

Bedroom 3
10¹⁰ x 11⁰

OPT. DOOR

Foyer
13'-5" CEILING

W./ D.

K.S.

SHWR.

W.i.c.

Living Room / Opt. Bedroom 4
11⁰ x 12²

COVERED ENTRY

Dining Room
12¹ x 12⁰
13'-5" HIGH CEILING

STAIRS UP

STAIRS TO OPT. BSMT.

LINEN

W.i.c.

Storage

Garage
21⁰ x 21⁹

copyright © 1995 frank betz associates, inc.

**First Floor
2,193 Sq. Ft.**

W.i.c.

Bath

STAIRS DN

Opt. Bonus
11⁰ x 20⁰

**Optional
Second Floor
400 Sq. Ft.**

PLAN DATA

Total Living Area:	2,193
Bedrooms:	3
Baths:	3
Garage:	2-car

Foundation Types:
 Basement
 Crawl space
 Slab
Please specify when ordering
Features:
 13'-5" ceilings in
 foyer, dining and
 family rooms

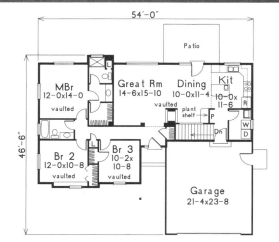

54'-0"

46'-6"

Patio

MBr
12-0x14-0
vaulted

Great Rm
14-6x15-10
vaulted

Dining
10-0x11-4

Kit
10-0x
11-6

plant
shelf

Br 2
12-0x10-8
vaulted

Br 3
10-2x
10-8
vaulted

Garage
21-4x23-8

PLAN DATA

Total Living Area:	1,428
Bedrooms:	3
Baths:	2
Garage:	2-car

Foundation Types:
Basement standard
Crawl space

Features:
- 2" x 6" exterior walls
- 10' ceilings in entry and hallway

PLAN DATA

Total Living Area:	2,648
Bedrooms:	4
Baths:	2
Garage:	2-car

Foundation Types:
Basement
Crawl space
Slab
Please specify when ordering

Features:
Varied ceiling heights

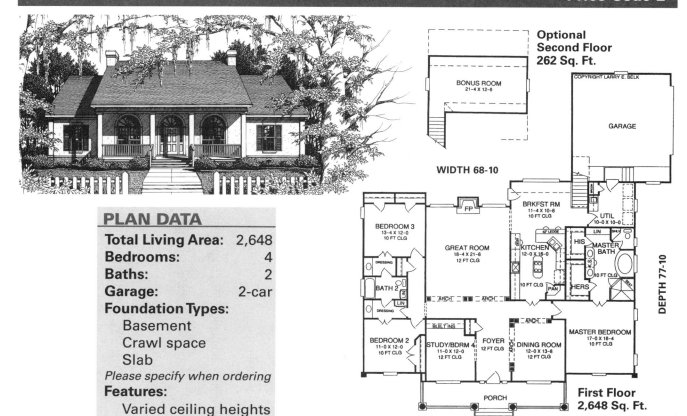

Optional Second Floor 262 Sq. Ft.

BONUS ROOM
21-4 X 12-6

COPYRIGHT LARRY E. BELK

GARAGE

WIDTH 68-10

DEPTH 77-10

BRKFST RM
11-4 X 10-6
10 FT CLG

UTIL
10-0 X 10-0

BEDROOM 3
13-4 X 12-0
10 FT CLG

GREAT ROOM
18-4 X 21-6
12 FT CLG

KITCHEN
12-0 X 15-0

MASTER BATH

10 FT CLG

BATH 2

BEDROOM 2
11-0 X 12-0
10 FT CLG

STUDY/BDRM 4
11-0 X 12-0
12 FT CLG

FOYER
12 FT CLG

DINING ROOM
12-0 X 13-8
12 FT CLG

MASTER BEDROOM
17-0 X 16-4
10 FT CLG

PORCH

First Floor 2,648 Sq. Ft.

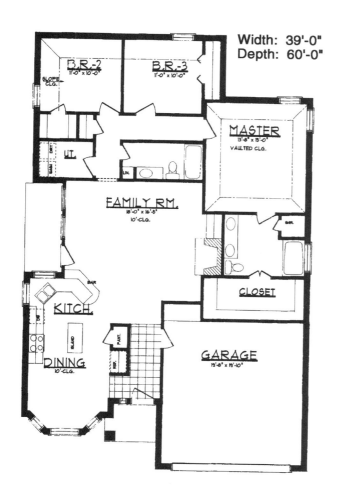

Width: 39'-0"
Depth: 60'-0"

PLAN DATA

Total Living Area:	1,605
Bedrooms:	3
Baths:	2
Garage:	2-car
Foundation Type:	
Slab	

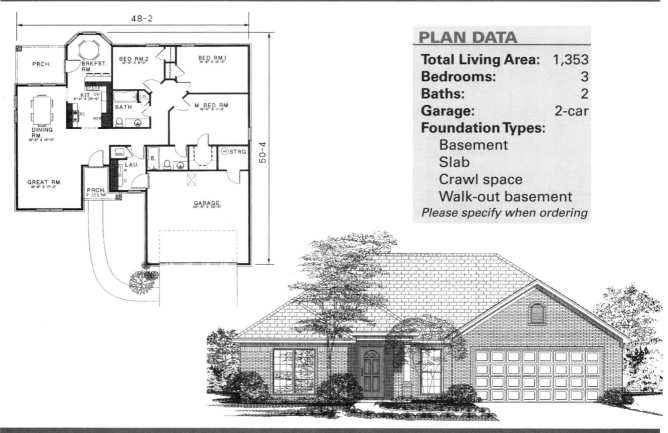

PLAN DATA

Total Living Area: 1,353
Bedrooms: 3
Baths: 2
Garage: 2-car
Foundation Types:
 Basement
 Slab
 Crawl space
 Walk-out basement
Please specify when ordering

PLAN DATA

Total Living Area: 1,370
Bedrooms: 3
Baths: 2
Garage: 2-car
Foundation Type:
 Basement

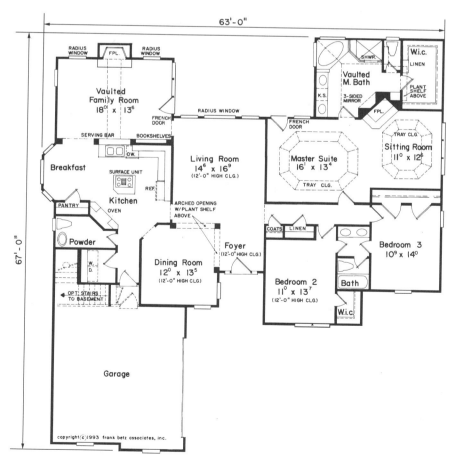

PLAN DATA

Total Living Area:	2,236
Bedrooms:	3
Baths:	2 1/2
Garage:	2-car

Foundation Types:
Basement
Crawl space
Please specify when ordering

Features:
Varied ceiling heights

PLAN DATA

Total Living Area: 1,781
Bedrooms: 3
Baths: 2
Garage: 2-car
Foundation Types:
  Slab
  Crawl space
Please specify when ordering

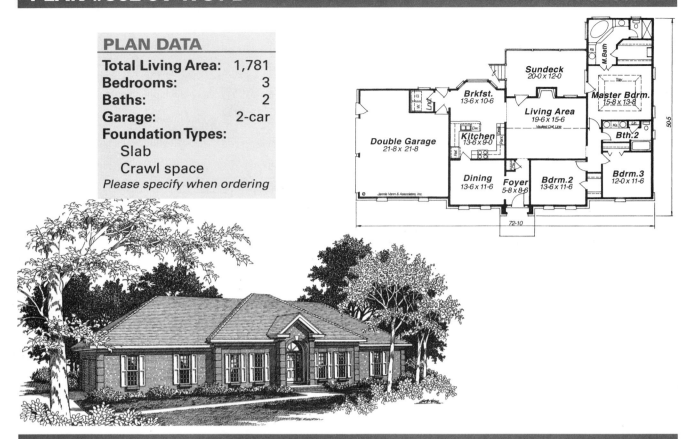

PLAN DATA

Total Living Area: 1,996
Bedrooms: 2
Baths: 2
Garage: 2-car carport
Foundation Type:
  Slab

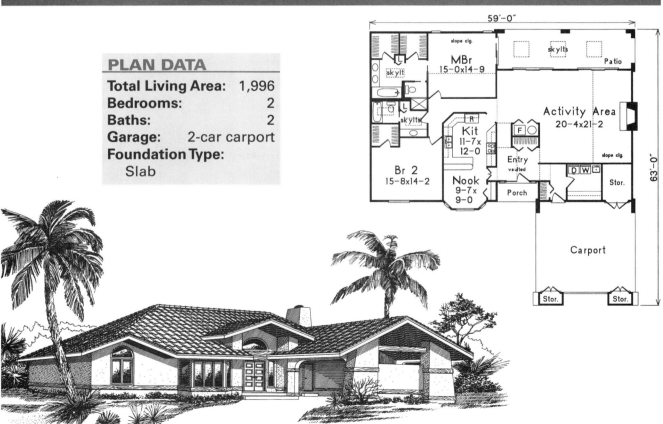

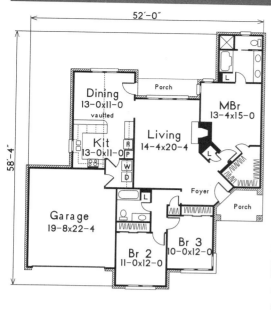

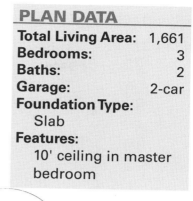

PLAN DATA

Total Living Area:	1,661
Bedrooms:	3
Baths:	2
Garage:	2-car
Foundation Type:	
Slab	
Features:	
10' ceiling in master bedroom	

PLAN #562-DDI-92-103

Price Code AA

PLAN DATA

Total Living Area:	960
Bedrooms:	2
Bath:	1
Foundation Type:	
Crawl space	

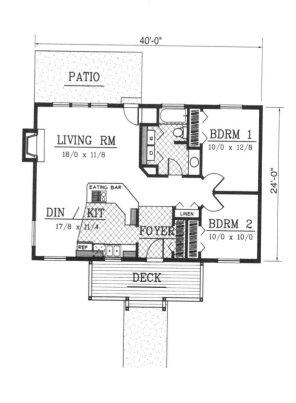

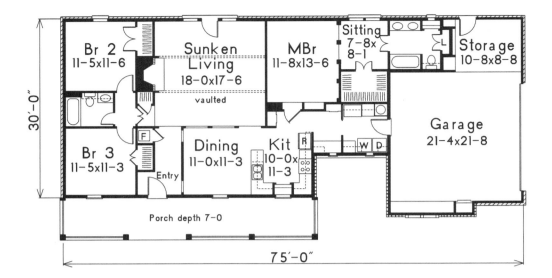

Br 2
11-5x11-6

Sunken Living
18-0x17-6
vaulted

MBr
11-8x13-6

Sitting
7-8x
8-1

Storage
10-8x8-8

Garage
21-4x21-8

Br 3
11-5x11-3

Entry

Dining
11-0x11-3

Kit
10-0x
11-3

30'-0"

Porch depth 7-0

75'-0"

PLAN DATA

Total Living Area:	1,600
Bedrooms:	3
Baths:	2
Garage:	2-car

Foundation Types:
   Slab standard
   Crawl space
   Basement

Features:
   - 2" x 6" exterior walls
   - Sunken living room
     with 16' ceiling

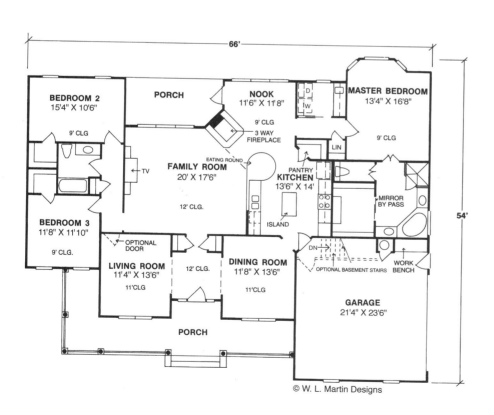

BEDROOM 2
15'4" X 10'6"

9' CLG

PORCH

NOOK
11'6" X 11'8"

9' CLG

MASTER BEDROOM
13'4" X 16'8"

D

W

9' CLG

3 WAY
FIREPLACE

EATING ROUND

FAMILY ROOM
20' X 17'6"

TV

12' CLG.

LIN

PANTRY

KITCHEN
13'6" X 14'

ISLAND

MIRROR
BY PASS

BEDROOM 3
11'8" X 11'10"

9' CLG.

OPTIONAL
DOOR

LIVING ROOM
11'4" X 13'6"

11'CLG

12' CLG.

DINING ROOM
11'8" X 13'6"

11'CLG

DN

OPTIONAL BASEMENT STAIRS

WORK
BENCH

PORCH

GARAGE
21'4" X 23'6"

66'

54'

© W. L. Martin Designs

PLAN DATA

Total Living Area:	2,126
Bedrooms:	3
Baths:	2
Garage:	2-car

Foundation Types:
  Basement
  Crawl space
  Slab
Please specify when ordering
Features:
  Varied ceiling heights

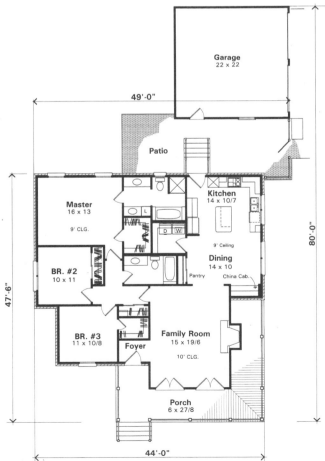

Garage
22 x 22

49'-0"

Patio

Master
16 x 13

9' CLG.

BR. #2
10 x 11

BR. #3
11 x 10/8

Foyer

Kitchen
14 x 10/7

9' Ceiling

Dining
14 x 10

Pantry

China Cab.

Family Room
15 x 19/6

10' CLG.

47'-6"

80'-0"

Porch
6 x 27/8

44'-0"

PLAN DATA

Total Living Area: 1,507
Bedrooms: 3
Baths: 2
Garage: 2-car
Foundation Types:
  Crawl space
  Slab
Please specify when ordering
Features:
  Varied ceiling heights

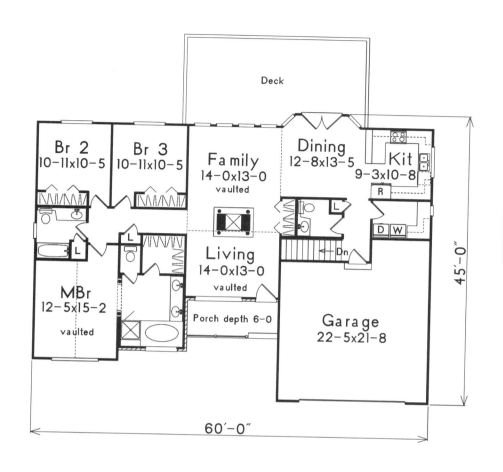

Deck

Br 2
10-11x10-5

Br 3
10-11x10-5

Family
14-0x13-0
vaulted

Dining
12-8x13-5

Kit
9-3x10-8

R

Living
14-0x13-0
vaulted

L

D W

Dn

MBr
12-5x15-2
vaulted

Porch depth 6-0

Garage
22-5x21-8

45'-0"

60'-0"

PLAN DATA

Total Living Area:	1,684
Bedrooms:	3
Baths:	2 1/2
Garage:	2-car
Foundation Type:	
Basement	

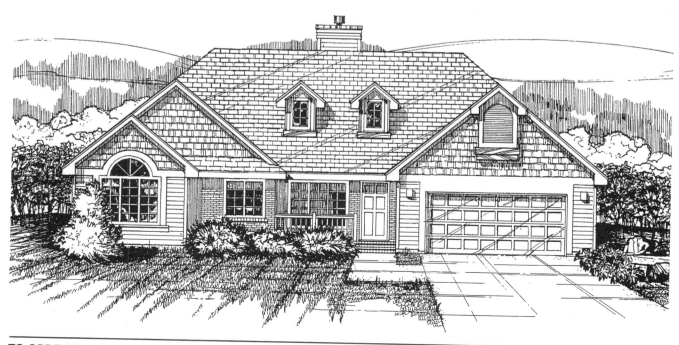

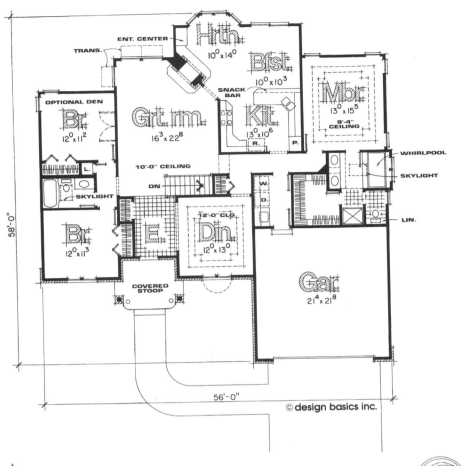

OPTIONAL DEN
Br 12⁰ x 11²

ENT. CENTER
TRANS.

Hrth. 10⁰ x 14⁰

Bfst. 10⁰ x 10³

Mbr 13⁰ x 15⁵
9'-4" CEILING

Grt. rm. 16³ x 22⁸

SNACK BAR

Kit. 13⁰ x 10⁶

WHIRLPOOL

SKYLIGHT

10'-0" CEILING

DN

SKYLIGHT

Br 12⁰ x 11³

L.

W. D.

LIN.

12'-0" CLG
Dn 12⁰ x 13⁰

COVERED STOOP

Gar 21⁴ x 21⁸

58'-0"

56'-0"

© design basics inc.

PLAN DATA

Total Living Area:	1,911
Bedrooms:	3
Baths:	2
Garage:	2-car
Foundation Types:	
Basement	
Slab	
Please specify when ordering	
Features:	
Varied ceiling heights	

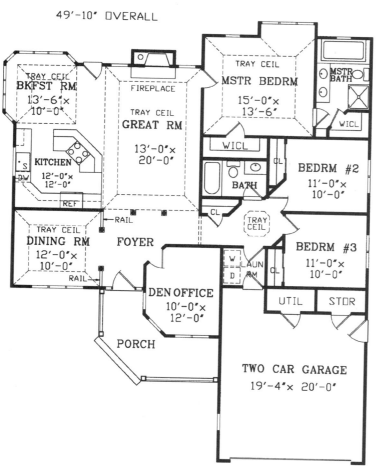

49'-10" OVERALL

60'-6" OVERALL

TRAY CEIL
BKFST RM
13'-6" x
10'-0"

FIREPLACE

TRAY CEIL
GREAT RM
13'-0" x
20'-0"

TRAY CEIL
MSTR BEDRM
15'-0" x
13'-6"

MSTR BATH

WICL

WICL

KITCHEN
12'-0" x
12'-0"

S
DW
REF

BATH
CL

BEDRM #2
11'-0" x
10'-0"

RAIL

CL

TRAY CEIL

TRAY CEIL
DINING RM
12'-0" x
10'-0"

FOYER

BEDRM #3
11'-0" x
10'-0"

W
D
LAUN RM

CL

RAIL

DEN OFFICE
10'-0" x
12'-0"

UTIL

STOR

PORCH

TWO CAR GARAGE
19'-4" x 20'-0"

PLAN DATA

Total Living Area:	1,699
Bedrooms:	3
Baths:	2
Garage:	2-car

Foundation Types:
  Basement
  Crawl space
  Slab
Please specify when ordering

PLAN #562-0693

PLAN DATA
Total Living Area: 1,013
Bedrooms: 2
Bath: 1
Foundation Type:
 Slab

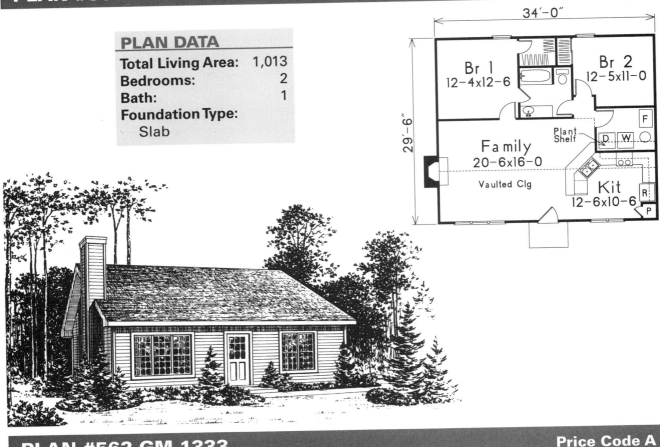

PLAN #562-GM-1333

PLAN DATA
Total Living Area: 1,333
Bedrooms: 3
Baths: 2
Garage: 2-car carport
Foundation Types:
 Slab
 Crawl space
Please specify when ordering
Features:
 Storage in carport

Width: 55'-6"
Depth: 64'-3"

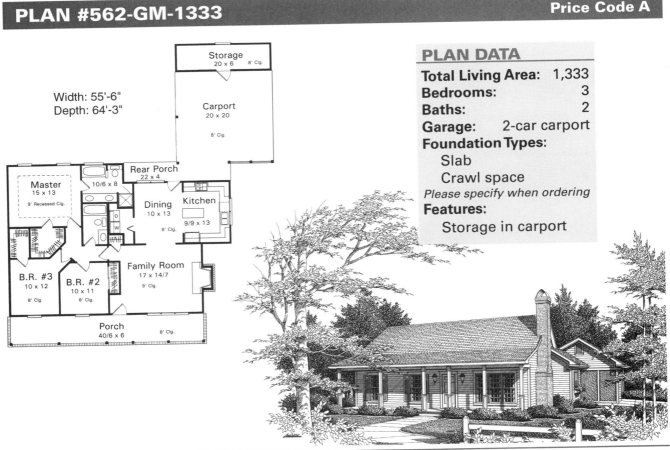

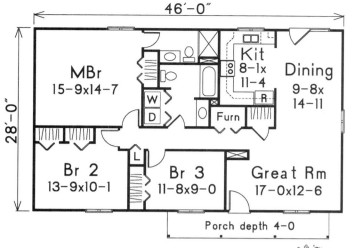

46'-0"

28'-0"

MBr
15-9x14-7

Kit
8-1x
11-4

Dining
9-8x
14-11

W
D

Furn

Br 2
13-9x10-1

L

Br 3
11-8x9-0

Great Rm
17-0x12-6

Porch depth 4-0

PLAN DATA

Total Living Area: 1,288
Bedrooms: 3
Baths: 2
Foundation Types:
  Crawl space standard
  Basement
  Slab

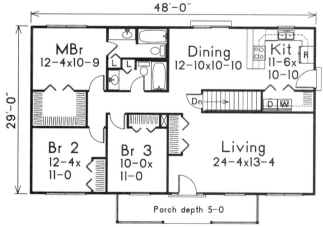

48'-0"

29'-0"

MBr
12-4x10-9

L L

Dining
12-10x10-10

Kit
11-6x
10-10

R

Dn

D W

Br 2
12-4x
11-0

Br 3
10-0x
11-0

Living
24-4x13-4

Porch depth 5-0

PLAN DATA

Total Living Area: 1,364
Bedrooms: 3
Baths: 2
Foundation Types:
  Basement
  Crawl space
Features:
  Optional 2-car garage

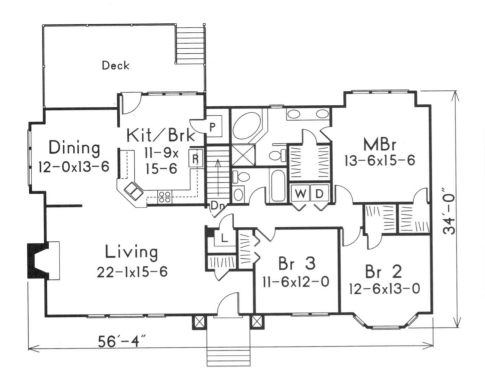

Deck

Dining
12-0x13-6

Kit/Brk
11-9x
15-6

P

R

Dn

MBr
13-6x15-6

W D

Living
22-1x15-6

L

Br 3
11-6x12-0

Br 2
12-6x13-0

34'-0"

56'-4"

PLAN DATA

Total Living Area:	1,698
Bedrooms:	3
Baths:	2
Garage:	2-car
Foundation Type:	
Basement	
Features:	
Drive-under garage	

PLAN DATA

Total Living Area: 1,615
Bedrooms: 3
Baths: 2
Garage: 2-car
Foundation Types:
  Basement
  Crawl space
  Slab
Plese specify when ordering

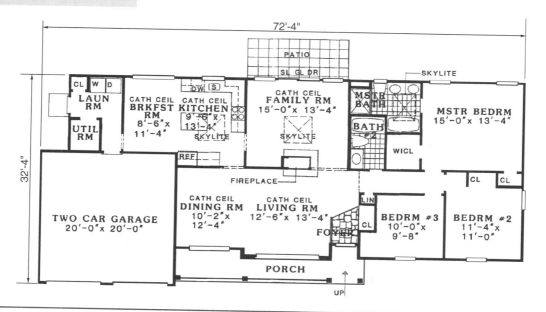

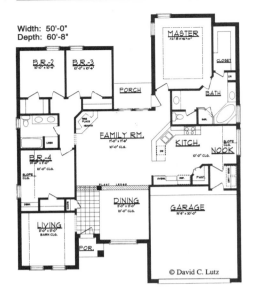

Width: 50'-0"
Depth: 60'-8"

© David C. Lutz

PLAN DATA

Total Living Area:	2,060
Bedrooms:	4
Baths:	2
Garage:	2-car
Foundation Type:	
Slab	
Features:	
Varied ceiling heights	

PLAN DATA

Total Living Area:	1,960
Bedrooms:	3
Baths:	2
Garage:	2-car
Foundation Type:	
Slab	
Features:	
Varied ceiling heights	

Width: 50'-0"
Depth: 60'-8"

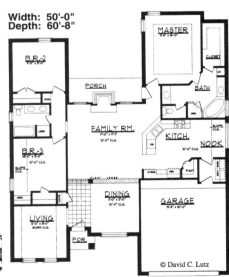

© David C. Lutz

PLAN #562-0694

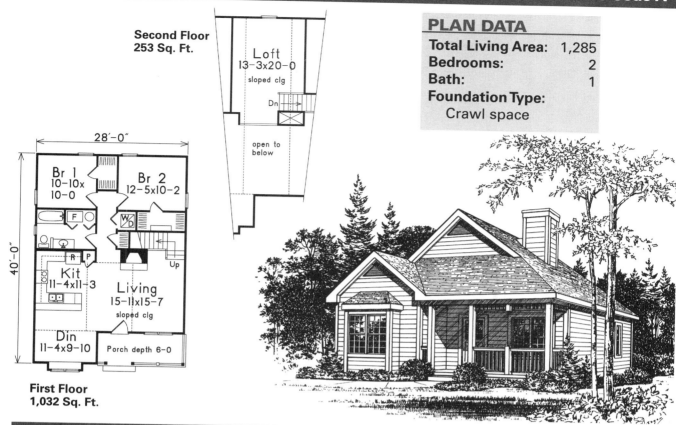

**Second Floor
253 Sq. Ft.**

Loft
13-3x20-0
sloped clg

Dn

open to
below

28'-0"

40'-0"

Br 1
10-10x
10-0

Br 2
12-5x10-2

F

W/D

R   P

Up

Kit
11-4x11-3

Living
15-11x15-7
sloped clg

Din
11-4x9-10

Porch depth 6-0

**First Floor
1,032 Sq. Ft.**

PLAN DATA
Total Living Area: 1,285
Bedrooms: 2
Bath: 1
Foundation Type:
 Crawl space

PLAN #562-1124

Price Code A

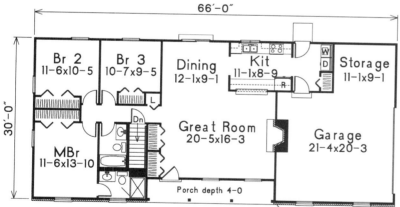

66'-0"

30'-0"

Br 2
11-6x10-5

Br 3
10-7x9-5

Dining
12-1x9-1

Kit
11-1x8-9

W
D

Storage
11-1x9-1

L

Dn

R

MBr
11-6x13-10

Great Room
20-5x16-3

Garage
21-4x20-3

Porch depth 4-0

PLAN DATA
Total Living Area: 1,345
Bedrooms: 3
Baths: 2
Garage: 2-car
Foundation Types:
 Basement
 Crawl space
 Slab
Please specify when ordering

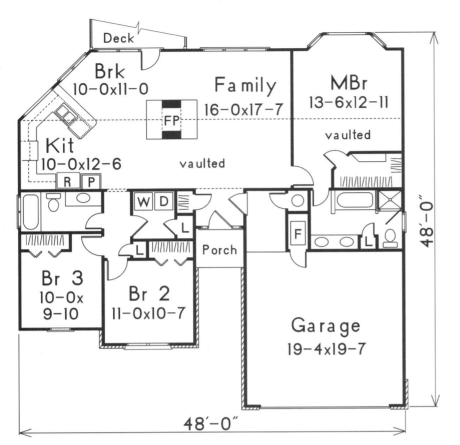

Deck

Brk
10-0x11-0

Family
16-0x17-7

MBr
13-6x12-11

vaulted

FP

Kit
10-0x12-6

vaulted

R P

48'-0"

W D

L

L

Porch

F

L

Br 3
10-0x
9-10

Br 2
11-0x10-7

Garage
19-4x19-7

48'-0"

PLAN DATA

Total Living Area: 1,408
Bedrooms: 3
Baths: 2
Garage: 2-car
Foundation Types:
Crawl space standard
Slab

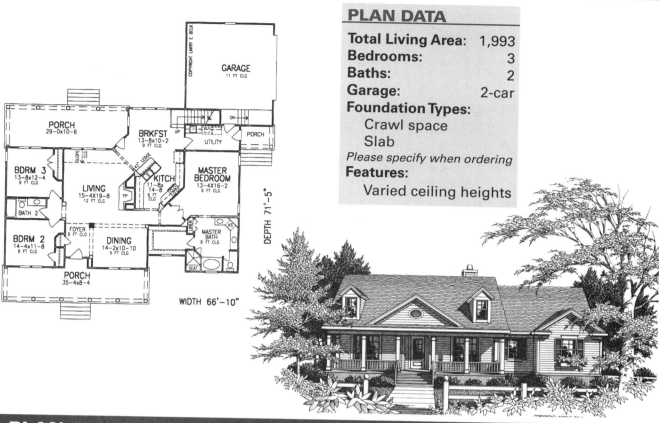

PLAN DATA

Total Living Area: 1,993
Bedrooms: 3
Baths: 2
Garage: 2-car
Foundation Types:
　Crawl space
　Slab
Please specify when ordering
Features:
　Varied ceiling heights

PLAN DATA

Total Living Area: 1,643
Bedrooms: 3
Baths: 2
Garage: 2-car
Foundation Types:
　Basement
　Crawl space
　Slab
Please specify when ordering

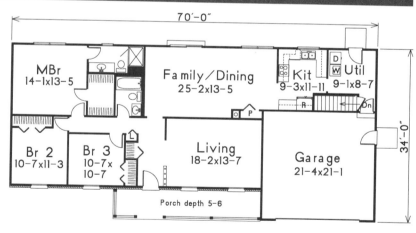

PLAN DATA

Total Living Area: 2,018
Bedrooms: 3
Baths: 2
Garage: 2-car
Foundation Types:
  Basement
  Crawl space
  Slab
Please specify when ordering
Features:
  Varied ceiling heights

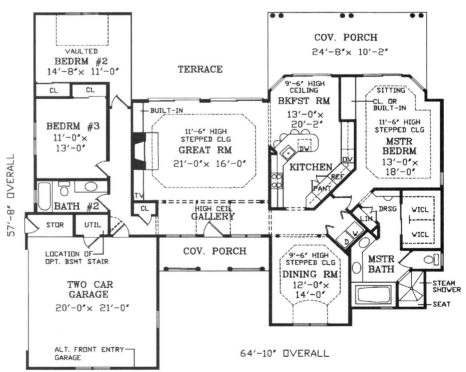

PLAN DATA

Total Living Area: 1,730
Bedrooms: 3
Baths: 2
Garage: 2-car
Foundation Type:
Partial basement/
crawl space

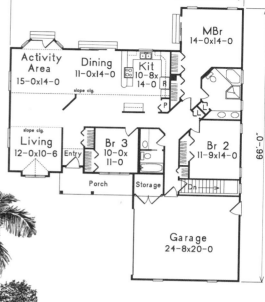

PLAN DATA

Total Living Area: 1,000
Bedrooms: 3
Bath: 1
Foundation Types:
Crawl space standard
Basement
Slab

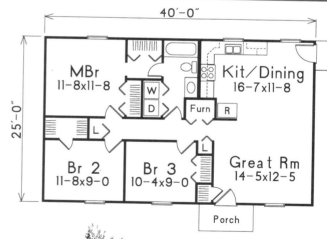

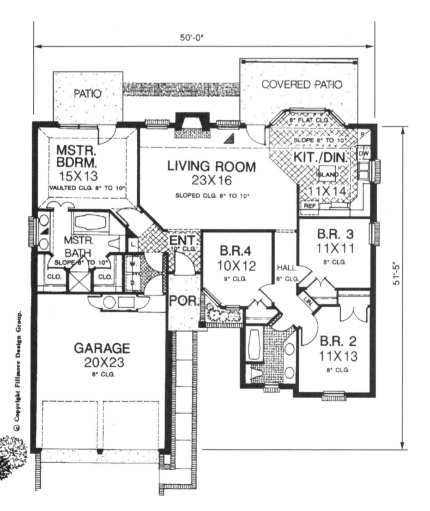

50'-0"

PATIO

COVERED PATIO

MSTR. BDRM.
15X13
VAULTED CLG. 8" TO 10"

LIVING ROOM
23X16
SLOPED CLG. 8" TO 10"

KIT./DIN.
8" FLAT CLG.
SLOPE 8" TO 10"
ISLAND
11X14
REF

MSTR. BATH
SLOPE 8" TO 10"
CLO.   CLO.
W.   D.

ENT.
10" CLG.

B.R.4
10X12
9" CLG.

HALL
8" CLG.

B.R. 3
11X11
8" CLG.

POR.

B.R. 2
11X13
8" CLG.

GARAGE
20X23
8" CLG.

51'-5"

© Copyright Fillmore Design Group.

PLAN DATA

Total Living Area: 1,584
Bedrooms: 4
Baths: 2
Garage: 2-car
Foundation Type:
  Slab
Features:
  Varied ceiling heights

PLAN DATA

Total Living Area: 2,109
Bedrooms: 3
Baths: 2
Garage: 2-car
Foundation Types:
  Slab standard
  Crawl space
Features:
  12' ceilings in living
  and dining rooms

Rear View

PLAN DATA

Total Living Area:	2,334
Bedrooms:	3
Baths:	2
Garage:	2-car
Foundation Type:	
Walk-out basement	

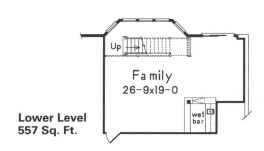

Family
26-9x19-0

Up

wet bar

Lower Level
557 Sq. Ft.

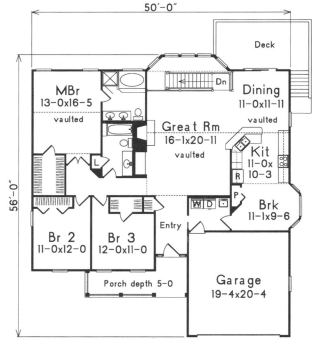

50'-0"

Deck

MBr
13-0x16-5
vaulted

Dining
11-0x11-11
vaulted

Great Rm
16-1x20-11
vaulted

Kit
11-0x
10-3

Dn

56'-0"

L

R

Br 2
11-0x12-0

Br 3
12-0x11-0

Entry

W D

P

Brk
11-1x9-6

Porch depth 5-0

Garage
19-4x20-4

First Floor
1,777 Sq. Ft.

83'-0"

42'-0"

Covered Porch

Brk
11-5x12-0

Atrium Below

Dn

Great Rm
16-0x16-10
vaulted

MBr
16-0x14-0
vaulted

Garage
29-4x21-4

Kit
11-5x
12-0

vaulted

Dining
11-0x11-6

Br 3
11-1x13-3

Br 2
11-0x12-9

Porch
27-8x5-0

PLAN DATA

Total Living Area:	1,721
Bedrooms:	3
Baths:	2
Garage:	3-car

Foundation Types:
Walk-out basement
standard
Crawl space
Slab

Rear View

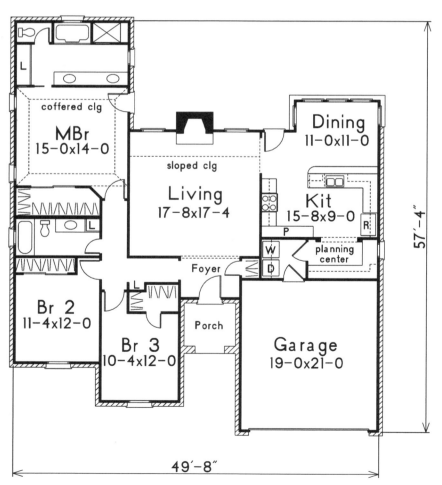

PLAN DATA

Total Living Area:	1,770
Bedrooms:	3
Baths:	2
Garage:	2-car
Foundation Type:	
Slab	

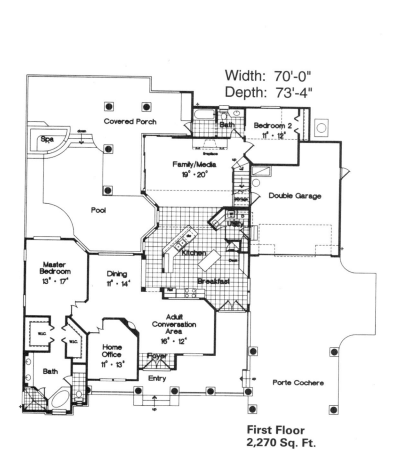

Width: 70'-0"
Depth: 73'-4"

Covered Porch

Spa

Pool

Bath

Bedroom 2
11' · 12'

Family/Media
19' · 20'

Double Garage

Master
Bedroom
13' · 17'

Dining
11' · 14'

Kitchen

Breakfast

Utility

Adult
Conversation
Area
16' · 12'

W.I.C.

W.I.C.

Home
Office
11' · 13'

Bath

Foyer

Entry

Porte Cochere

**First Floor
2,270 Sq. Ft.**

**Second Floor
461 Sq. Ft.**

Attic

Balcony

storage

storage

Bedroom 3
14' · 26'

W.I.C.

storage

storage

PLAN DATA

Total Living Area:	2,731
Bedrooms:	3
Baths:	3
Garage:	2-car
Foundation Type:	
Slab	

PLAN DATA

Total Living Area: 2,483
Bedrooms: 3
Baths: 2
Garage: 2-car
Foundation Type:
  Basement

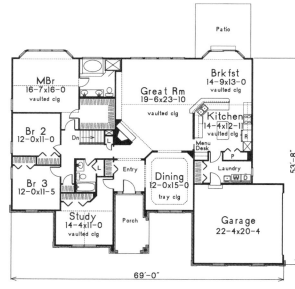

PLAN #562-0477

Price Code AA

PLAN DATA

Total Living Area: 1,140
Bedrooms: 3
Baths: 2
Garage: 2-car
Foundation Type:
  Basement
Features:
  Drive-under garage

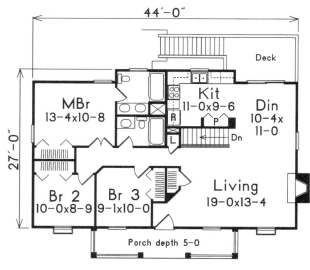

PLAN #562-0195

PLAN DATA

Total Living Area:	988
Bedrooms:	3
Bath:	1
Garage:	1-car
Foundation Types:	
Basement standard	
Crawl space	

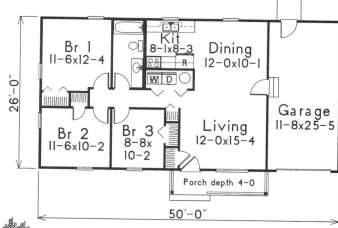

Br 1
11-6x12-4

Kit
8-1x8-3

Dining
12-0x10-1

W D

Br 2
11-6x10-2

Br 3
8-8x
10-2

Living
12-0x15-4

Garage
11-8x25-5

26'-0"

Porch depth 4-0

50'-0"

PLAN #562-VL1267

PLAN DATA

Total Living Area:	1,267
Bedrooms:	3
Baths:	2
Garage:	2-car
Foundation Types:	
Slab	
Crawl space	
Please specify when ordering	
Features:	
10' vaulted ceiling in great room	

52'

49'

PATIO

BEDRM
11 × 11

MASTER SUITE
15 × 12

BATH

UTIL

KITCHEN
10 × 11

DINING
10 × 11

CLOS

BATH

STORAGE

CLOSET

GREAT RM
15 × 17

BEDRM
11 × 11

GARAGE
22 × 21

PORCH

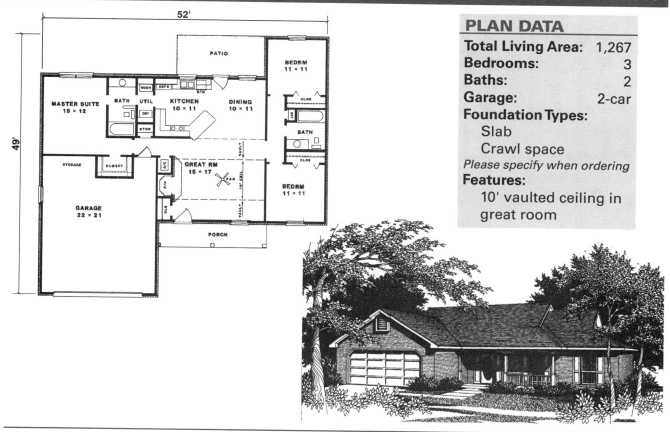

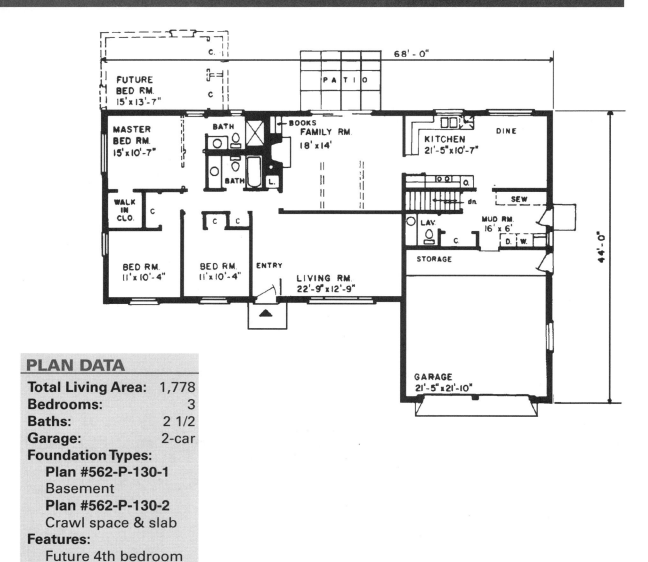

68' - 0"

FUTURE BED RM. 15'x13'-7"

PATIO

MASTER BED RM. 15'x10'-7"

BATH

BOOKS

FAMILY RM. 18'x14'

KITCHEN 21'-5"x10'-7"

DINE

BATH

WALK IN CLO.

C

SEW

dn

MUD RM. 16' x 6'

44'-0"

BED RM. 11'x10'-4"

BED RM. 11'x10'-4"

ENTRY

LIVING RM. 22'-9"x12'-9"

LAV.

STORAGE

D. W.

GARAGE 21'-5"x21'-10"

PLAN DATA

Total Living Area: 1,778
Bedrooms: 3
Baths: 2 1/2
Garage: 2-car
Foundation Types:
   Plan #562-P-130-1
   Basement
   Plan #562-P-130-2
   Crawl space & slab
Features:
   Future 4th bedroom
   has 266 sq. ft.

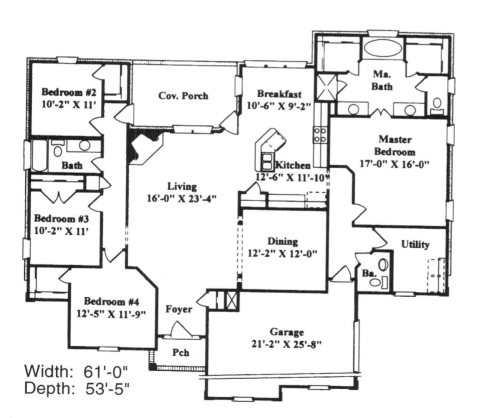

Bedroom #2
10'-2" X 11'

Cov. Porch

Breakfast
10'-6" X 9'-2"

Ma.
Bath

Bath

Master
Bedroom
17'-0" X 16'-0"

Living
16'-0" X 23'-4"

Kitchen
12'-6" X 11'-10"

Bedroom #3
10'-2" X 11'

Dining
12'-2" X 12'-0"

Utility

Bedroom #4
12'-5" X 11'-9"

Foyer

Ba.

Pch

Garage
21'-2" X 25'-8"

Width: 61'-0"
Depth: 53'-5"

PLAN DATA

Total Living Area:	2,246
Bedrooms:	4
Baths:	2 1/2
Garage:	2-car
Foundation Type:	
Slab	

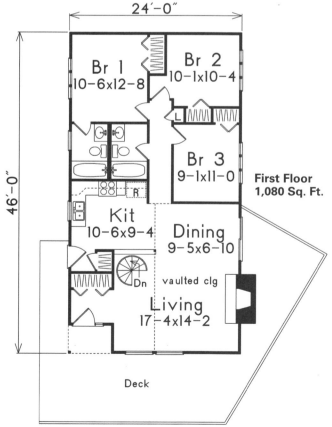

24'-0"

46'-0"

Br 1
10-6x12-8

Br 2
10-1x10-4

Br 3
9-1x11-0

**First Floor
1,080 Sq. Ft.**

L

Kit
10-6x9-4

Dining
9-5x6-10

R

Dn

vaulted clg

Living
17-4x14-2

Deck

PLAN DATA

Total Living Area: 1,584
Bedrooms: 3
Baths: 2
Foundation Types:
  Basement standard
  Slab
  Crawl space

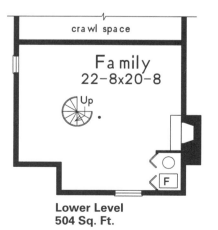

crawl space

Family
22-8x20-8

Up

F

**Lower Level
504 Sq. Ft.**

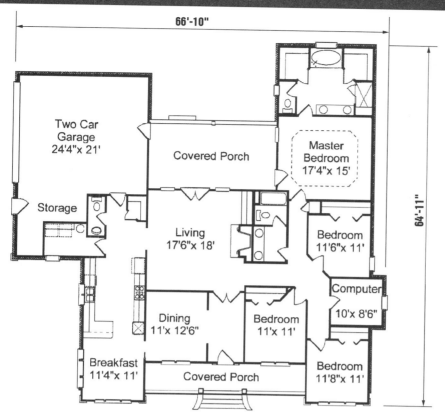

Two Car Garage
24'4"x 21'

Storage

Covered Porch

Master Bedroom
17'4"x 15'

Living
17'6"x 18'

Bedroom
11'6"x 11'

Computer
10'x 8'6"

Dining
11'x 12'6"

Bedroom
11'x 11'

Breakfast
11'4"x 11'

Covered Porch

Bedroom
11'8"x 11'

66'-10"

64'-11"

PLAN DATA

Total Living Area:	2,450
Bedrooms:	4
Baths:	2 1/2
Garage:	2-car
Foundation Type:	
Basement	

PLAN DATA

Total Living Area: 3,671
Bedrooms: 3
Baths: 2 full, 2 half
Garage: 4-car
Foundation Type:
  Crawl space
Features:
  Varied ceiling heights

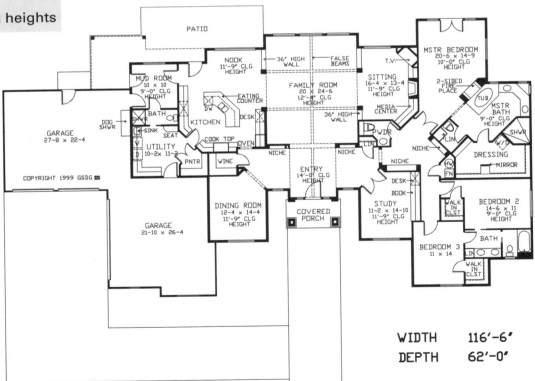

WIDTH 116'-6'
DEPTH 62'-0'

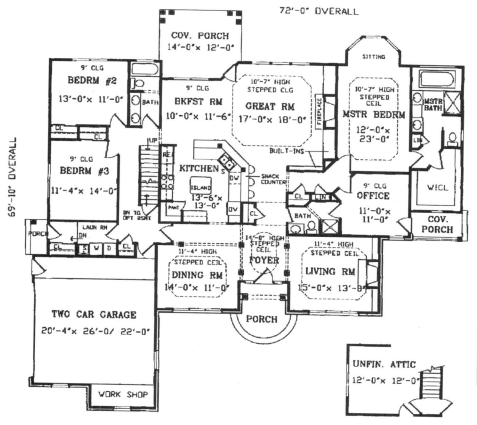

72'-0" OVERALL

COV. PORCH
14'-0"x 12'-0"

9' CLG
BEDRM #2
13'-0"x 11'-0"

BATH

BKFST RM
9' CLG
10'-0"x 11'-6"

10'-7" HIGH
STEPPED CLG
GREAT RM
17'-0"x 18'-0"

SITTING

10'-7" HIGH
STEPPED CEIL
MSTR BEDRM
12'-0"x
23'-0"

MSTR
BATH

CL   CL

FIREPLACE

BUILT-INS

9' CLG
BEDRM #3
11'-4"x 14'-0"

UP

KITCHEN

ISLAND
13'-6"x
13'-0"

DW
SNACK
COUNTER

WICL

9' CLG
OFFICE
11'-0"x
11'-0"

CL LIN

OV

CL

BATH

COV.
PORCH

PORCH

LAUN RM
DN
S W D
CL   CL

DN TO
OPT BSMT

PANT

14'-0" HIGH
STEPPED CEIL
FOYER

11'-4" HIGH
STEPPED CEIL
DINING RM
14'-0"x 11'-0"

11'-4" HIGH
STEPPED CEIL
LIVING RM
15'-0"x 13'-0"

TWO CAR GARAGE
20'-4"x 26'-0/ 22'-0"

PORCH

WORK SHOP

UNFIN. ATTIC
12'-0"x 12'-0"

69'-10" OVERALL

PLAN DATA

Total Living Area: 2,585
Bedrooms: 3
Baths: 2 1/2
Garage: 2-car
Foundation Types:
  Basement
  Crawl space
  Slab
Please specify when ordering

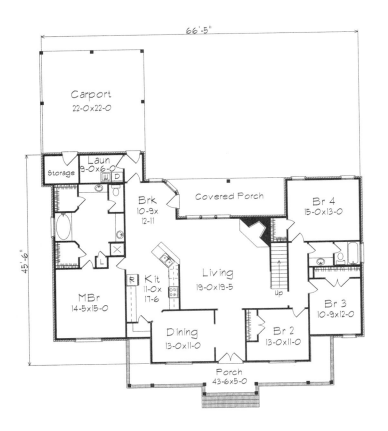

Carport
22-0x22-0

Laun
9-0x6-0

Storage

W D

Brk
10-9x
12-11

Covered Porch

Br 4
15-0x13-0

Kit
11-0x
17-6

Living
19-0x19-5

Up

MBr
14-5x15-0

Br 3
10-9x12-0

Dining
13-0x11-0

Br 2
13-0x11-0

Porch
43-6x5-0

66'-5"

45'-6"

PLAN DATA

Total Living Area: 2,365
Bedrooms: 4
Baths: 2
Garage: 2-car carport
Foundation Type:
  Slab
Features:
  9' ceilings

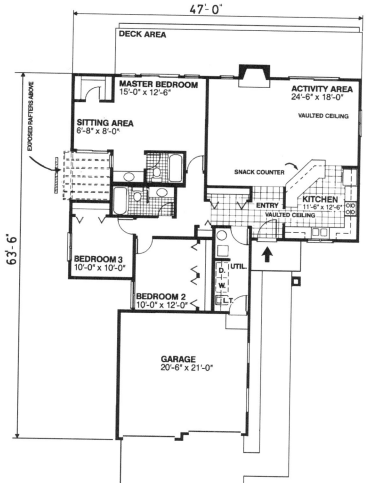

47'-0"

DECK AREA

EXPOSED RAFTERS ABOVE

63'-6"

MASTER BEDROOM
15'-0" x 12'-6"

ACTIVITY AREA
24'-6" x 18'-0"

VAULTED CEILING

SITTING AREA
6'-8" x 8'-0"

SNACK COUNTER

KITCHEN
11'-6" x 12'-6"

ENTRY

VAULTED CEILING

BEDROOM 3
10'-0" x 10'-0"

D. UTIL.

W.

L.T.

BEDROOM 2
10'-0" x 12'-0"

GARAGE
20'-6" x 21'-0"

PLAN DATA

Total Living Area: 1,533
Bedrooms: 3
Baths: 2
Garage: 2-car
Foundation Types:
  Plan #562-1276-1
  Partial basement/
  crawl space
  Plan #562-1276-2
  Slab

PLAN #562-FB1119

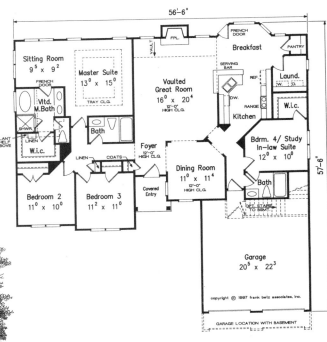

PLAN DATA

Total Living Area: 1,915
Bedrooms: 4
Baths: 3
Garage: 2-car
Foundation Types:
   Basement
   Crawl space
Please specify when ordering
Features:
   Varied ceiling heights

PLAN #562-0263

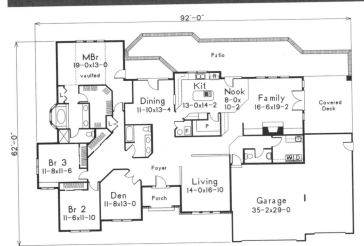

PLAN DATA

Total Living Area: 3,003
Bedrooms: 3
Baths: 2 1/2
Garage: 3-car
Foundation Type:
   Crawl space
Features:
   12' ceiling in living room

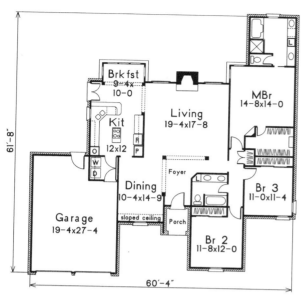

PLAN DATA

Total Living Area:	1,846
Bedrooms:	3
Baths:	2
Garage:	2-car
Foundation Type:	
Slab	
Features:	
Storage in garage	

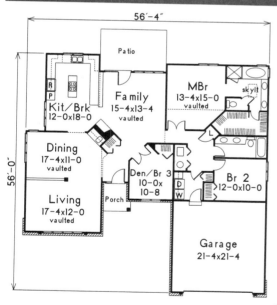

PLAN DATA

Total Living Area:	1,847
Bedrooms:	3
Baths:	2
Garage:	2-car
Foundation Type:	
Slab	

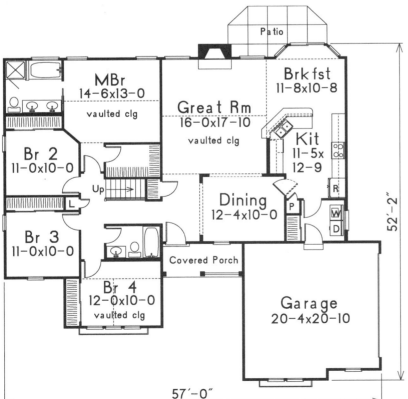

PLAN DATA

Total Living Area:	1,761
Bedrooms:	4
Baths:	2
Garage:	2-car
Foundation Type:	
Basement	

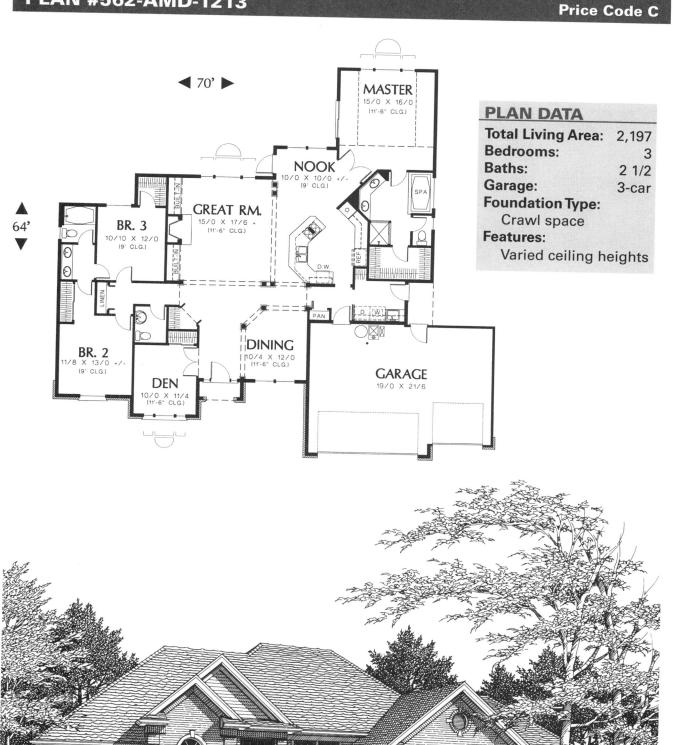

◄ 70' ►

▲
64'
▼

MASTER
15/0 X 16/0
(11'-6" CLG.)

NOOK
10/0 X 10/0 +/-
(9' CLG.)

GREAT RM.
15/0 X 17/6 +
(11'-6" CLG.)

BR. 3
10/10 X 12/0
(9' CLG.)

SPA

REF

D.W.

LINEN

BUILT-IN

BUILT-IN

BUILT-IN

BR. 2
11/8 X 13/0 +/-
(9' CLG.)

DEN
10/0 X 11/4
(11'-6" CLG.)

DINING
10/4 X 12/0
(11'-6" CLG.)

PAN

D W

GARAGE
19/0 X 21/6

PLAN DATA

Total Living Area:	2,197
Bedrooms:	3
Baths:	2 1/2
Garage:	3-car
Foundation Type:	
Crawl space	
Features:	
Varied ceiling heights	

Width: 60'-0"
Depth: 58'-1"

© David C. Lutz

PLAN DATA

Total Living Area:	1,905
Bedrooms:	3
Baths:	2
Garage:	2-car
Foundation Type:	
Slab	
Features:	
Varied ceiling heights	

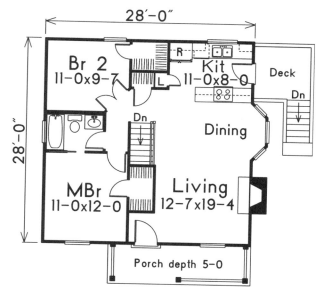

28'-0"

28'-0"

Br 2
11-0x9-7

R

Kit
11-0x8-0

Deck

L

Dn

MBr
11-0x12-0

Dn

Dining

Living
12-7x19-4

Porch depth 5-0

PLAN DATA

Total Living Area:	796
Bedrooms:	2
Bath:	1
Garage:	2-car
Foundation Type:	
Basement	

Features:
- Drive-under garage
- Optional 118 sq. ft. on lower level

PLAN #562-0485

Price Code AA

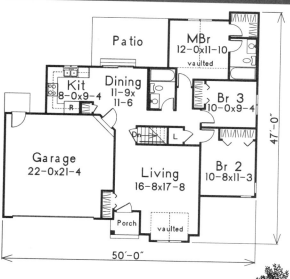

Patio

MBr
12-0x11-10
vaulted

Kit
8-0x9-4

R

Dining
11-9x
11-6

Br 3
10-0x9-4

Dn

L

Garage
22-0x21-4

Living
16-8x17-8

Br 2
10-8x11-3

Porch

vaulted

47'-0"

50'-0"

PLAN DATA

Total Living Area:	1,195
Bedrooms:	3
Baths:	2
Garage:	2-car
Foundation Type:	
Basement	

PLAN #562-1230-1 & 2

Price Code A

PLAN DATA

Total Living Area: 1,288
Bedrooms: 3
Baths: 2
Foundation Types:
   Plan #562-1230-1
   Basement
   Plan #562-1230-2
   Crawl space & slab

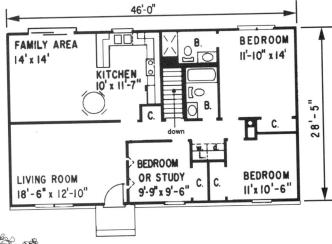

FAMILY AREA 14' x 14'
KITCHEN 10' x 11'-7"
BEDROOM 11'-10" x 14'
46'-0"
28'-5"
down
LIVING ROOM 18'-6" x 12'-10"
BEDROOM OR STUDY 9'-9" x 9'-6"
BEDROOM 11' x 10'-6"
B.
B.
C.
C.
C.
C.
C.

PLAN #562-DL-17104L1

Price Code B

PLAN DATA

Total Living Area: 1,710
Bedrooms: 4
Baths: 2
Garage: 2-car
Foundation Type:
   Slab
Features:
   10' ceiling in family
   room

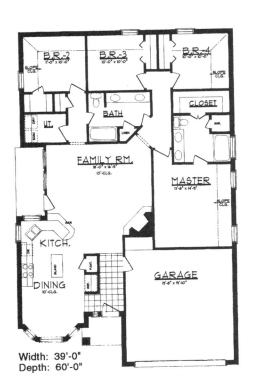

B.R.-2
B.R.-3
B.R.-4
BATH
CLOSET
UT.
FAMILY RM.
MASTER
KITCH.
DINING
GARAGE

Width: 39'-0"
Depth: 60'-0"

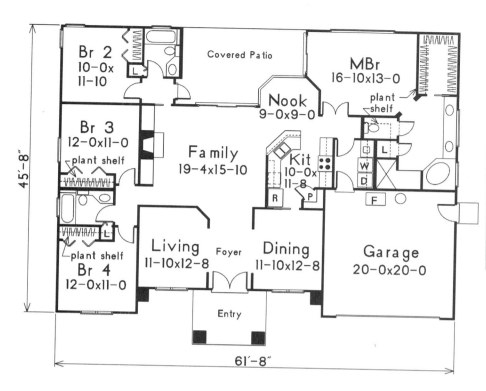

Br 2
10-0x
11-10

Covered Patio

MBr
16-10x13-0

plant shelf

Nook
9-0x9-0

Br 3
12-0x11-0

plant shelf

Family
19-4x15-10

Kit
10-0x
11-8

L

W
D

R

P

F

45-8"

plant shelf

Br 4
12-0x11-0

Living
11-10x12-8

Foyer

Dining
11-10x12-8

Garage
20-0x20-0

Entry

61'-8"

PLAN DATA
Total Living Area: 2,089
Bedrooms: 4
Baths: 3
Garage: 2-car
Foundation Type:
Slab

N.HANSEN.P.L.

PLAN DATA

Total Living Area: 1,474
Bedrooms: 3
Baths: 2
Garage: 2-car detached
Foundation Types:
  Slab
  Crawl space
Please specify when ordering
Features:
  Varied ceiling heights

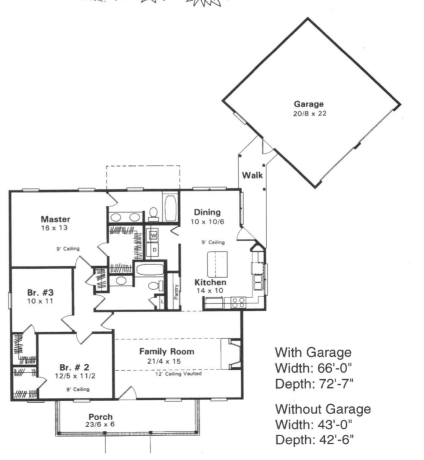

Garage
20/8 x 22

Walk

Master
16 x 13

9' Ceiling

Dining
10 x 10/6

9' Ceiling

Kitchen
14 x 10

Br. #3
10 x 11

Pantry

Family Room
21/4 x 15

12' Ceiling Vaulted

Br. # 2
12/5 x 11/2

9' Ceiling

Porch
23/6 x 6

With Garage
Width: 66'-0"
Depth: 72'-7"

Without Garage
Width: 43'-0"
Depth: 42'-6"

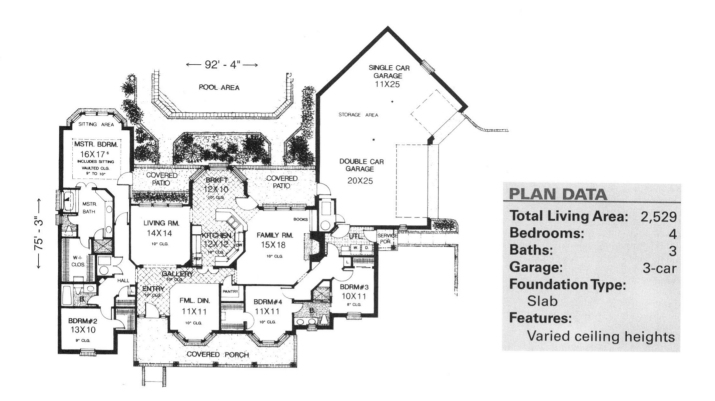

← 92' - 4" →

POOL AREA

SINGLE CAR GARAGE
11X25

STORAGE AREA

DOUBLE CAR GARAGE
20X25

SITTING AREA

MSTR. BDRM.
16X17⁶
INCLUDES SITTING
VAULTED CLG.
9" TO 10"

COVERED PATIO

BRKFT.
12X10
10" CLG.

COVERED PATIO

MSTR. BATH

75' - 3"

LIVING RM.
14X14
10" CLG.

KITCHEN
12X12
10" CLG.

FAMILY RM.
15X18
10" CLG.

BOOKS

UTL.
W D

SERVICE POR.

W-I CLOS.

HALL

GALLERY
10" CLG.

ENTRY
10" CLG.

PANTRY

BDRM#4
11X11
10" CLG.

BDRM#3
10X11
8" CLG.

BDRM#2
13X10
9" CLG.

FML. DIN.
11X11
10" CLG.

B

COVERED PORCH

PLAN DATA

Total Living Area:	2,529
Bedrooms:	4
Baths:	3
Garage:	3-car
Foundation Type:	
Slab	
Features:	
Varied ceiling heights	

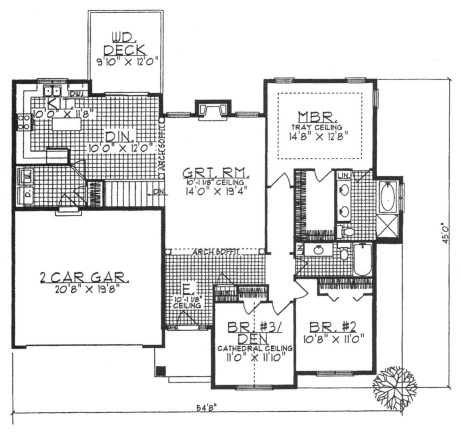

PLAN DATA

Total Living Area:	1,600
Bedrooms:	3
Baths:	2
Garage:	2-car
Foundation Type:	
Basement	

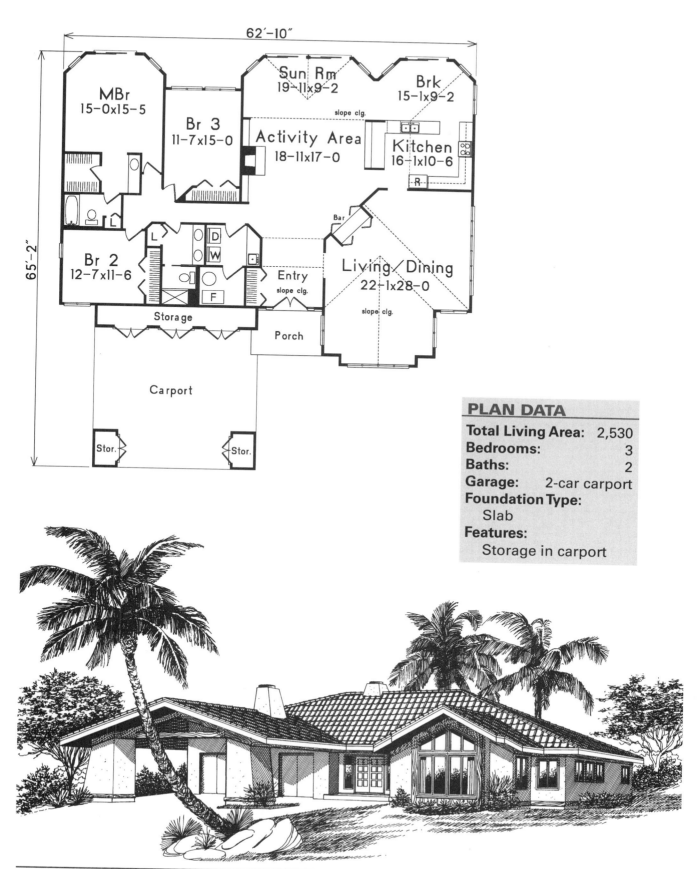

62'-10"

65'-2"

MBr
15-0x15-5

Br 3
11-7x15-0

Sun Rm
19-11x9-2

Brk
15-1x9-2

slope clg.

Activity Area
18-11x17-0

Kitchen
16-1x10-6

R

Bar

Br 2
12-7x11-6

L

D
W

F

Entry

slope clg.

Living/Dining
22-1x28-0

slope clg.

Storage

Porch

Carport

Stor.

Stor.

PLAN DATA

Total Living Area: 2,530
Bedrooms: 3
Baths: 2
Garage: 2-car carport
Foundation Type:
Slab
Features:
Storage in carport

PLAN #562-BF-1718

PLAN DATA

Total Living Area: 2,665
Bedrooms: 3
Baths: 2
Garage: 2-car
Foundation Types:
   Slab
   Crawl space
Please specify when ordering
Features:
   12' ceilings in living
   and dining areas and
   breakfast/kitchen

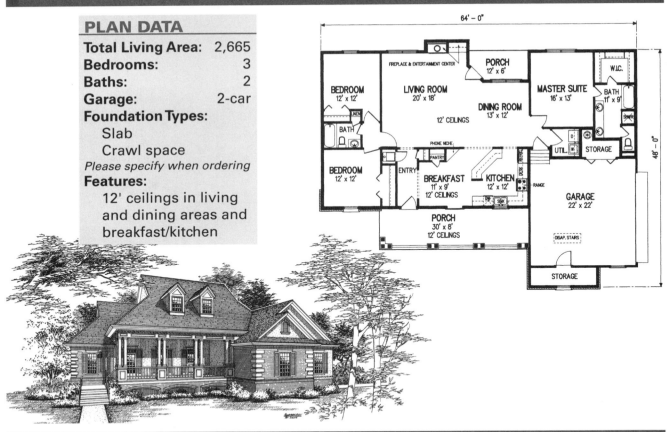

PLAN #562-0799

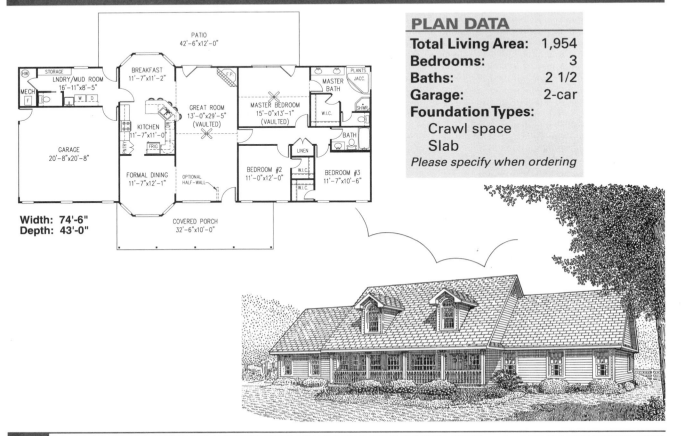

Width: 74'-6"
Depth: 43'-0"

PLAN DATA

Total Living Area: 1,954
Bedrooms: 3
Baths: 2 1/2
Garage: 2-car
Foundation Types:
   Crawl space
   Slab
Please specify when ordering

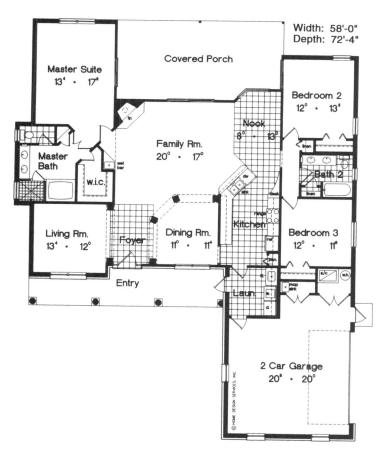

Width: 58'-0"
Depth: 72'-4"

Master Suite
13⁴ · 17⁸

Covered Porch

Bedroom 2
12⁰ · 13⁸

Master Bath

Nook
8⁰ · 13⁰

Family Rm.
20⁰ · 17⁰

wet bar

w.i.c.

Bath 2

Living Rm.
13⁴ · 12⁰

Foyer

Dining Rm.
11⁰ · 11⁴

Kitchen

Bedroom 3
12⁰ · 11⁸

Entry

Laun.

2 Car Garage
20⁸ · 20⁰

PLAN DATA

Total Living Area:	1,993
Bedrooms:	3
Baths:	2
Garage:	2-car
Foundation Type:	
Slab	

Family Room Interior View

PLAN DATA

Total Living Area: 947
Bedrooms: 2
Bath: 1
Foundation Types:
  Crawl space
  Slab
Please specify when ordering
Features:
  Future option has
  392 sq. ft. with 3
  bedrooms and 2 baths

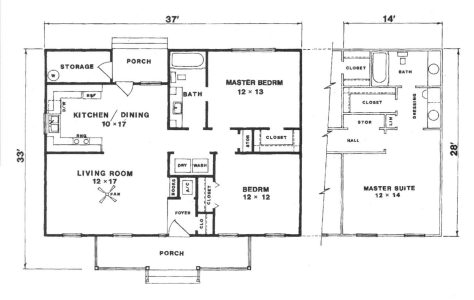

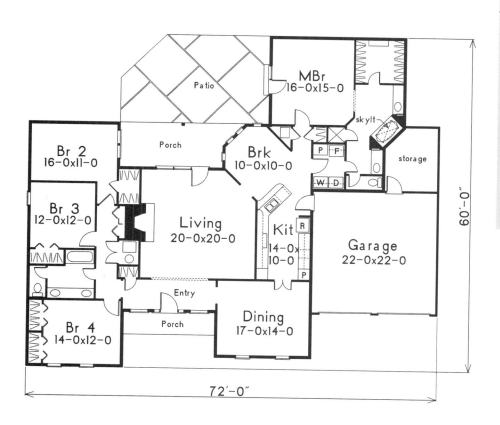

PLAN DATA

Total Living Area: 2,396
Bedrooms: 4
Baths: 2
Garage: 2-car
Foundation Types:
  Slab standard
  Basement
  Crawl space
Features:
  - 2" x 6" exterior walls
  - 12' ceiling in living room

PLAN DATA

Total Living Area: 2,350
Bedrooms: 3
Baths: 2
Garage: 2-car
Foundation Type:
Slab
Features:
- 2" x 6" exterior walls
- 8" x 8" exposed headers at architectural openings

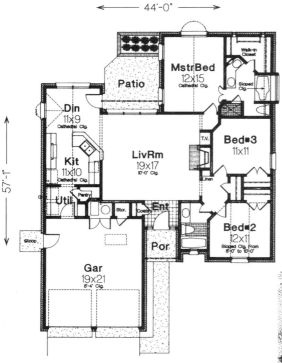

PLAN DATA

Total Living Area: 1,431
Bedrooms: 3
Baths: 2
Garage: 2-car
Foundation Type:
Slab
Features:
10' ceiling in living room

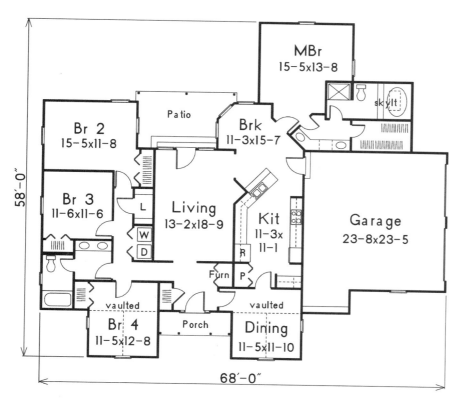

PLAN DATA

Total Living Area: 2,080
Bedrooms: 4
Baths: 2
Garage: 2-car
Foundation Types:
  Crawl space standard
  Basement
  Slab

PLAN DATA

Total Living Area: 1,720
Bedrooms: 3
Baths: 1 full, 2 half
Garage: 2-car
Foundation Type:
   Basement
Features:
   Drive-under garage

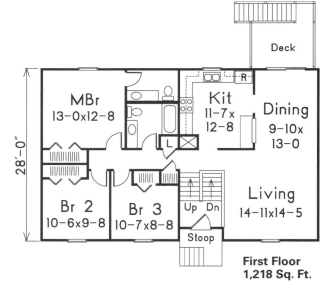

First Floor
1,218 Sq. Ft.

MBr 13-0x12-8
Kit 11-7x 12-8
Dining 9-10x 13-0
Br 2 10-6x9-8
Br 3 10-7x8-8
Living 14-11x14-5
Up Dn
Stoop
Deck
R
L
28'-0"

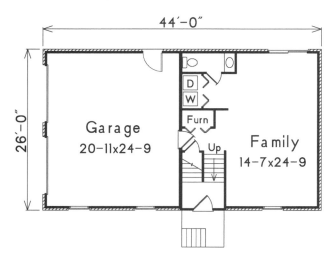

Garage 20-11x24-9
Family 14-7x24-9
Furn
D
W
Up
44'-0"
26'-0"

Lower Level
502 Sq. Ft.

PLAN DATA

Total Living Area:	2,162
Bedrooms:	3
Baths:	2
Garage:	2-car

Foundation Types:
Crawl space
Slab
Please specify when ordering

Features:
10' ceilings in great room, dining room, master suite and foyer

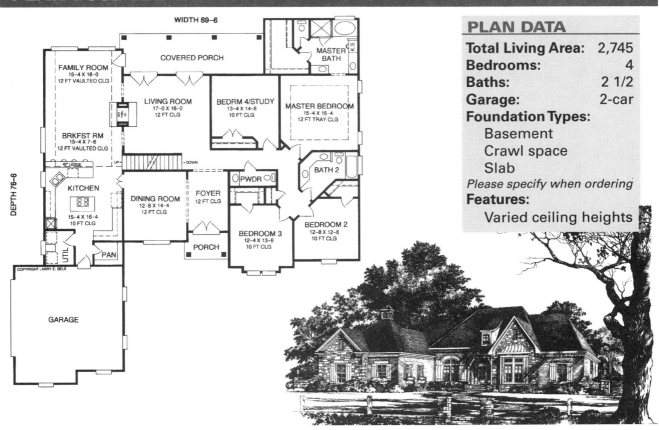

PLAN DATA

Total Living Area:	2,745
Bedrooms:	4
Baths:	2 1/2
Garage:	2-car

Foundation Types:
Basement
Crawl space
Slab
Please specify when ordering

Features:
Varied ceiling heights

PLAN DATA

Total Living Area: 1,604
Bedrooms: 3
Baths: 2
Garage: 2-car
Foundation Type:
  Slab
Features:
  Varied ceiling heights

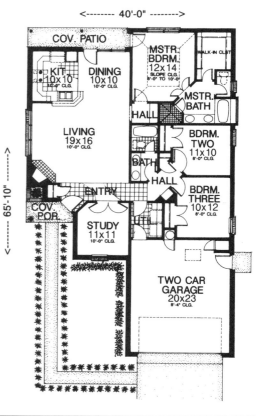

PLAN DATA

Total Living Area: 1,604
Bedrooms: 3
Baths: 2
Garage: 2-car
Foundation Types:
  Basement
  Slab
Please specify when ordering
Features:
  Varied ceiling heights

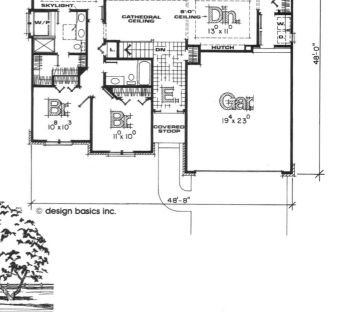

© design basics inc.

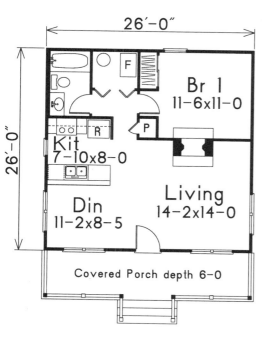

26'-0"

26'-0"

Br 1
11-6x11-0

Kit
7-10x8-0

Din
11-2x8-5

Living
14-2x14-0

F

R

P

Covered Porch depth 6-0

PLAN DATA
Total Living Area: 676
Bedroom: 1
Bath: 1
Foundation Type:
Crawl space

PLAN DATA
Total Living Area: 1,347
Bedrooms: 3
Baths: 2
Garage: 2-car
Foundation Type:
Basement
Features:
- 9'-4" ceiling in master bedroom
- 10' ceiling in great room

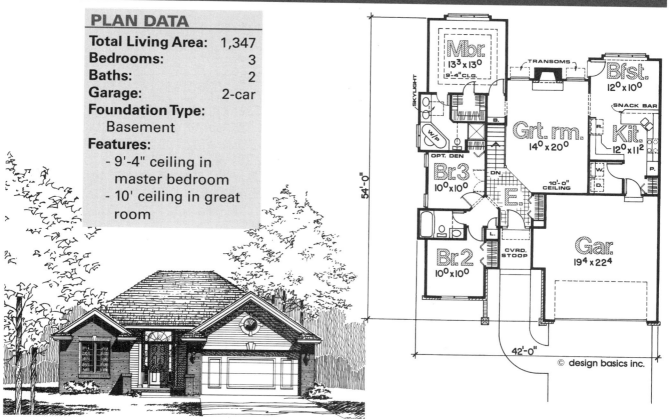

Mbr.
13^3 x 13^0
9'-4" CLG.

TRANSOMS

Bfst.
12^0 x 10^0

SKYLIGHT

B.

SNACK BAR

Grt. rm.
14^0 x 20^0

Kit.
12^0 x 11^2

R.

OPT. DEN

W/P

Br.3
10^0 x 10^0

DN

W.

D.

P.

$10'-0"$ CEILING

L.

Br.2
10^0 x 10^0

CVRD. STOOP

Gar.
19^4 x 22^4

54'-0"

42'-0"

© design basics inc.

PLAN DATA

Total Living Area: 1,393
Bedrooms: 3
Baths: 2
Garage: 2-car detached
Foundation Types:
 Crawl space standard
 Slab

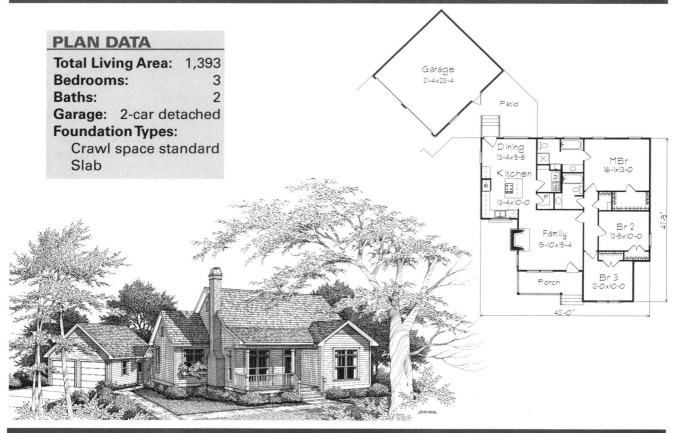

© W. L. Martin Designs

PLAN DATA

Total Living Area: 1,395
Bedrooms: 3
Baths: 2
Garage: 2-car
Foundation Types:
 Basement
 Crawl space
 Slab
Please specify when ordering
Features:
 Varied ceiling heights

PLAN #562-0661

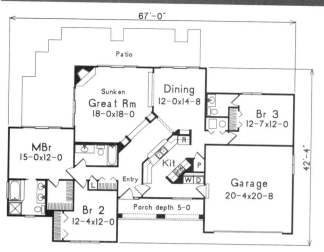

67'-0"

Patio

Sunken
Great Rm
18-0x18-0

Dining
12-0x14-8

Br 3
12-7x12-0

MBr
15-0x12-0

Kit

42'-4"

Br 2
12-4x12-0

Entry

Porch depth 5-0

Garage
20-4x20-8

PLAN DATA

Total Living Area:	1,712
Bedrooms:	3
Baths:	2 1/2
Garage:	2-car
Foundation Type:	
Crawl space	

PLAN #562-0676

PLAN DATA

Total Living Area:	1,367
Bedrooms:	3
Baths:	2
Garage:	2-car
Foundation Types:	
Basement standard	
Slab	

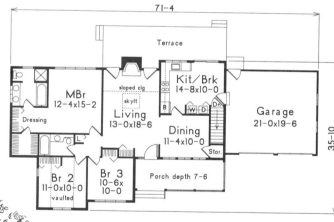

71-4

Terrace

MBr
12-4x15-2

sloped clg
skylt

Kit/Brk
14-8x10-0

Garage
21-0x19-6

35-10

Dressing

Living
13-0x18-6

Dining
11-4x10-0

Stor.

Br 2
11-0x10-0
vaulted

Br 3
10-6x
10-0

Porch depth 7-6

First Floor

PLAN DATA

Total Living Area: 1,617
Bedrooms: 3
Baths: 2
Garage: 2-car
Foundation Types:
   Basement
   Partial crawl space
Please specify when ordering
Features:
   Drive-under garage

Lower Level

PLAN DATA

Total Living Area: 1,984
Bedrooms: 3
Baths: 2
Garage: 2-car
Foundation Types:
  Slab
  Crawl space
Please specify when ordering

PLAN #562-1248

Price Code B

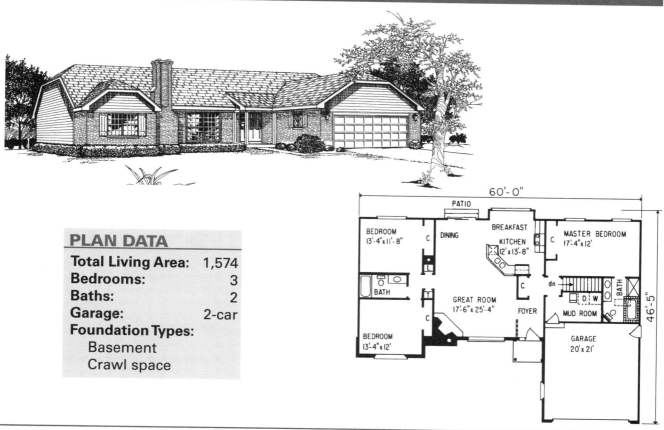

PLAN DATA

Total Living Area: 1,574
Bedrooms: 3
Baths: 2
Garage: 2-car
Foundation Types:
  Basement
  Crawl space

PLAN DATA

Total Living Area: 1,984
Bedrooms: 3
Baths: 2
Garage: 2-car
Foundation Type:
 Basement

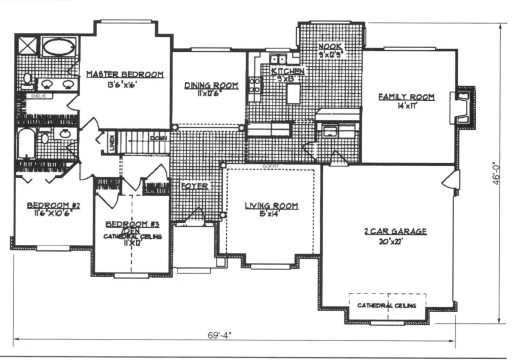

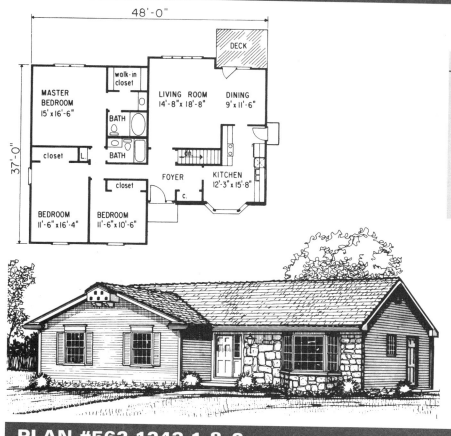

48'-0"

DECK

MASTER BEDROOM
15' x 16'-6"

walk-in closet

LIVING ROOM
14'-8" x 18'-8"

DINING
9' x 11'-6"

BATH

BATH

closet

37'-0"

dn.

FOYER

KITCHEN
12'-3" x 15'-8"

closet

c.

BEDROOM
11'-6" x 16'-4"

BEDROOM
11'-6" x 10'-6"

PLAN DATA

Total Living Area: 1,610
Bedrooms: 3
Baths: 2
Foundation Types:
  Plan #562-1229-1
  Basement
  Plan #562-12292
  Crawl space & slab

PLAN DATA

Total Living Area: 2,705
Bedrooms: 3
Baths: 2 1/2
Garage: 2-car
Foundation Types:
  Plan #562-1243-1
  Partial basement/
  crawl space
  Plan #562-1243-2
  Crawl space

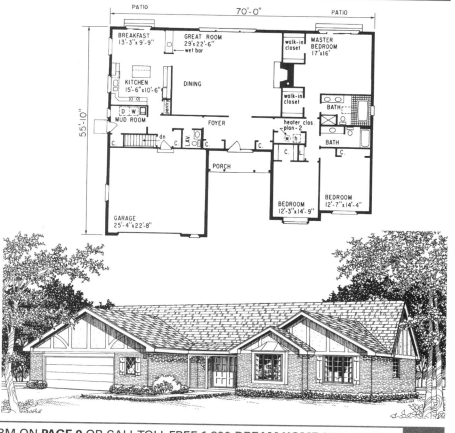

PATIO

70'-0"

PATIO

BREAKFAST
13'-3" x 9'-9"

GREAT ROOM
29' x 22'-6"
← wet bar

walk-in closet

MASTER BEDROOM
17' x 16'

KITCHEN
15'-6" x 10'-6"

DINING

walk-in closet

BATH

55'-10"

D W

pantry

MUD ROOM

FOYER

heater clos.
plan-2

BATH

dn

c.

LAV.

c.

c.

c.

c.

PORCH

BEDROOM
12'-3" x 14'-9"

BEDROOM
12'-7" x 14'-4"

GARAGE
25'-4" x 22'-8"

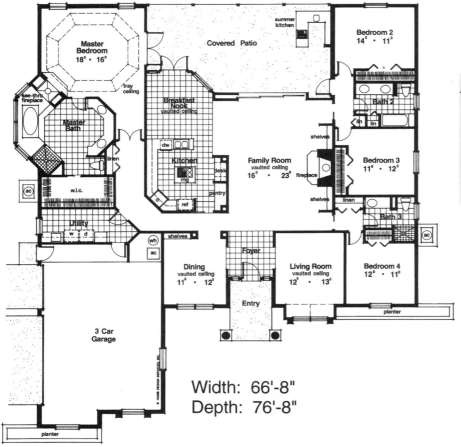

PLAN DATA

Total Living Area:	2,962
Bedrooms:	4
Baths:	3
Garage:	3-car
Foundation Type: Slab	

Width: 66'-8"
Depth: 76'-8"

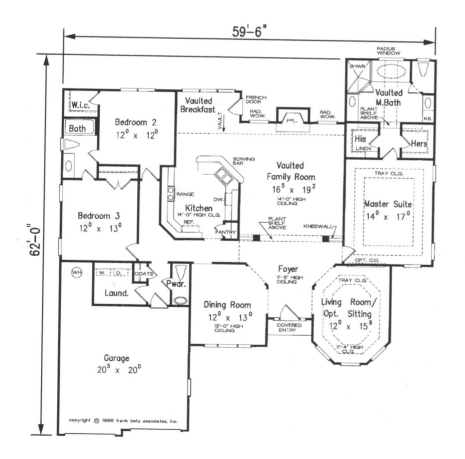

59'-6"

62'-0"

RADIUS WINDOW

W.i.c.

Bath

Bedroom 2
12⁰ x 12⁰

Vaulted Breakfast

FRENCH DOOR

RAD. WDW.

FPL.

RAD. WDW.

SHWR.

Vaulted M.Bath

PLANT SHELF ABOVE

K.S.

His

LINEN

Hers

SERVING BAR

VAULT

Vaulted Family Room
16⁵ x 19²
14'-0" HIGH CEILING

TRAY CLG.

RANGE

DW.

Kitchen
14'-0" HIGH CLG.

REF.

PANTRY

PLANT SHELF ABOVE

KNEEWALL

Master Suite
14⁰ x 17⁰

Bedroom 3
12⁰ x 13⁰

WH

W.

D.

COATS

Pwdr.

Laund.

Foyer
11'-5" HIGH CEILING

OPT. C.Q.

TRAY CLG.

Dining Room
12⁰ x 13⁰
13'-0" HIGH CEILING

COVERED ENTRY

Living Room/
Opt. Sitting
12⁰ x 15⁹
11'-4" HIGH CLG.

Garage
20⁵ x 20⁰

copyright © 1996 frank betz associates, inc.

PLAN DATA

Total Living Area: 2,201
Bedrooms: 3
Baths: 2 1/2
Garage: 2-car
Foundation Types:
   Basement
   Crawl space
Please specify when ordering
Features:
   Varied ceiling heights

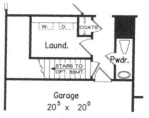

W.

D.

COATS

Laund.

STAIRS TO OPT. BSMT.

Pwdr.

Garage
20⁵ x 20⁰

OPT. BSMT. STAIR LOCATION

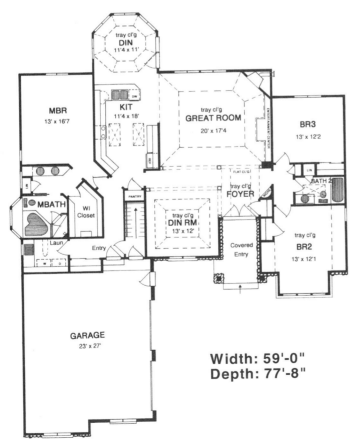

tray cl'g
DIN
11'4 x 11'

MBR
13' x 16'7

KIT
11'4 x 18'

tray cl'g
GREAT ROOM
20' x 17'4

BR3
13' x 12'2

MBATH

WI
Closet

PANTRY

tray cl'g
FOYER

FLAT CL'G

BATH 2

LIN

Laun

Entry

tray cl'g
DIN RM
13' x 12'

Covered
Entry

tray cl'g
BR2
13' x 12'1

W D

GARAGE
23' x 27'

Width: 59'-0"
Depth: 77'-8"

PLAN DATA

Total Living Area:	2,178
Bedrooms:	3
Baths:	2
Garage:	2-car
Foundation Type:	
Basement	

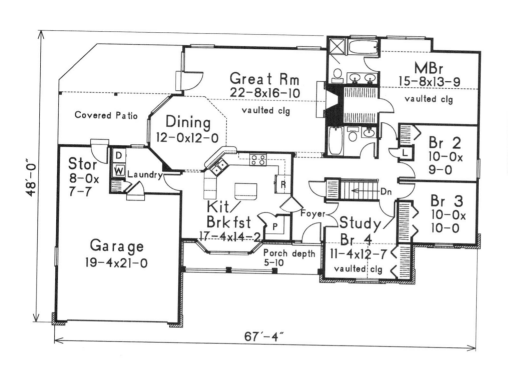

Great Rm
22-8x16-10
vaulted clg

Covered Patio

Dining
12-0x12-0

MBr
15-8x13-9
vaulted clg

Br 2
10-0x
9-0

Stor
8-0x
7-7

D
W
Laundry

Kit/
Brkfst
17-4x14-2

R

L

Dn

Br 3
10-0x
10-0

Foyer

P

Study
Br 4
11-4x12-7
vaulted clg

Garage
19-4x21-0

Porch depth
5-10

48'-0"

67'-4"

PLAN DATA

Total Living Area: 1,791
Bedrooms: 4
Baths: 2
Garage: 2-car
Foundation Type:
  Basement
Features:
  Storage in garage

PLAN #562-FDG-7773

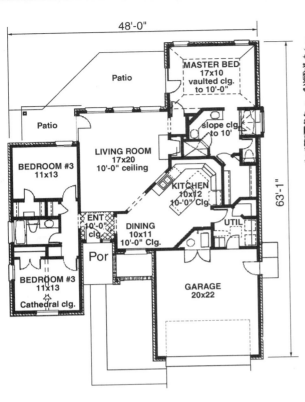

48'-0"

Patio

Patio

MASTER BED
17x10
vaulted clg.
to 10'-0"

slope clg.
to 10'

LIVING ROOM
17x20
10'-0" ceiling

BEDROOM #3
11x13

KITCHEN
10x12
10'-0" Clg.

ENT
10'-0"
clg.

DINING
10x11
10'-0" Clg.

UTIL

Por

BEDROOM #3
11x13
Cathedral clg.

GARAGE
20x22

63'-1"

PLAN DATA

Total Living Area:	1,653
Bedrooms:	3
Baths:	2
Garage:	2-car
Foundation Type:	
Slab	
Features:	
Varied ceiling heights	

PLAN #562-0583

PLAN DATA

Total Living Area:	1,000
Bedrooms:	3
Bath:	1
Foundation Types:	
Crawl space standard	
Basement	
Slab	

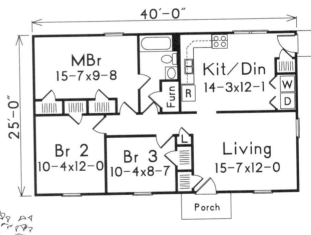

40'-0"

MBr
15-7x9-8

Kit/Din
14-3x12-1

Furn

R

W
D

25'-0"

Br 2
10-4x12-0

Br 3
10-4x8-7

L

Living
15-7x12-0

Porch

PLAN DATA

Total Living Area: 2,049
Bedrooms: 3
Baths: 2 1/2
Garage: 3-car
Foundation Type:
  Basement
Features:
  Varied ceiling heights

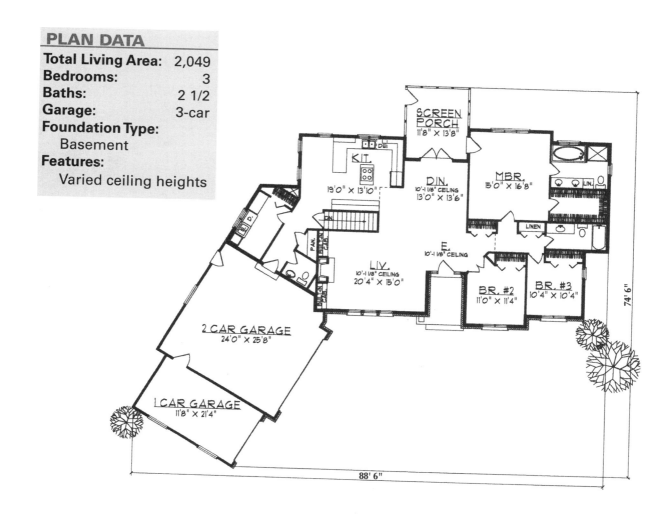

SCREEN PORCH
11'8" X 13'8"

KIT.
19'0" X 13'10"

DIN.
10'-1 1/8" CEILING
13'0" X 13'6"

MBR.
15'0" X 16'8"

LINEN

LIV.
10'-1 1/8" CEILING
20'4" X 15'0"

E.
10'-1 1/8" CEILING

BR. #2
11'0" X 11'4"

BR. #3
10'4" X 10'4"

2 CAR GARAGE
24'0" X 25'8"

1 CAR GARAGE
11'8" X 21'4"

74' 6"

88' 6"

PLAN DATA

Total Living Area: 1,540
Bedrooms: 3
Baths: 2
Garage: 2-car
Foundation Types:
  Basement
  Crawl space
  Slab
Please specify when ordering

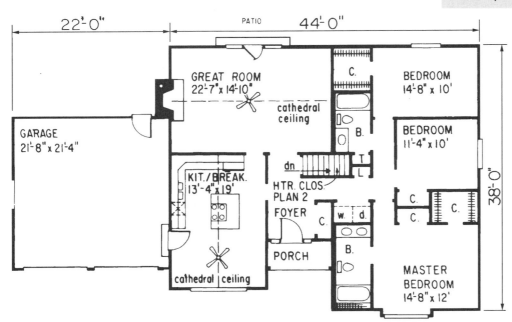

22'-0"

PATIO 44'-0"

GREAT ROOM
22'-7" x 14'-10"

cathedral ceiling

C.

BEDROOM
14'-8" x 10'

B.

BEDROOM
11'-4" x 10'

GARAGE
21'-8" x 21'-4"

dn

T.
L

KIT./BREAK.
13'-4" x 19'

HTR. CLOS.
PLAN 2

C.

C.

C.

FOYER

C.

w. d.

38'-0"

PORCH

B.

cathedral ceiling

MASTER
BEDROOM
14'-8" x 12'

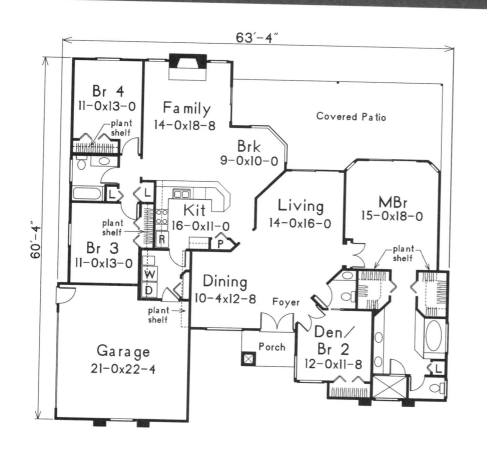

63'-4"

60'-4"

Br 4
11-0x13-0

Family
14-0x18-8

Covered Patio

plant shelf

Brk
9-0x10-0

L
L

Kit
16-0x11-0

Living
14-0x16-0

MBr
15-0x18-0

plant shelf

plant shelf

R

Br 3
11-0x13-0

P

plant shelf

W
D

Dining
10-4x12-8

Foyer

plant shelf

Garage
21-0x22-4

Porch

Den/
Br 2
12-0x11-8

L

PLAN DATA

Total Living Area:	2,287
Bedrooms:	4
Baths:	2 1/2
Garage:	2-car
Foundation Type:	
Slab	

J.N. HANSEN P.T.L

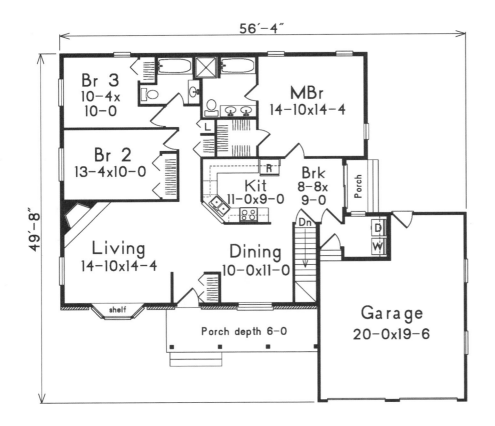

56'−4"

49'−8"

Br 3
10-4x
10-0

MBr
14-10x14-4

Br 2
13-4x10-0

L

R

Kit
11-0x9-0

Brk
8-8x
9-0

Porch

Dn

D
W

Living
14-10x14-4

Dining
10-0x11-0

shelf

Porch depth 6-0

Garage
20-0x19-6

PLAN DATA

Total Living Area:	1,466
Bedrooms:	3
Baths:	2
Garage:	2-car
Foundation Types:	
Basement standard	
Slab	
Features:	
2" x 6" exterior walls	

STORAGE
10' x 6'

STORAGE
10' x 6'

CARPORT
22' x 20'

ATTIC STAIRS

PATIO

64'

UTILITY
11' x 6'

WH BRM/STO

WASH DRY

SHV'S

PANT.

RANGE

KITCHEN
12' x 11'

SINK D.W.

REF

BAR

PANT

EATING
12' x 10'

LIVING
20' x 18'

12' HIGH CEILING

SLOPE

SLOPE

SHV

CLO.

BATH

LIN

LIN

LIN

BATH

HEAT & A.C.

W.H.

HALL

SHV

CLO.

MASTER SUITE
16' x 14'

CLO.

CLO.

DINING
12' x 12'

ENTRY

PORCH

BED RM.
14' x 12'

BED RM.
14' x 12'

58'

PLAN DATA
Total Living Area: 2,424
Bedrooms: 3
Baths: 2
Garage: 2-car carport
Foundation Types:
  Slab
  Crawl space
Please specify when ordering
Features:
  Storage in garage

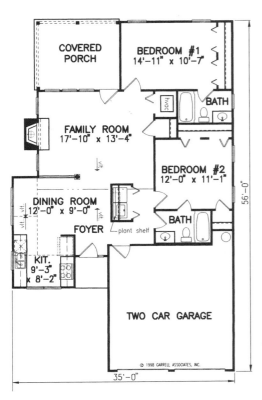

PLAN DATA

Total Living Area:	1,093
Bedrooms:	2
Baths:	2
Garage:	2-car
Foundation Type:	
Basement	

PLAN DATA

Total Living Area:	987
Bedrooms:	3
Bath:	1
Foundation Type:	
Basement	

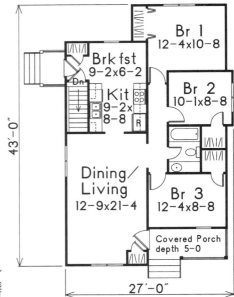

PLAN #562-LBD-13-1A

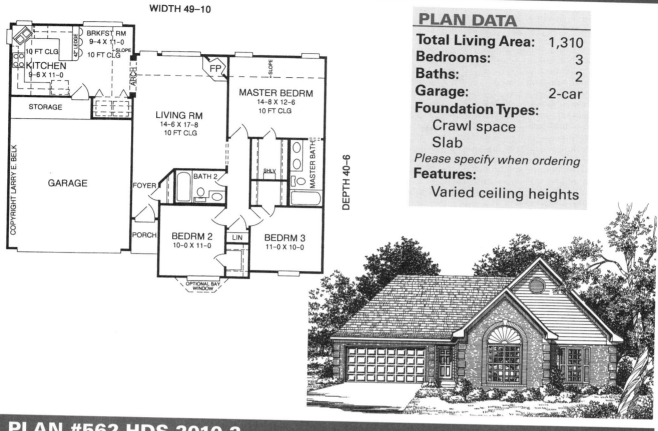

WIDTH 49–10

BRKFST RM 9–4 X 11–0
10 FT CLG — SLOPE

10 FT CLG
42" LEDGE

KITCHEN 9–6 X 11–0

STORAGE

ARCH

FP

SLOPE

MASTER BEDRM 14–8 X 12–6
10 FT CLG

COPYRIGHT LARRY E. BELK

GARAGE

LIVING RM 14–6 X 17–8
10 FT CLG

FOYER

BATH 2

SHLV

MASTER BATH

DEPTH 40–6

PORCH

BEDRM 2 10–0 X 11–0

LIN

BEDRM 3 11–0 X 10–0

OPTIONAL BAY WINDOW

PLAN DATA
Total Living Area: 1,310
Bedrooms: 3
Baths: 2
Garage: 2-car
Foundation Types:
  Crawl space
  Slab
Please specify when ordering
Features:
  Varied ceiling heights

PLAN #562-HDS-2010-2

PLAN DATA
Total Living Area: 2,010
Bedrooms: 4
Baths: 2
Garage: 2-car
Foundation Type:
  Slab

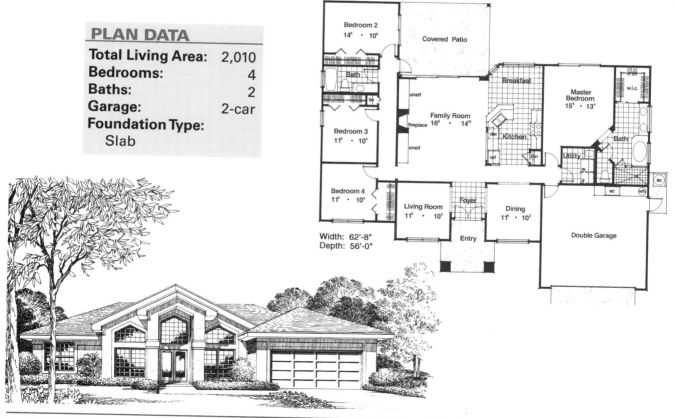

Bedroom 2 14⁰ · 10⁰

Covered Patio

Bath

Breakfast

Master Bedroom 15⁸ · 13⁴

w.i.c.

shelf

lin

Family Room 16⁸ · 14¹⁰

Kitchen
dw

Bath

Bedroom 3 11⁰ · 10⁴

fireplace
shelf

ref
pan

Utility
w
d

ac
wh

ac

Bedroom 4 11⁰ · 10⁴

Living Room 11⁰ · 10²

Foyer

Dining 11⁰ · 10²

Double Garage

Width: 62'-8"
Depth: 56'-0"

Entry

WIDTH 65–0

MASTER BEDRM
12-8 X 14-6
10 FT CLG

MASTER BATH
10 FT CLG

BATH 2

FP

BRKFST RM
12-0 X 10-0
10 FT CLG

GREAT ROOM
18-6 X 15-6
10 FT CLG

UTIL
6-8 X 8-6

LIN

BEDRM 2
11-0 X 13-6

KITCHEN
12-6 X 14-0
10 FT CLG

PAN

FOYER
10 FT CLG

ARCH

ARCH

BEDRM 3
12-6 X 13-4

DINING ROOM
12-2 X 14-0
10 FT CLG

DEPTH 58–8

PORCH

GARAGE

COPYRIGHT LARRY E. BELK

PLAN DATA

Total Living Area: 1,955
Bedrooms: 3
Baths: 2
Garage: 2-car
Foundation Types:
   Crawl space
   Slab
Please specify when ordering
Features:
   Varied ceiling heights

PLAN #562-0198

PLAN DATA

Total Living Area: 1,416
Bedrooms: 3
Baths: 2
Garage: 2-car
Foundation Types:
  Basement standard
  Crawl space

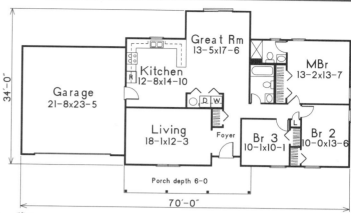

Great Rm
13-5x17-6

Kitchen
12-8x14-10

MBr
13-2x13-7

Garage
21-8x23-5

Living
18-1x12-3

Foyer

Br 3
10-1x10-1

Br 2
10-0x13-6

34'-0"

Porch depth 6-0

70'-0"

PLAN #562-JFD-10-1456-2

DIN
10'8 x 9'
cath cl'g

MBATH

WI Closet

SNACK BAR OPT.

KIT
10'4 x 10'6
cath cl'g

GREAT ROOM
13'2 x 17'4
cath cl'g

BR2
12' x 10'2

LINEN

BATH 2

MBR
12' x 14'8

Entry

FOYER
cath cl'g

DIN RM
10'2 x 12'
cath cl'g

STUDY/ BR 3
9'6 x 11'

Covered Entry

GARAGE
19'4 x 21'4

Width: 49'-0"
Depth: 51'-8"

PLAN DATA

Total Living Area: 1,456
Bedrooms: 3
Baths: 2
Garage: 2-car
Foundation Type:
  Basement

PLAN DATA

Total Living Area: 1,595
Bedrooms: 3
Baths: 2
Garage: 2-car
Foundation Types:
  Basement
  Crawl space
  Slab
Features:
  Storage in garage

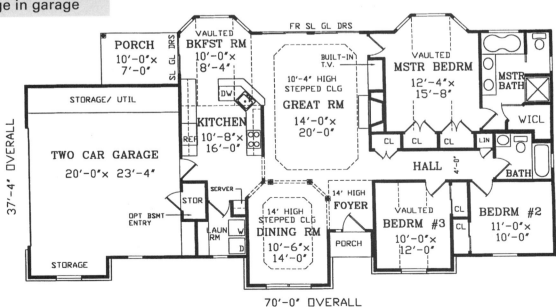

PLAN DATA

Total Living Area: 1,978
Bedrooms: 3
Baths: 2 1/2
Garage: 2-car
Foundation Types:
Basement
Crawl space
Please specify when ordering
Features:
12'-6" ceilings in foyer, family and dining rooms

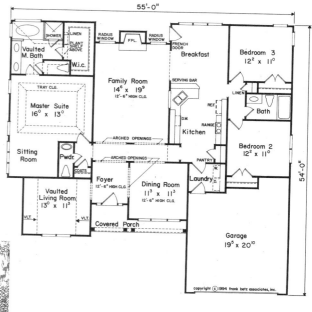

PLAN DATA

Total Living Area: 1,580
Bedrooms: 3
Baths: 2
Garage: 2-car
Foundation Type:
Basement
Features:
Bedroom 2 easily converts to Den

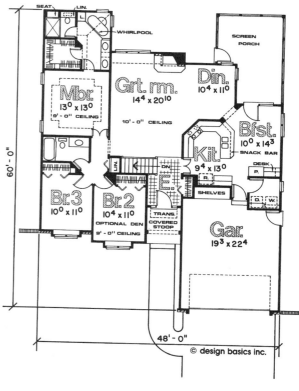

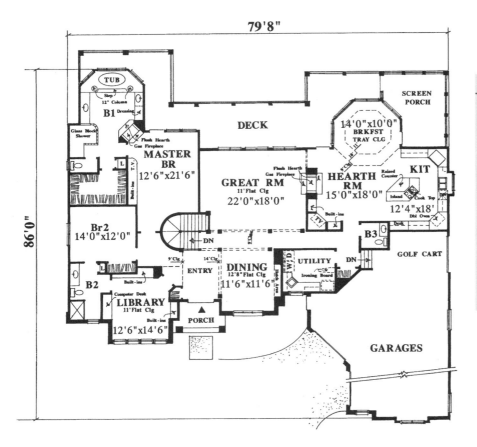

PLAN DATA

Total Living Area:	2,900
Bedrooms:	2
Baths:	2 1/2
Garage:	3-car

Foundation Types:
  Walk-out basement
  Basement

Features:
  - Varied ceiling heights
  - Golf cart door in garage

PLAN DATA

Total Living Area:	924
Bedrooms:	2
Bath:	1
Foundation Type:	
Slab	

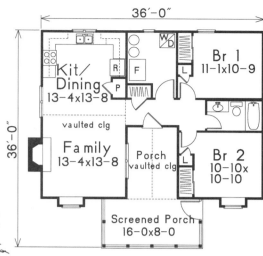

Kit/Dining 13-4x13-8

vaulted clg

Family 13-4x13-8

Porch vaulted clg

Br 1 11-1x10-9

Br 2 10-10x 10-10

36'-0"

36'-0"

Screened Porch 16-0x8-0

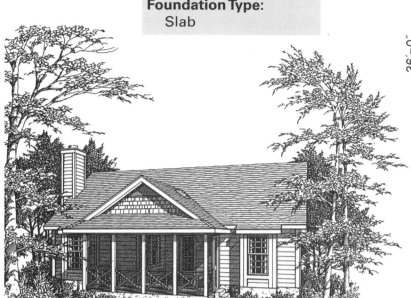

PLAN #562-1120-1 & 2
Price Code A

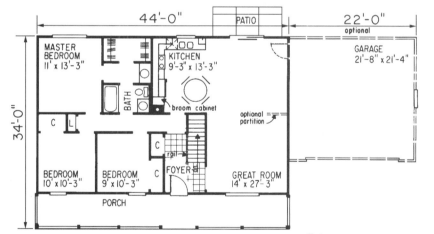

44'-0"

22'-0" optional

PATIO

GARAGE 21'-8" x 21'-4"

MASTER BEDROOM 11' x 13'-3"

KITCHEN 9'-3" x 13'-3"

BATH

broom cabinet

optional partition

34'-0"

C L

BEDROOM 10' x 10'-3"

BEDROOM 9' x 10'-3"

C

C

FOYER

rail

GREAT ROOM 14' x 27'-3"

PORCH

PLAN DATA

Total Living Area:	1,232
Bedrooms:	3
Bath:	1

Foundation Types:
Plan #562-1120-1
Basement
Plan #562-1120-2
Crawl space & slab
Features:
Optional 2-car garage

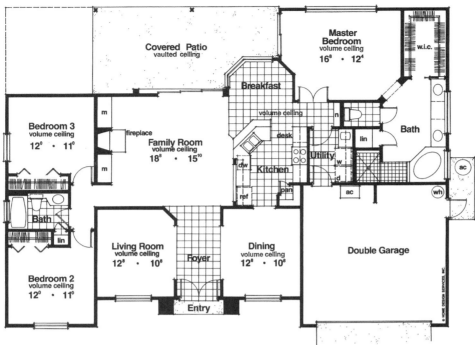

Width: 60'-0"
Depth: 45'-0"

PLAN DATA

Total Living Area:	1,783
Bedrooms:	3
Baths:	2
Garage:	2-car
Foundation Type:	
Slab	

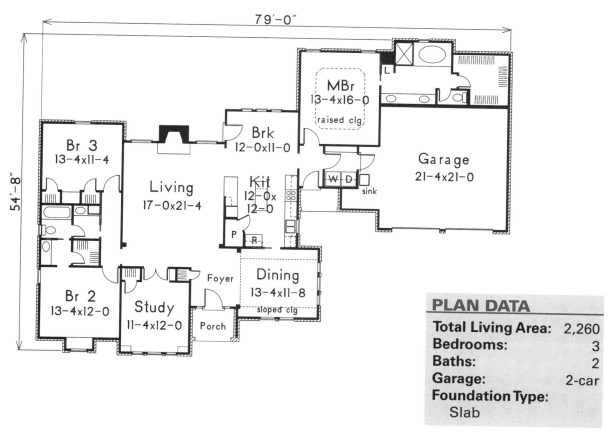

79'-0"

54'-8"

Br 3
13-4x11-4

Living
17-0x21-4

Brk
12-0x11-0

MBr
13-4x16-0
raised clg

L

Garage
21-4x21-0

Kit
12-0x
12-0

W D

sink

P

R

Br 2
13-4x12-0

Study
11-4x12-0

Foyer

Porch

Dining
13-4x11-8
sloped clg

PLAN DATA

Total Living Area:	2,260
Bedrooms:	3
Baths:	2
Garage:	2-car
Foundation Type:	
Slab	

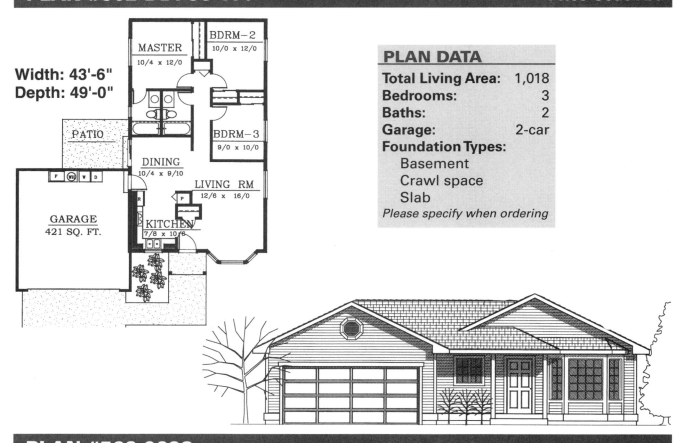

Width: 43'-6"
Depth: 49'-0"

MASTER
10/4 x 12/0

BDRM-2
10/0 x 12/0

BDRM-3
9/0 x 10/0

PATIO

DINING
10/4 x 9/10

LIVING RM
12/6 x 16/0

GARAGE
421 SQ. FT.

KITCHEN
7/8 x 10/6

PLAN DATA

Total Living Area:	1,018
Bedrooms:	3
Baths:	2
Garage:	2-car

Foundation Types:
Basement
Crawl space
Slab
Please specify when ordering

PLAN #562-0698

Price Code AA

PLAN DATA

Total Living Area:	1,143
Bedrooms:	2
Bath:	1

Foundation Type:
Crawl space

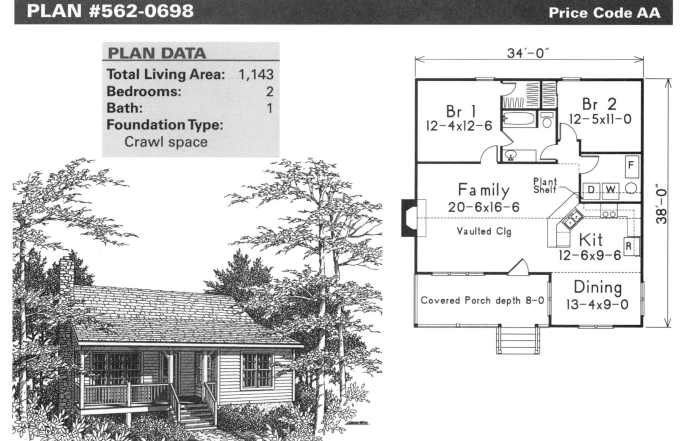

34'-0"

38'-0"

Br 1
12-4x12-6

Br 2
12-5x11-0

Family
20-6x16-6

Plant Shelf

F

D W

Vaulted Clg

Kit
12-6x9-6

R

Covered Porch depth 8-0

Dining
13-4x9-0

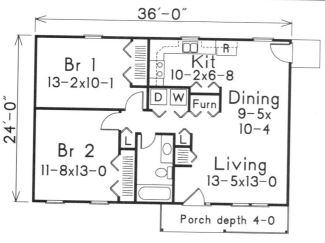

36'-0"

24'-0"

Br 1
13-2x10-1

Kit
10-2x6-8

R

D W Furn

Dining
9-5x
10-4

Br 2
11-8x13-0

L L

Living
13-5x13-0

Porch depth 4-0

PLAN DATA

Total Living Area: 864
Bedrooms: 2
Bath: 1
Foundation Types:
Crawl space standard
Basement
Slab

PLAN DATA

Total Living Area: 1,220
Bedrooms: 3
Baths: 2
Garage: 2-car
Foundation Type:
Basement
Features:
Drive-under garage

Deck

28'-0"

L

Br 3
10-0x
10-1

D
W

Kit/Din
18-3x10-1

R

vaulted

MBr
11-6x14-8

Dn

Living
19-7x12-11

vaulted

Br 2
11-1x10-0

Porch

50'-4"

PLAN DATA

Total Living Area: 1,950
Bedrooms: 4
Baths: 2
Garage: 3-car
Foundation Type:
  Crawl space

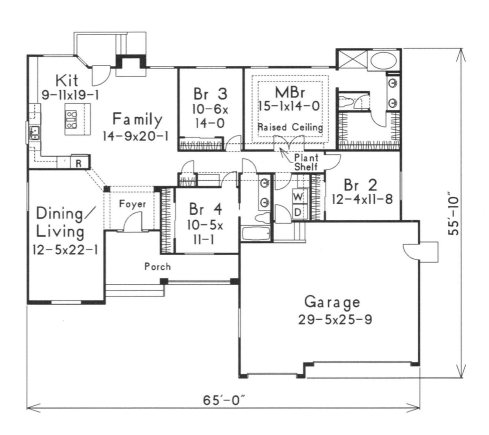

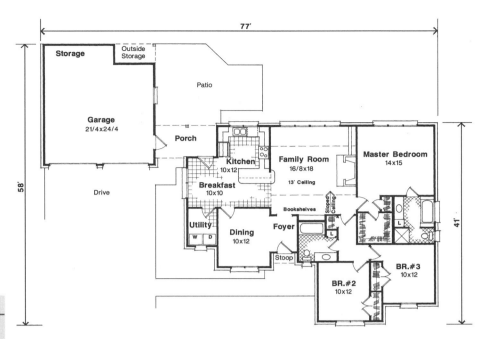

PLAN DATA

Total Living Area:	1,572
Bedrooms:	3
Baths:	2
Garage:	2-car
Foundation Type:	
Slab	
Features:	
9' ceilings	

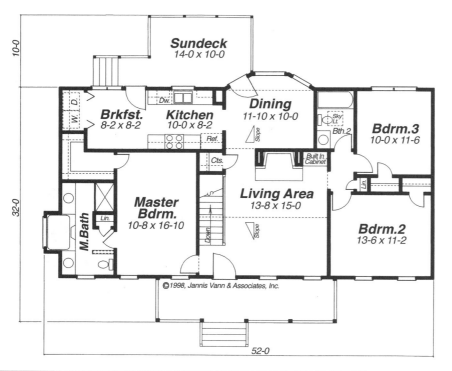

Sundeck
14-0 x 10-0

Brkfst.
8-2 x 8-2

Kitchen
10-0 x 8-2

Dw.

Dining
11-10 x 10-0

Ref.

Sky. Lt.

Bth.2

Bdrm.3
10-0 x 11-6

Cts.

Slope

Built In Cabinet

Lin.

Master Bdrm.
10-8 x 16-10

Living Area
13-8 x 15-0

Down

Slope

M.Bath

Lin.

W. D.

Bdrm.2
13-6 x 11-2

©1998, Jannis Vann & Associates, Inc.

52-0

32-0

10-0

PLAN DATA

Total Living Area: 1,325
Bedrooms: 3
Baths: 2
Garage: 2-car
Foundation Type:
 Basement
Features:
 Drive-under garage

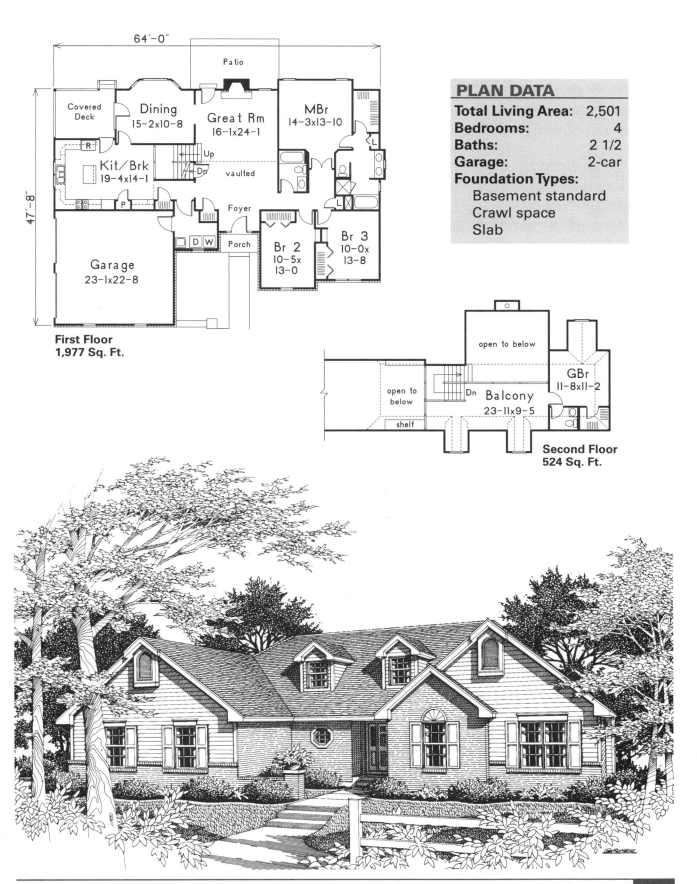

64'-0"

Patio

Covered Deck

Dining
15-2x10-8

Great Rm
16-1x24-1

MBr
14-3x13-10

L

47'-8"

Kit/Brk
19-4x14-1

Up
Dn

vaulted

R

P

Foyer

Garage
23-1x22-8

D W

Porch

Br 2
10-5x
13-0

Br 3
10-0x
13-8

L

L

First Floor
1,977 Sq. Ft.

PLAN DATA

Total Living Area:	2,501
Bedrooms:	4
Baths:	2 1/2
Garage:	2-car
Foundation Types:	
Basement standard	
Crawl space	
Slab	

open to below

open to below

GBr
11-8x11-2

open to below

Dn

Balcony
23-11x9-5

shelf

Second Floor
524 Sq. Ft.

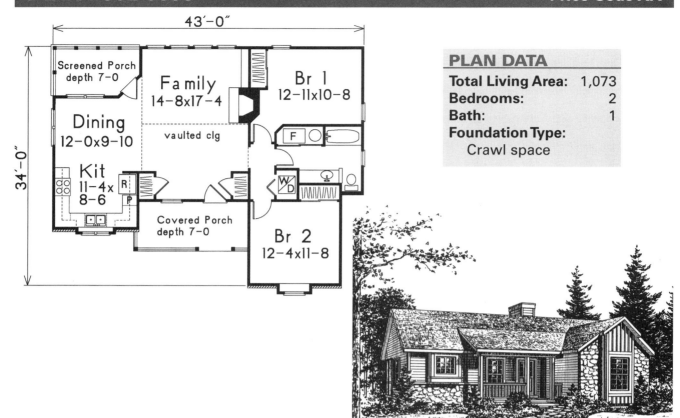

43'-0"

34'-0"

Screened Porch
depth 7-0

Family
14-8x17-4

vaulted clg

Br 1
12-11x10-8

Dining
12-0x9-10

Kit
11-4x
8-6

R
P

F

W
D

Covered Porch
depth 7-0

Br 2
12-4x11-8

PLAN DATA

Total Living Area: 1,073
Bedrooms: 2
Bath: 1
Foundation Type:
   Crawl space

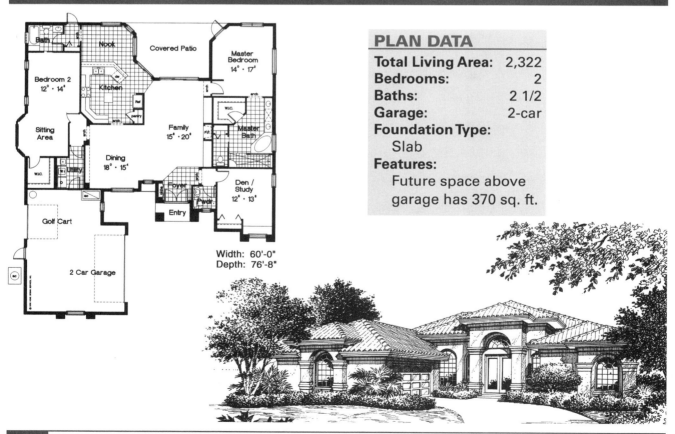

Bath

Nook

Covered Patio

Master
Bedroom
14° · 17²

Bedroom 2
12° · 14°

Kitchen

W.I.C.

Sitting
Area

W.I.C.

Utility

Family
15° · 20°

Master
Bath

pantry

Dining
18° · 15°

Foyer

Den /
Study
12° · 13°

Pwdr

Entry

Golf Cart

2 Car Garage

Width: 60'-0"
Depth: 76'-8"

PLAN DATA

Total Living Area: 2,322
Bedrooms: 2
Baths: 2 1/2
Garage: 2-car
Foundation Type:
   Slab
Features:
   Future space above
   garage has 370 sq. ft.

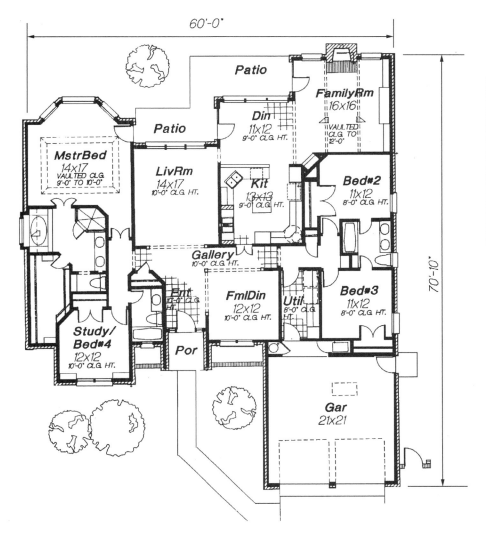

60'-0"

70'-10"

Patio

Patio

MstrBed
14x17
VAULTED CLG
9'-0" TO 10'-0"

LivRm
14x17
10'-0" CLG HT.

Din
11x12
9'-0" CLG HT.

FamilyRm
16x16
VAULTED
CLG TO
12'-0"

Kit
13x13
9'-0" CLG HT.

Bed#2
11x12
8'-0" CLG HT.

Gallery
10'-0" CLG HT.

Ent
10'-0"
HT.

FmlDin
12x12
10'-0" CLG HT.

Util
8'-0" CLG

Bed#3
11x12
8'-0" CLG HT.

Study/
Bed#4
12x12
10'-0" CLG HT.

Por

Gar
21x21

PLAN DATA

Total Living Area: 2,506
Bedrooms: 4
Baths: 3
Garage: 2-car
Foundation Type:
Slab
Features:
Varied ceiling heights

WIDTH 65-10

PLAN DATA

Total Living Area:	1,890
Bedrooms:	3
Baths:	2
Garage:	2-car

Foundation Types:
Crawl space
Slab
Please specify when ordering

Features:
Varied ceiling heights

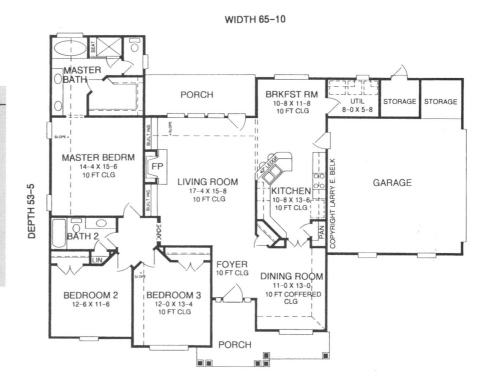

DEPTH 53-5

MASTER BATH

SEAT

PORCH

BRKFST RM
10-8 X 11-8
10 FT CLG

UTIL
8-0 X 5-8

STORAGE

STORAGE

SLOPE

BUILT INS

SLOPE

MASTER BEDRM
14-4 X 15-6
10 FT CLG

FP

BUILT INS

LIVING ROOM
17-4 X 15-8
10 FT CLG

42" EDGE

KITCHEN
10-8 X 13-6
10 FT CLG

PAN

GARAGE

COPYRIGHT LARRY E. BELK

BATH 2

LIN

PORCH

FOYER
10 FT CLG

DINING ROOM
11-0 X 13-0
10 FT COFFERED
CLG

SLOPE

BEDROOM 2
12-6 X 11-6

BEDROOM 3
12-0 X 13-4
10 FT CLG

PORCH

PLAN #562-N297-1 & 2

Price Code AA

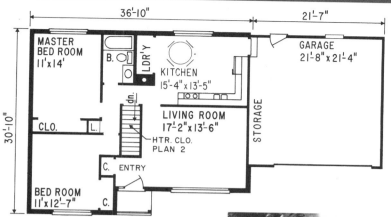

MASTER BED ROOM 11'x14'
B.
LDR'Y
KITCHEN 15'-4"x13'-5"
GARAGE 21'-8"x21'-4"
36'-10"
21'-7"
30'-10"
CLO.
L.
dn.
LIVING ROOM 17'-2"x13'-6"
STORAGE
HTR. CLO. PLAN 2
C. ENTRY
BED ROOM 11'x12'-7"
C.

PLAN DATA

Total Living Area:	1,042
Bedrooms:	2
Bath:	1
Garage:	2-car

Foundation Types:
Plan #562-N297-1
Basement
Plan #562-N297-2
Crawl space & slab

PLAN #562-0582

Price Code AAA

PLAN DATA

Total Living Area:	800
Bedrooms:	2
Bath:	1

Foundation Types:
Crawl space standard
Basement
Slab

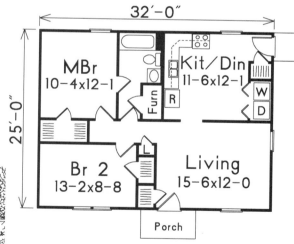

32'-0"
25'-0"
MBr 10-4x12-1
Kit/Din 11-6x12-1
Furn
R
W
D
Br 2 13-2x8-8
L
Living 15-6x12-0
Porch

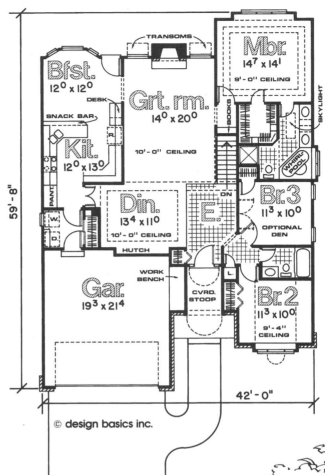

PLAN DATA

Total Living Area: 1,636
Bedrooms: 3
Baths: 2
Garage: 2-car
Foundation Types:
　Basement
　Slab
Please specify when ordering
Features:
　Varied ceiling heights

Bfst. 12^0 x 12^0

Mbr. 14^7 x 14^1 9'-0" CEILING

TRANSOMS

SKYLIGHT

DESK

SNACK BAR

Grt. rm. 14^0 x 20^0 10'-0" CEILING

BOOKS

Kit. 12^0 x 13^0

PANT.

WHIRL POOL

Br.3 11^3 x 10^0

OPTIONAL DEN

Din. 13^4 x 11^0 10'-0" CEILING

DN

W. D.

HUTCH

Gar. 19^3 x 21^4

WORK BENCH

CVRD. STOOP

Br.2 11^3 x 10^0 9'-4" CEILING

59'-8"

42'-0"

© design basics inc.

G. MacDonald

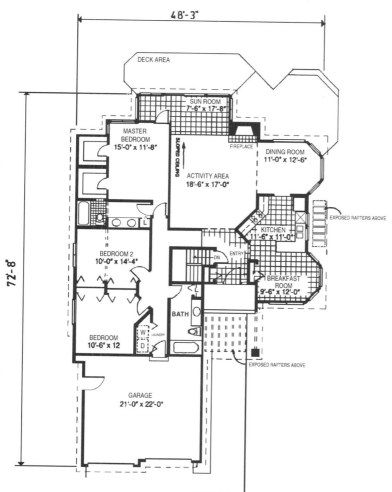

48'-3"

DECK AREA

SUN ROOM
7'-6" x 17'-8"

MASTER
BEDROOM
15'-0" x 11'-8"

SLOPED CEILING

FIREPLACE

DINING ROOM
11'-0" x 12'-6"

ACTIVITY AREA
18'-6" x 17'-0"

EXPOSED RAFTERS ABOVE

KITCHEN
11'-6" x 11'-0"

BEDROOM 2
10'-0" x 14'-4"

DN   ENTRY

BREAKFAST
ROOM
9'-6" x 12'-0"

BATH

BEDROOM
10'-6" x 12

W
D   LAUNDRY

EXPOSED RAFTERS ABOVE

72'-8"

GARAGE
21'-0" x 22'-0"

PLAN DATA

Total Living Area:	1,907
Bedrooms:	3
Baths:	2
Garage:	2-car
Foundation Type:	
Partial basement/ crawl space	

PLAN DATA

Total Living Area: 2,403
Bedrooms: 3
Baths: 2 1/2
Garage: 2-car
Foundation Types:
  Basement
  Walk-out basement
  Crawl space
  Slab
Please specify when ordering
Features:
  Varied ceiling heights

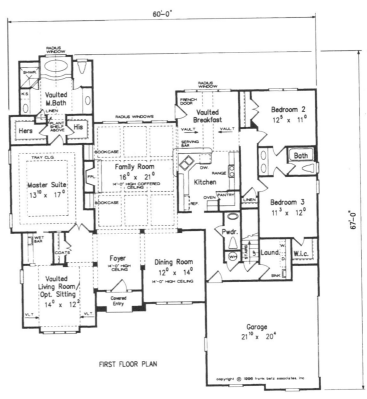

FIRST FLOOR PLAN

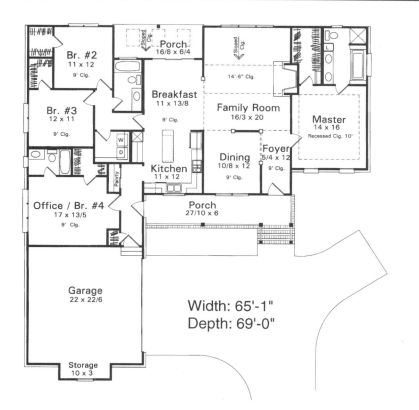

Br. #2
11 x 12
9' Clg.

Br. #3
12 x 11
9' Clg.

Office / Br. #4
17 x 13/5
9' Clg.

Porch
16/8 x 6/4

Breakfast
11 x 13/8
9' Clg.

Family Room
16/3 x 20
14'-6" Clg.

Master
14 x 16
Recessed Clg. 10'

Kitchen
11 x 12

Dining
10/8 x 12
9' Clg.

Foyer
5/4 x 12
9' Clg.

Porch
27/10 x 6

Garage
22 x 22/6

Storage
10 x 3

Width: 65'-1"
Depth: 69'-0"

PLAN DATA

Total Living Area:	2,158
Bedrooms:	4
Baths:	3
Garage:	2-car

Foundation Types:
   Crawl space
   Slab
Please specify when ordering
Features:
   Varied ceiling heights

Width: 50'-0"
Depth: 55'-0"

PLAN DATA
Total Living Area: 1,735
Bedrooms: 3
Baths: 2
Garage: 2-car
Foundation Type:
 Basement
Features:
 Varied ceiling heights

PLAN #562-1400-1 & 2

60'-5"

30'-10"

MASTER
BEDROOM
11'-4" x 14'-4"

MASTER
BATH

D.

W.

KITCHEN
17'-11" x 11'-11"

REF.

DN.

LIN.

HEATER CLOSET
FOR PLAN 2

LIVING ROOM
19'-8" x 13'-10"

GARAGE
22'-0" x 21'-4"

BEDROOM 2
11'-4" x 13'-0"

PLAN DATA

Total Living Area: 1,102
Bedrooms: 2
Bath: 1
Garage: 2-car
Foundation Types:
 Plan #562-1400-1
 Basement
 Plan #562-1400-2
 Crawl space

PLAN #562-0273

PLAN DATA

Total Living Area: 988
Bedrooms: 2
Baths: 1
Garage: 2-car
Foundation Type:
 Basement

38'-0"

46'-0"

MBr
14-0x12-6

Deck

Br 2
12-0x10-0

Kit/Din
13-0x11-4
vaulted

P
R

Dn

Garage
20-0x20-0

Great Rm
17-8x13-8
vaulted

PLAN DATA

Total Living Area:	1,467
Bedrooms:	3
Baths:	2
Garage:	2-car
Foundation Type:	
Crawl space	

◄49'►

43'

VAULTED DINING 11/0 X 14/0
VAULTED LIVING 15/8 X 14/0
VAULTED MASTER 13/0 X 11/8 +
8/0 X 12/8
PANTRY DESK
PLANT SHELF OVER AT 9'
GARAGE 19/4 X 19/8 +
LINEN
BR. 3 10/8 X 10/4
BR. 2 12/0 X 10/0
©Alan Mascord Design Associates, Inc.

HERS HIS
SIT MASTER BATH 11 FT TRAY CLG
FP
PORCH 9 FT CLG
FAMILY ROOM 13-6 X 16-6 9 FT CLG
MASTER BEDRM 15-0 X 17-4 11 FT TRAY CLG
BEDRM 4 14-8 X 12-8 9 FT CLG
COVERED PORCH 9 FT CLG
BRKFST RM 10-8 X 11-6 9 FT CLG
DEPTH 67-9
42" LEDGE
BATH 2
LIVING ROOM 18-4 X 18-6 11 FT CLG
KITCHEN 13-6 X 11-4 9 FT CLG
PWDR
UTIL 12-6 X 5-8 9 FT CLG
PAN
BEDRM 3 11-0 X 13-4 9 FT CLG
BEDRM 2/ STUDY 11-6 X 13-0 11 FT TRAY CLG
FOYER 11 FT CLG
ARCH
DINING ROOM 14-0 X 13-6 11 FT CLG
GARAGE
PORCH 9 FT CLG
COPYRIGHT LARRY E. BELK

WIDTH 70-2

PLAN DATA

Total Living Area:	2,678
Bedrooms:	4
Baths:	2 1/2
Garage:	2-car
Foundation Types:	
Crawl space	
Slab	
Please specify when ordering	
Features:	
Varied ceiling heights	

Garage
21-5x21-5

Covered Porch

D
W Utility

Covered Porch

MBr
14-7x12-9

P

Kit/Din
22-1x12-9

L
L

Dn

R

Br 3
12-1x10-11

Family
18-3x14-4

Br 2
12-1x10-11

Covered Porch
33-4x6-8

64'-0"

48'-0"

PLAN DATA

Total Living Area:	1,501
Bedrooms:	3
Baths:	2
Garage:	2-car
Foundation Types:	
Basement standard	
Crawl space	
Slab	

PLAN DATA

Total Living Area: 1,433
Bedrooms: 3
Baths: 2
Garage: 2-car
Foundation Types:
  Basement
  Crawl space
  Slab
Please specify when ordering

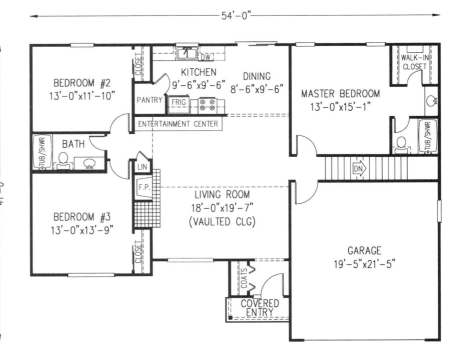

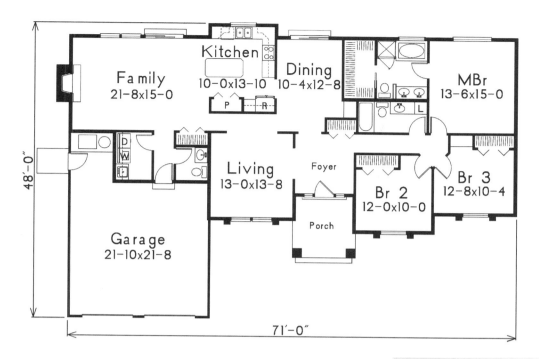

Family
21-8x15-0

Kitchen
10-0x13-10

Dining
10-4x12-8

MBr
13-6x15-0

48'-0"

P   R

D
W

Living
13-0x13-8

Foyer

Br 2
12-0x10-0

Br 3
12-8x10-4

Garage
21-10x21-8

Porch

71'-0"

PLAN DATA

Total Living Area:	1,941
Bedrooms:	3
Baths:	2 1/2
Garage:	2-car
Foundation Type:	
Crawl space	

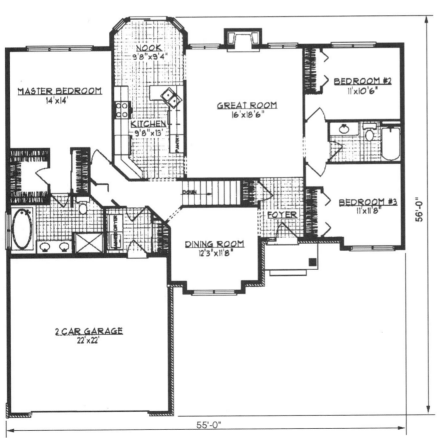

NOOK
9'8"x9'4"

MASTER BEDROOM
14'x14'

GREAT ROOM
16'x18'6"

BEDROOM #2
11'x10'6"

KITCHEN
9'8"x13'

BEDROOM #3
11'x11'8"

DOWN

FOYER

DINING ROOM
12'3"x11'8"

2 CAR GARAGE
22'x22'

56'-0"

55'-0"

PLAN DATA

Total Living Area: 1,730
Bedrooms: 3
Baths: 2
Garage: 2-car
Foundation Type:
 Basement
Features:
 2" x 6" exterior walls

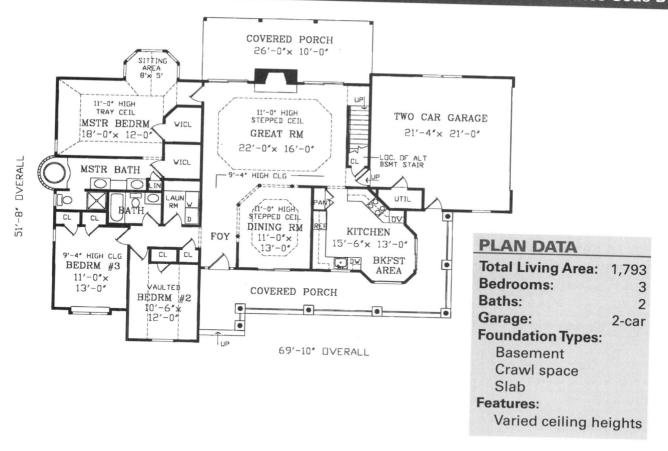

COVERED PORCH
26'-0" x 10'-0"

SITTING
AREA
8' x 5'

11'-0" HIGH
TRAY CEIL
MSTR BEDRM
18'-0" x 12'-0"

WICL

11'-0" HIGH
STEPPED CEIL
GREAT RM
22'-0" x 16'-0"

UP

TWO CAR GARAGE
21'-4" x 21'-0"

WICL

MSTR BATH

CL

LOC. OF ALT
BSMT STAIR

9'-4" HIGH CLG

UP

51'-8" OVERALL

LIN

BATH

LAUN
RM
W
D

UTIL

PANT

DV

FOY

11'-0" HIGH
STEPPED CEIL
DINING RM
11'-0" x
13'-0"

REF

KITCHEN
15'-6" x 13'-0"

9'-4" HIGH CLG
BEDRM #3
11'-0" x
13'-0"

CL

CL

DV

BKFST
AREA

VAULTED
BEDRM #2
10'-6" x
12'-0"

COVERED PORCH

UP

69'-10" OVERALL

PLAN DATA

Total Living Area: 1,793
Bedrooms: 3
Baths: 2
Garage: 2-car
Foundation Types:
 Basement
 Crawl space
 Slab
Features:
 Varied ceiling heights

PLAN DATA

Total Living Area: 1,969
Bedrooms: 3
Baths: 2
Garage: 2-car
Foundation Types:
  Crawl space standard
  Slab

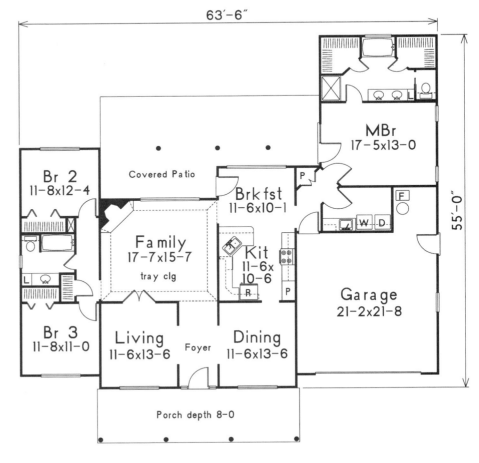

63'-6"

55'-0"

MBr
17-5x13-0

Br 2
11-8x12-4

Covered Patio

Brk fst
11-6x10-1

Family
17-7x15-7
tray clg

Kit
11-6x
10-6

P

W D

F

Garage
21-2x21-8

Br 3
11-8x11-0

Living
11-6x13-6

Foyer

Dining
11-6x13-6

Porch depth 8-0

PLAN DATA

Total Living Area: 2,532
Bedrooms: 3
Baths: 4
Garage: 3-car
Foundation Types:
  Basement
  Crawl space
  Slab
Please specify when ordering
Features:
  Varied ceiling heights

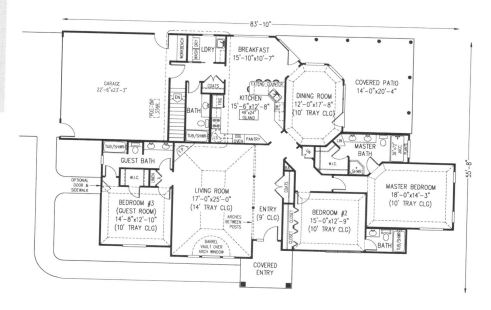

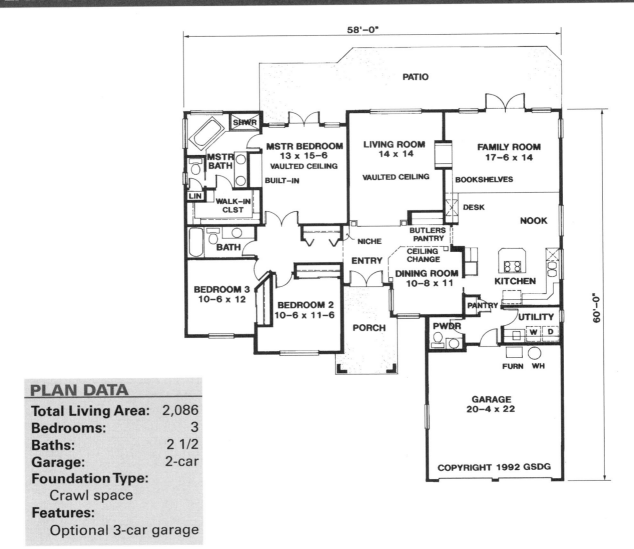

58'-0"

60'-0"

PATIO

MSTR BEDROOM
13 x 15-6
VAULTED CEILING

BUILT-IN

LIVING ROOM
14 x 14

VAULTED CEILING

FAMILY ROOM
17-6 x 14

BOOKSHELVES

SHWR

MSTR
BATH

LIN

WALK-IN
CLST

DESK

NOOK

BUTLERS
PANTRY

NICHE

CEILING
CHANGE

BATH

ENTRY

DINING ROOM
10-8 x 11

KITCHEN

BEDROOM 3
10-6 x 12

BEDROOM 2
10-6 x 11-6

PORCH

PANTRY

PWDR

UTILITY

W   D

FURN   WH

GARAGE
20-4 x 22

COPYRIGHT 1992 GSDG

PLAN DATA

Total Living Area: 2,086
Bedrooms: 3
Baths: 2 1/2
Garage: 2-car
Foundation Type:
  Crawl space
Features:
  Optional 3-car garage

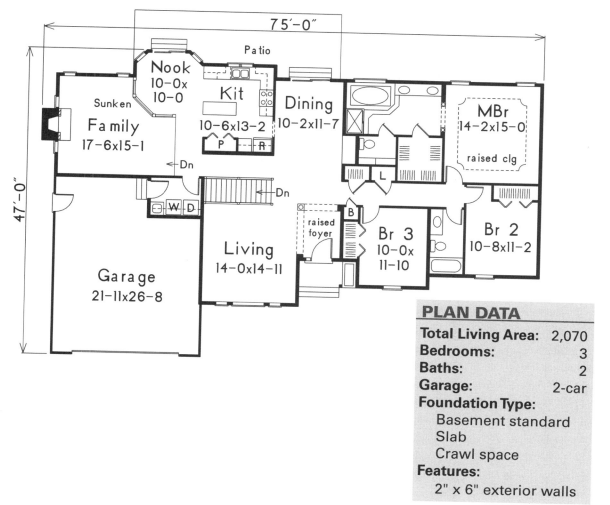

75'-0"

47'-0"

Patio

Nook
10-0x
10-0

Kit
10-6x13-2

Dining
10-2x11-7

MBr
14-2x15-0
raised clg

Sunken

Family
17-6x15-1

P   R

←Dn

L

←Dn

W D

Living
14-0x14-11

raised foyer

B

Br 3
10-0x
11-10

Br 2
10-8x11-2

Garage
21-11x26-8

PLAN DATA

Total Living Area: 2,070
Bedrooms: 3
Baths: 2
Garage: 2-car
Foundation Type:
  Basement standard
  Slab
  Crawl space
Features:
  2" x 6" exterior walls

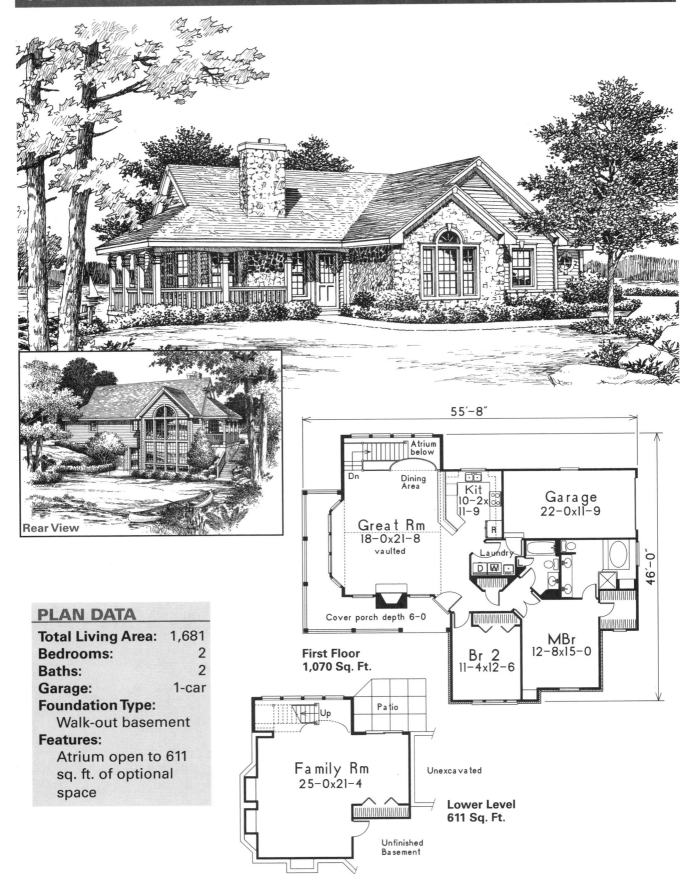

Rear View

55'-8"

46'-0"

Atrium below

Dn

Dining Area

Kit
10-2x
11-9

Garage
22-0x11-9

Great Rm
18-0x21-8
vaulted

Laundry

D W

R

First Floor
1,070 Sq. Ft.

Cover porch depth 6-0

Br 2
11-4x12-6

MBr
12-8x15-0

PLAN DATA

Total Living Area: 1,681
Bedrooms: 2
Baths: 2
Garage: 1-car
Foundation Type:
   Walk-out basement
Features:
   Atrium open to 611
   sq. ft. of optional
   space

Up

Patio

Unexcavated

Family Rm
25-0x21-4

Lower Level
611 Sq. Ft.

Unfinished
Basement

PLAN DATA

Total Living Area:	1,134
Bedrooms:	2
Bath:	1
Garage:	2-car
Foundation Type:	
Basement	

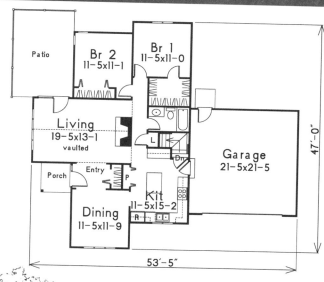

PLAN #562-N294-1 & 2

Price Code AA

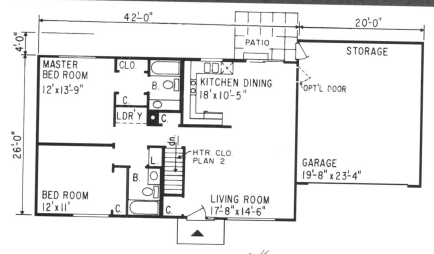

PLAN DATA

Total Living Area:	1,092
Bedrooms:	2
Baths:	2
Garage:	2-car
Foundation Types:	
Plan #562-N294-1	
Basement	
Plan #562-N294-2	
Crawl space & slab	

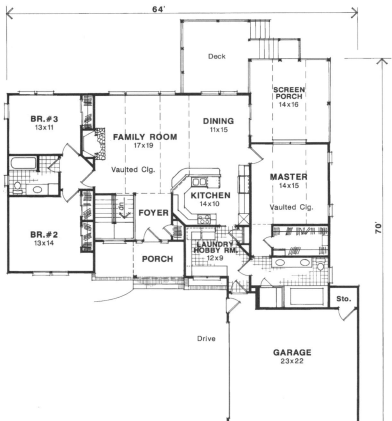

64'

Deck

SCREEN PORCH
14 x 16

BR.#3
13 x 11

DINING
11 x 15

FAMILY ROOM
17 x 19

Vaulted Clg.

MASTER
14 x 15

KITCHEN
14 x 10

Vaulted Clg.

FOYER

BR.#2
13 x 14

LAUNDRY
HOBBY RM.
12 x 9

PORCH

Sto.

Drive

GARAGE
23 x 22

70'

PLAN DATA

Total Living Area:	1,892
Bedrooms:	3
Baths:	2
Garage:	2-car
Foundation Type:	
Basement	

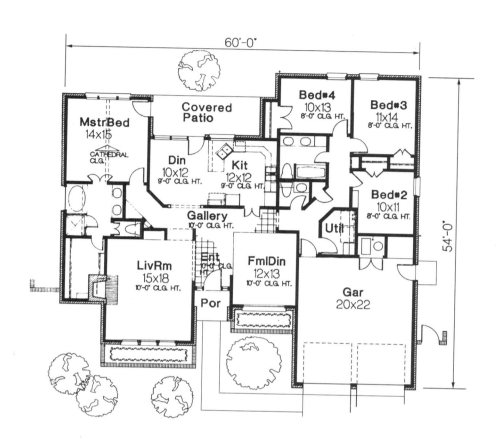

60'-0"

MstrBed
14x15
CATHEDRAL CLG.

Covered Patio

Bed#4
10x13
8'-0" CLG. HT.

Bed#3
11x14
8'-0" CLG. HT.

Din
10x12
9'-0" CLG. HT.

Kit
12x12
9'-0" CLG. HT.

Bed#2
10x11
8'-0" CLG. HT.

Gallery
10'-0" CLG. HT.

Util

LivRm
15x18
10'-0" CLG. HT.

Ent
10'-0" CLG HT.

FmlDin
12x13
10'-0" CLG. HT.

Por

Gar
20x22

54'-0"

PLAN DATA
Total Living Area: 2,030
Bedrooms: 4
Baths: 2 1/2
Garage: 2-car
Foundation Type:
Slab

PLAN DATA

Total Living Area:	3,034
Bedrooms:	3
Baths:	2 1/2
Garage:	3-car
Foundation Type:	
Basement	
Features:	
Varied ceiling heights	

PLAN DATA

Total Living Area: 1,097
Bedrooms: 3
Baths: 2
Foundation Types:
 Basement
 Crawl space
 Slab
Please specify when ordering
Features:
 Optional 2-car garage
 and alternate garage
 location

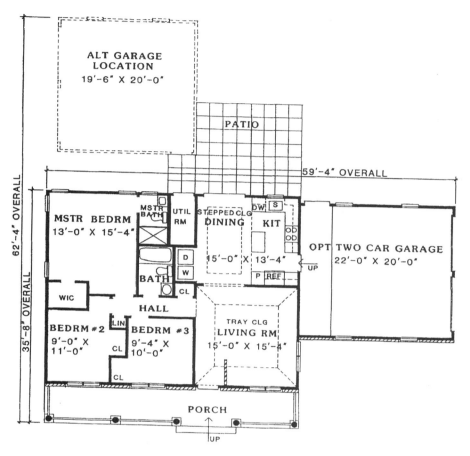

ALT GARAGE
LOCATION
19'-6" X 20'-0"

PATIO

62'-4" OVERALL

35'-8" OVERALL

59'-4" OVERALL

MSTR BEDRM
13'-0" X 15'-4"

MSTR
BATH

UTIL
RM

STEPPED CLG
DINING

KIT

DW S

OPT TWO CAR GARAGE
22'-0" X 20'-0"

15'-0" X 13'-4"

D

W

BATH

P REF

CL

WIC

HALL

UP

OD

BEDRM #2
9'-0" X
11'-0"

LIN

BEDRM #3
9'-4" X
10'-0"

CL

CL

TRAY CLG
LIVING RM
15'-0" X 15'-4"

CL

PORCH

UP

PLAN DATA

Total Living Area: 1,770
Bedrooms: 3
Baths: 2
Garage: 2-car
Foundation Types:
  Slab
  Crawl space
Please specify when ordering
Features:
  12' ceilings in break-
  fast/kitchen, living
  and dining areas

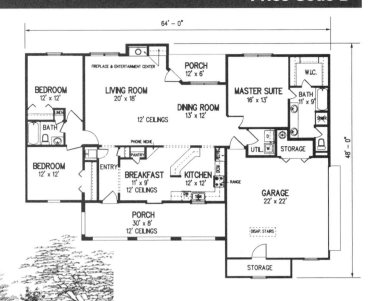

PLAN DATA

Total Living Area: 1,475
Bedrooms: 3
Baths: 2
Garage: 2-car
Foundation Types:
  Slab standard
  Crawl space

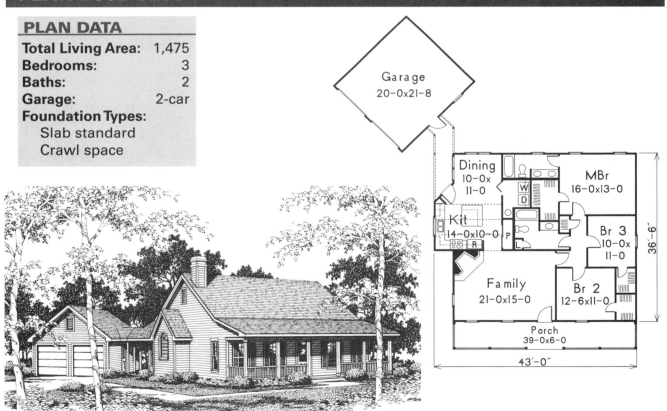

PLAN DATA

Total Living Area:	829
Bedroom:	1
Bath:	1
Foundation Type:	
Slab	

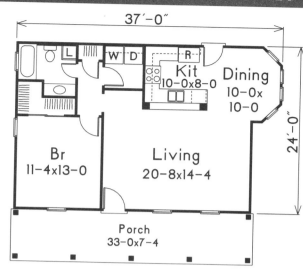

37'-0"

24'-0"

Kit 10-0x8-0

Dining 10-0x 10-0

Br 11-4x13-0

Living 20-8x14-4

Porch 33-0x7-4

PLAN #562-JFD-10-1724-2

Price Code B

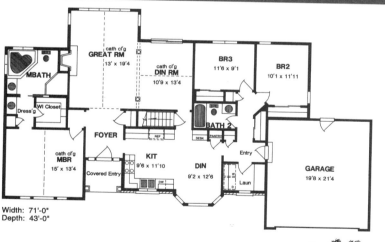

cath cl'g
GREAT RM
13' x 19'4

MBATH

WI Closet

Dress'g

cath cl'g
DIN RM
10'9 x 13'4

cath cl'g
MBR
15' x 13'4

FOYER

Covered Entry

BR3
11'6 x 9'1

BR2
10'1 x 11'11

BATH 2

REF

DESK PANTRY

KIT
9'6 x 11'10

DIN
9'2 x 12'6

Entry

Laun

GARAGE
19'8 x 21'4

Width: 71'-0"
Depth: 43'-0"

PLAN DATA

Total Living Area:	1,724
Bedrooms:	3
Baths:	2
Garage:	2-car
Foundation Type:	
Basement	

PLAN DATA

Total Living Area: 1,882
Bedrooms: 3
Baths: 2
Garage: 2-car
Foundation Type:
  Basement

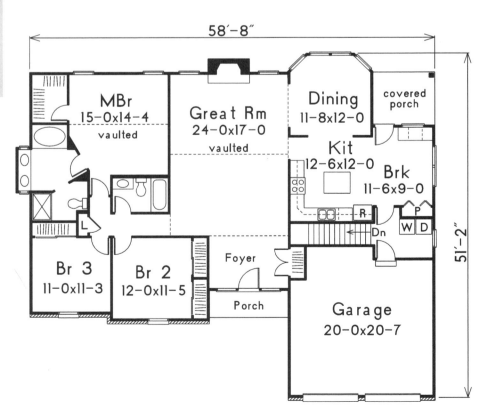

58'-8"

MBr
15-0x14-4
vaulted

Great Rm
24-0x17-0
vaulted

Dining
11-8x12-0

covered
porch

Kit
12-6x12-0

Brk
11-6x9-0

51'-2"

Br 3
11-0x11-3

Br 2
12-0x11-5

Foyer

Porch

Garage
20-0x20-7

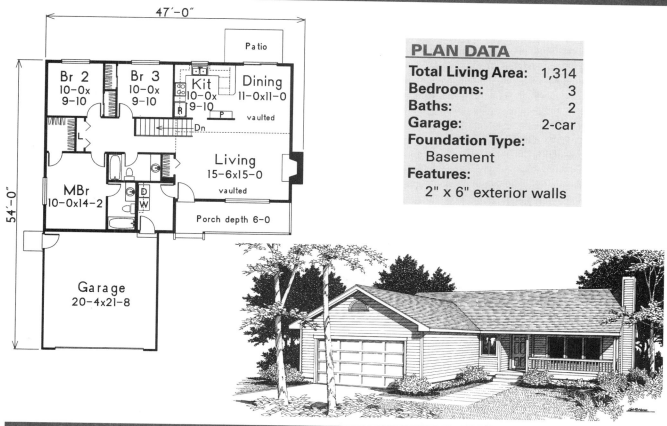

47'-0"

Patio

Br 2
10-0x
9-10

Br 3
10-0x
9-10

Kit
10-0x
9-10

Dining
11-0x11-0

vaulted

Dn

Living
15-6x15-0

vaulted

MBr
10-0x14-2

D
W

Porch depth 6-0

54'-0"

Garage
20-4x21-8

PLAN DATA

Total Living Area:	1,314
Bedrooms:	3
Baths:	2
Garage:	2-car

Foundation Type:
  Basement
Features:
  2" x 6" exterior walls

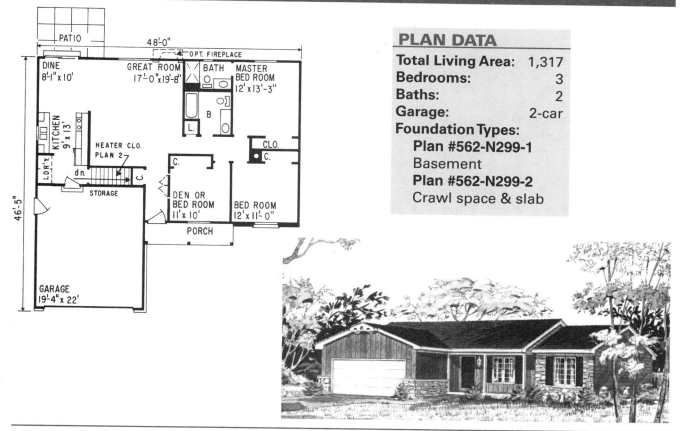

PATIO

48'-0"

OPT. FIREPLACE

DINE
8'-1" x 10'

GREAT ROOM
17'-0"x19'-8"

BATH

MASTER
BED ROOM
12' x13'-3"

KITCHEN
9' x 13'

B

HEATER CLO.
PLAN 2

L

CLO.

LDRY

dn.

c.

C.

STORAGE

DEN OR
BED ROOM
11' x 10'

BED ROOM
12' x11'-0"

46'-5"

PORCH

GARAGE
19'-4" x 22'

PLAN DATA

Total Living Area:	1,317
Bedrooms:	3
Baths:	2
Garage:	2-car

Foundation Types:
  Plan #562-N299-1
  Basement
  Plan #562-N299-2
  Crawl space & slab

PLAN DATA

Total Living Area:	1,629
Bedrooms:	3
Baths:	2
Garage:	2-car
Foundation Type:	
Basement	

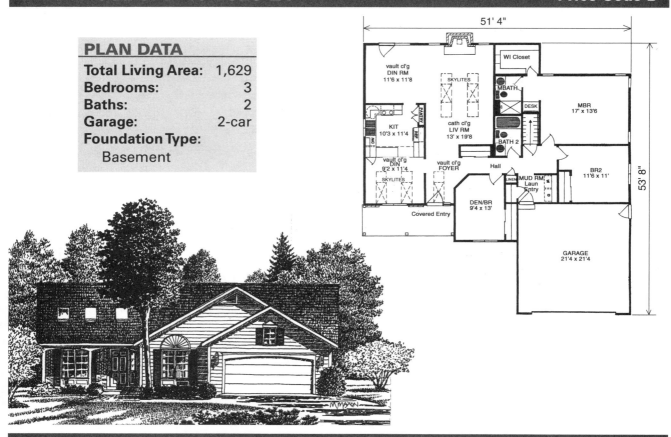

PLAN DATA

Total Living Area:	1,516
Bedrooms:	3
Baths:	2
Garage:	2-car
Foundation Type:	
Basement	

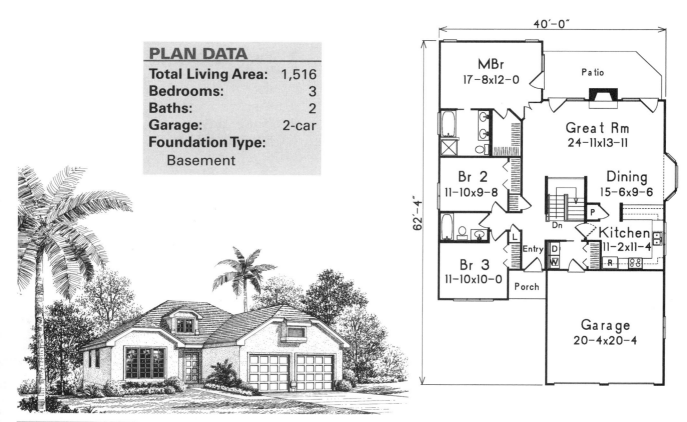

Width: 70'-4"
Depth: 69'-5"

First Floor
3,535 Sq. Ft.

© David C. Lutz

Optional
Second Floor
685 Sq. Ft.

PLAN DATA

Total Living Area:	3,535
Bedrooms:	5
Baths:	4
Garage:	3
Foundation Type: Slab	
Features: Varied ceiling heights	

PLAN DATA

Total Living Area:	1,444
Bedrooms:	3
Baths:	2
Garage:	2-car

Foundation Types:
  Slab standard
  Crawl space

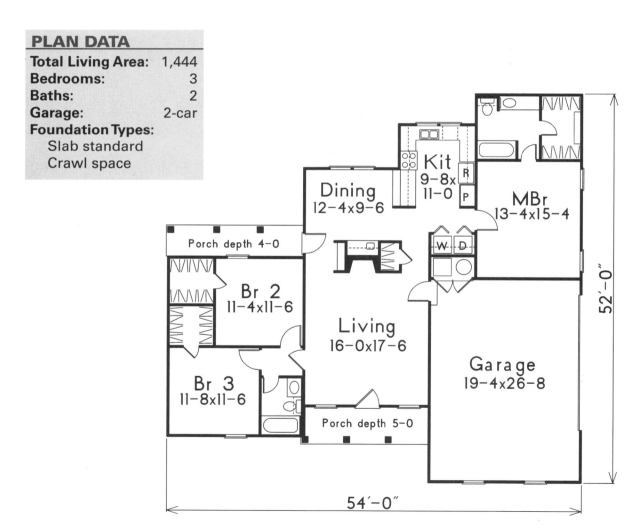

Porch depth 4-0

Dining
12-4x9-6

Kit
9-8x
11-0

R
P

MBr
13-4x15-4

W D

Br 2
11-4x11-6

Living
16-0x17-6

Br 3
11-8x11-6

Garage
19-4x26-8

Porch depth 5-0

52'-0"

54'-0"

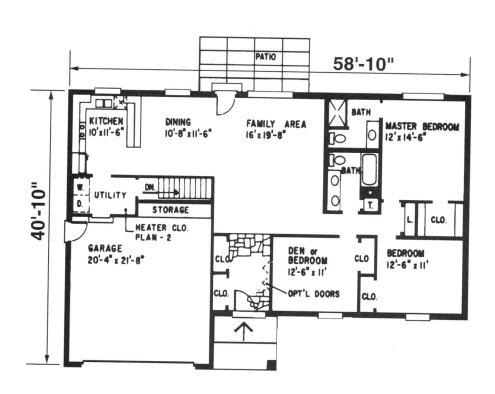

PATIO

58'-10"

40'-10"

KITCHEN
10'x11'-6"

DINING
10'-8"x11'-6"

FAMILY AREA
16'x19'-8"

BATH

MASTER BEDROOM
12'x14'-6"

BATH

T.

W.
D.

UTILITY

DN.

STORAGE

HEATER CLO.
PLAN - 2

GARAGE
20'-4" x 21'-8"

CLO.

DEN or
BEDROOM
12'-6" x 11'

CLO

L.

CLO.

BEDROOM
12'-6" x 11'

CLO.

OPT'L DOORS

CLO.

PLAN DATA

Total Living Area:	1,605
Bedrooms:	3
Baths:	2
Garage:	2-car

Foundation Types:
 Plan #562-ES-125-1
 Basement
 Plan #562-ES-125-2
 Crawl space & slab

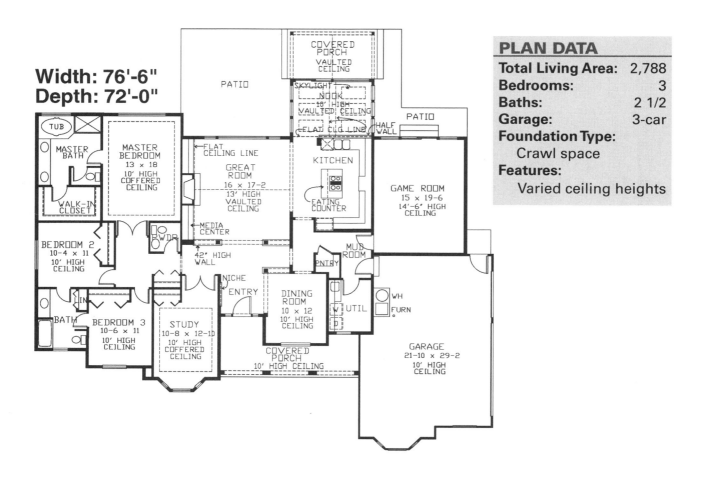

Width: 76'-6"
Depth: 72'-0"

PLAN DATA

Total Living Area:	2,788
Bedrooms:	3
Baths:	2 1/2
Garage:	3-car
Foundation Type:	
Crawl space	
Features:	
Varied ceiling heights	

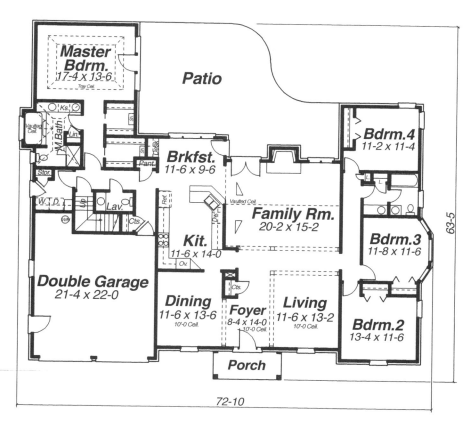

Master Bdrm.
17-4 x 13-6
Tray Ceil.

Patio

Vaulted Ceil.
M. Bath
Ks.
Lin.
Stor.

Brkfst.
11-6 x 9-6

Pant.

Bdrm.4
11-2 x 11-4

W.D.
Lav.
Cts.

Family Rm.
20-2 x 15-2
Vaulted Ceil.

Kit.
11-6 x 14-0
Ov.

Bdrm.3
11-8 x 11-6

Double Garage
21-4 x 22-0

Dining
11-6 x 13-6
10'-0 Ceil.

Foyer
8-4 x 14-0
10'-0 Ceil.

Living
11-6 x 13-2
10'-0 Ceil.

Bdrm.2
13-4 x 11-6

Porch

72-10

63-5

PLAN DATA

Total Living Area: 2,542
Bedrooms: 4
Baths: 2 1/2
Garage: 2-car
Foundation Types:
   Basement
   Crawl space
   Slab
Please specify when ordering
Features:
   10' ceilings in dining
   and living rooms

PLAN #562-CHP-1532-A-141

PLAN DATA

Total Living Area:	1,500
Bedrooms:	3
Baths:	2
Garage:	2-car
Foundation Type:	Slab

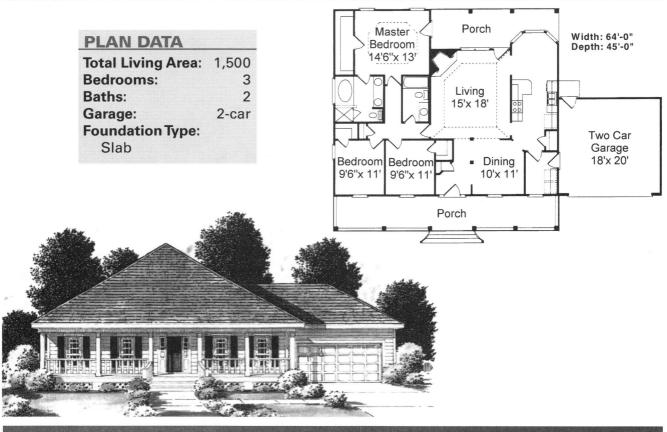

Width: 64'-0"
Depth: 45'-0"

Master Bedroom 14'6"x 13'

Porch

Living 15'x 18'

Two Car Garage 18'x 20'

Bedroom 9'6"x 11'

Bedroom 9'6"x 11'

Dining 10'x 11'

Porch

PLAN #562-1429

PLAN DATA

Total Living Area:	1,500
Bedrooms:	3
Baths:	2
Garage:	2-car
Foundation Type:	Basement

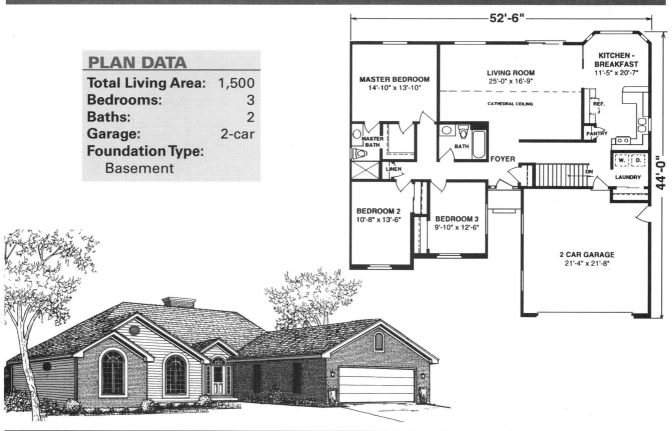

52'-6"

MASTER BEDROOM 14'-10" x 13'-10"

LIVING ROOM 25'-0" x 16'-9"

KITCHEN - BREAKFAST 11'-5" x 20'-7"

CATHEDRAL CEILING

REF.

MASTER BATH

LINEN

BATH

FOYER

PANTRY

W. D.

LAUNDRY

DN

44'-0"

BEDROOM 2 10'-8" x 13'-6"

BEDROOM 3 9'-10" x 12'-6"

2 CAR GARAGE 21'-4" x 21'-8"

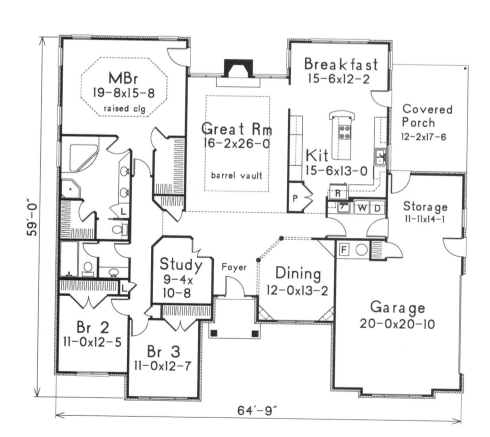

MBr
19-8x15-8
raised clg

Breakfast
15-6x12-2

Covered
Porch
12-2x17-6

Great Rm
16-2x26-0

barrel vault

Kit
15-6x13-0

Storage
11-11x14-1

Study
9-4x
10-8

Foyer

Dining
12-0x13-2

Garage
20-0x20-10

Br 2
11-0x12-5

Br 3
11-0x12-7

59'-0"

64'-9"

PLAN DATA

Total Living Area:	2,437
Bedrooms:	3
Baths:	2
Garage:	2-car
Foundation Types:	
Slab standard	
Crawl space	

PLAN DATA

Total Living Area: 1,742
Bedrooms: 3
Baths: 2
Garage: 2-car
Foundation Types:
  Slab standard
  Crawl space

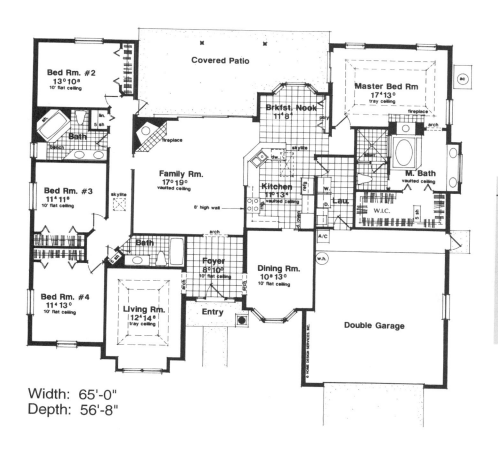

PLAN DATA

Total Living Area:	2,458
Bedrooms:	4
Baths:	3
Garage:	2-car
Foundation Type:	
Slab	
Features:	
Varied ceiling heights	

Width: 65'-0"
Depth: 56'-8"

PLAN DATA

Total Living Area:	2,456
Bedrooms:	3
Baths:	2 1/2
Garage:	3-car

Foundation Types:
  Basement
  Crawl space
  Slab
Please specify when ordering

Features:
  Varied ceiling heights

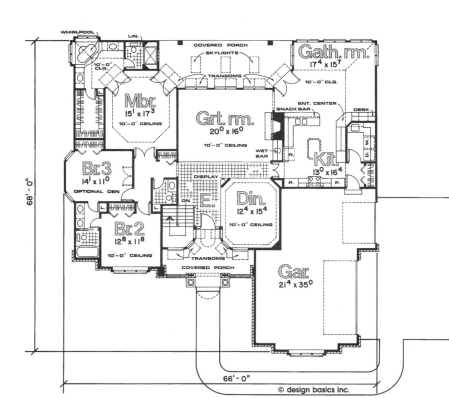

PLAN DATA

Total Living Area: 3,172
Bedrooms: 3
Baths: 2 1/2
Garage: 2-car
Foundation Types:
  Crawl space
  Slab
Please specify when ordering
Features:
  Storage in garage

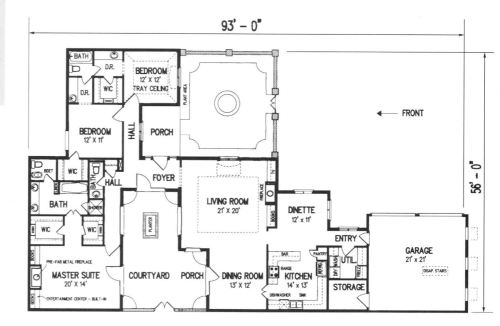

103'-3"

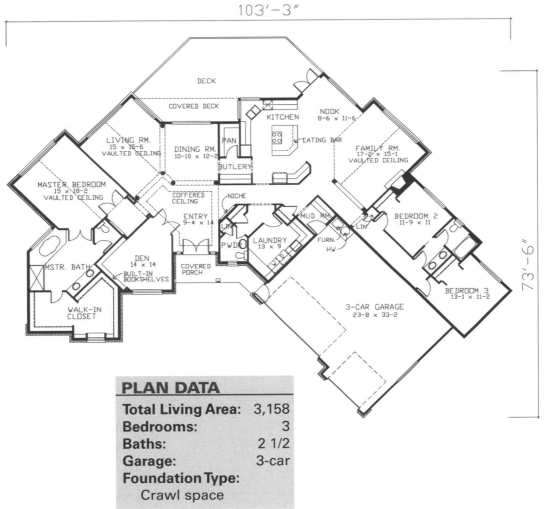

73'-6"

DECK

COVERED DECK

KITCHEN

NOOK
8-6 x 11-6

LIVING RM.
15 x 15-6
VAULTED CEILING

DINING RM.
10-10 x 12-2

PAN

EATING BAR

FAMILY RM.
17-2 x 15-1
VAULTED CEILING

BUTLERY

MASTER BEDROOM
15 x 18-2
VAULTED CEILING

COFFERED
CEILING

NICHE

LIN

MUD RM.

LIN

BEDROOM 2
11-9 x 11

ENTRY
9-4 x 14

PWDR

LAUNDRY
13 x 9

FURN.
HW

MSTR. BATH

DEN
14 x 14

BUILT-IN
BOOKSHELVES

COVERED
PORCH

WALK-IN
CLOSET

BEDROOM 3
13-1 x 11-2

3-CAR GARAGE
23-8 x 33-2

PLAN DATA

Total Living Area:	3,158
Bedrooms:	3
Baths:	2 1/2
Garage:	3-car
Foundation Type:	
Crawl space	

PLAN #562-0796

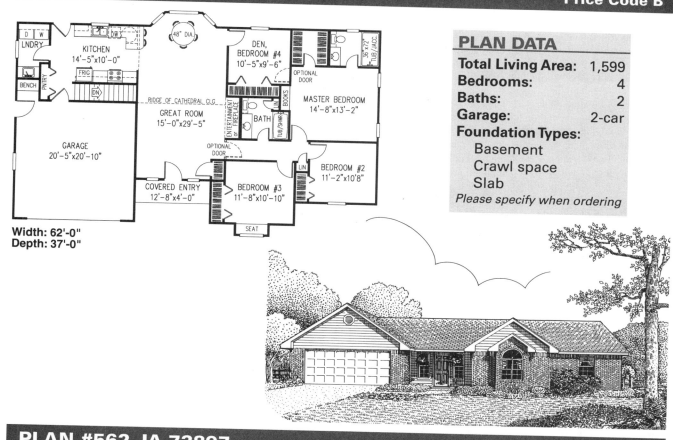

Width: 62'-0"
Depth: 37'-0"

PLAN DATA

Total Living Area:	1,599
Bedrooms:	4
Baths:	2
Garage:	2-car

Foundation Types:
   Basement
   Crawl space
   Slab
Please specify when ordering

PLAN #562-JA-73897

PLAN DATA

Total Living Area:	1,794
Bedrooms:	3
Baths:	2
Garage:	3-car

Foundation Type:
   Basement

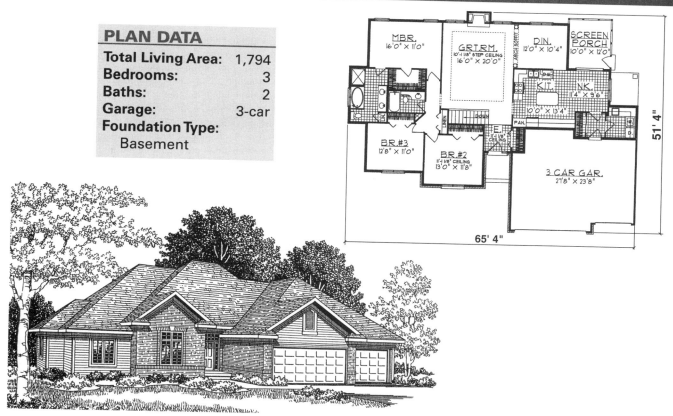

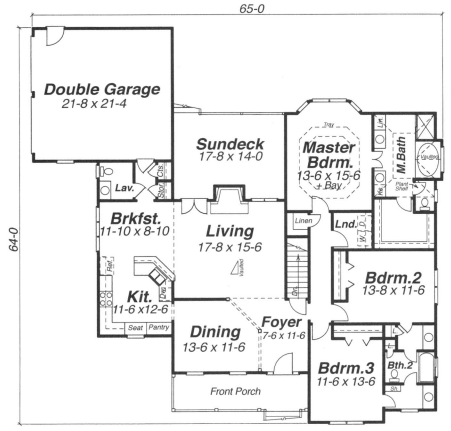

65-0

64-0

Double Garage
21-8 x 21-4

Sundeck
17-8 x 14-0

Tray

Lin.

Master Bdrm.
13-6 x 15-6
+ Bay

M. Bath

Vaulted

Lav.

Stor. Cts.

Brkfst.
11-10 x 8-10

Living
17-8 x 15-6

Linen

Lnd.

W. D.

Ref.

Vaulted

Dw.

Kit.
11-6 x12-6

Seat | Pantry

Dining
13-6 x 11-6

Foyer
7-6 x 11-6

Bdrm.2
13-8 x 11-6

Bdrm.3
11-6 x 13-6

Bth.2

Sh.

Front Porch

PLAN DATA

Total Living Area:	2,012
Bedrooms:	3
Baths:	2 1/2
Garage:	2-car
Foundation Type:	
Basement	

PLAN #562-DL-21644L1

PLAN DATA

Total Living Area: 2,164
Bedrooms: 4
Baths: 2 1/2
Garage: 2-car
Foundation Type:
Slab
Features:
Varied ceiling heights

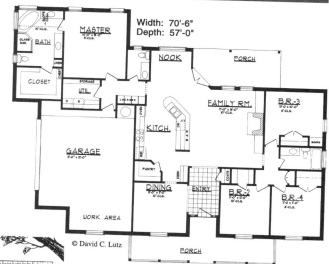

Width: 70'-6"
Depth: 57'-0"

© David C. Lutz

PLAN #562-DL-25454L1

Width: 74'-0"
Depth: 65'-0"

© David C. Lutz

PLAN DATA

Total Living Area: 2,545
Bedrooms: 4
Baths: 3
Garage: 3-car
Foundation Type:
Slab
Features:
Varied ceiling heights

PLAN #562-0246

PLAN DATA

Total Living Area: 1,539
Bedrooms: 3
Baths: 2
Garage: 2-car
Foundation Type:
  Slab
Features:
  - 9' ceilings
  - 10' ceiling in master
    bedroom

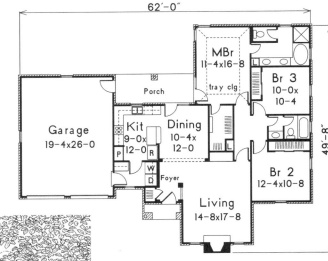

PLAN #562-VL2069

PLAN DATA

Total Living Area: 2,069
Bedrooms: 3
Baths: 2 1/2
Garage: 2-car
Foundation Types:
  Crawl space
  Slab
Please specify when ordering
Features:
  - 9' ceiling standard
  - 11' ceiling in living
    room

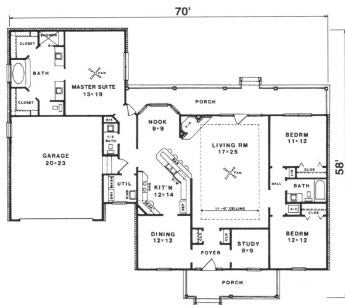

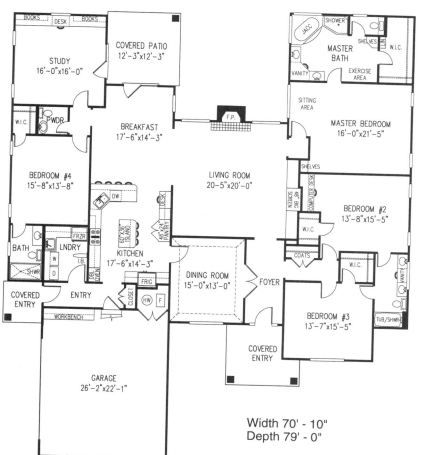

COVERED PATIO
12'-3"x12'-3"

STUDY
16'-0"x16'-0"

BOOKS | DESK | BOOKS

W.I.C.

PWDR

BREAKFAST
17'-6"x14'-3"

BEDROOM #4
15'-8"x13'-8"

DW

LIVING ROOM
20'-5"x20'-0"

F.P.

60"x36" ISLAND

48"x24" PANTRY

DESK

BATH

FRZR

LNDRY

W

D

I.B.

KITCHEN
17'-6"x14'-3"

DBL OVEN

COVERED ENTRY

ENTRY

CLOSET

FRIG

HW | F

WORKBENCH

DINING ROOM
15'-0"x13'-0"

FOYER

GARAGE
26'-2"x22'-1"

COVERED ENTRY

MASTER BATH

JACC

SHOWER

SHELVES

LIN

W.I.C.

VANITY

EXERCISE AREA

SITTING AREA

MASTER BEDROOM
16'-0"x21'-5"

SHELVES

48" BIG SCREEN

COMPUTER DESK

BEDROOM #2
13'-8"x15'-5"

W.I.C.

COATS

W.I.C.

VANITY

BEDROOM #3
13'-7"x15'-5"

TUB/SHWR

Width 70'-10"
Depth 79'-0"

PLAN DATA

Total Living Area:	3,366
Bedrooms:	4
Baths:	3 1/2
Garage:	2-car

Foundation Types:
  Crawl space
  Slab
Please specify when ordering

PLAN DATA

Total Living Area: 1,772
Bedrooms: 3
Baths: 2
Garage: 2-car detached
Foundation Types:
  Slab standard
  Crawl space

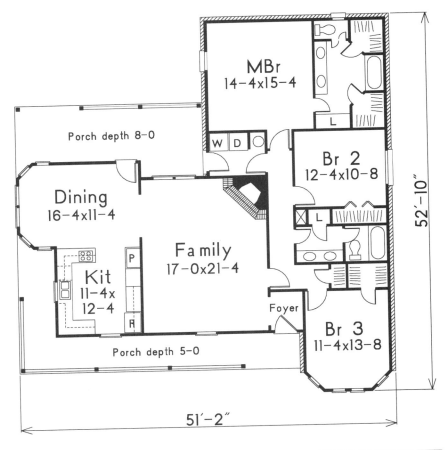

Porch depth 8-0

Dining
16-4x11-4

Kit
11-4x
12-4

Family
17-0x21-4

Foyer

Porch depth 5-0

MBr
14-4x15-4

Br 2
12-4x10-8

Br 3
11-4x13-8

W D

52'-10"

51'-2"

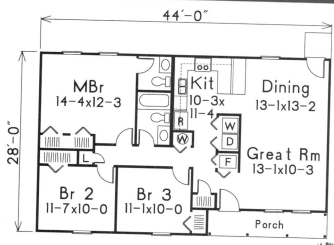

44'-0"

28'-0"

MBr
14-4x12-3

Kit
10-3x
11-4

Dining
13-1x13-2

Great Rm
13-1x10-3

Br 2
11-7x10-0

Br 3
11-1x10-0

Porch

PLAN DATA

Total Living Area: 1,160
Bedrooms: 3
Baths: 1 1/2
Foundation Types:
  Crawl space standard
  Basement
  Slab

PLAN DATA

Total Living Area: 1,253
Bedrooms: 3
Baths: 2
Garage: 2-car
Foundation Types:
  Crawl space
  Slab
Please specify when ordering

Rear Porch
16 x 5/9

Master
14 x 12
8' Clg.

Dining
10/9 x 11

Kitchen
9 x 11
8' clg.

Garage
20 x 22

Bedroom #3
10/4 x 10/7
8' Clg.

Pass
Thru

W
D

Stor.

Family Room
14 x 16/8
11'-4" Clg.

Bedroom #2
10 x 10/8
8' Clg.

Sloped Ceiling

Foyer

Width: 61'-3"
Depth: 40'-6"

Porch
34/8 x 6

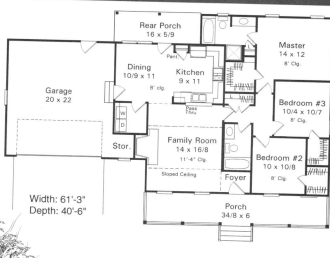

PLAN DATA

Total Living Area:	1,925
Bedrooms:	3
Baths:	2
Garage:	2-car

Foundation Types:
Crawl space
Slab
Please specify when ordering

Features:
2" x 6" exterior walls

PORCH
20' X 8'

BEDROOM
12' x 12'

WIC

LIVING ROOM
24' X 16'
SLOPED CEILINGS

MASTER SUITE
16' X 16'

DRESS. RM.

BATH

WIC

STORAGE
9' X 9'

FIREPLACE

BATH

HEAT & A/C

SHWR.

UTIL.
8' X 7'

HALL

EATING AREA
10' X 10'

GARAGE
23' X 22'

BEDROOM
12' x 12'

FOYER

DINING ROOM
12' x 12'

PANTRY

KITCHEN
12' x 12'

RANGE

DW   SINK

BALCONY
10' X 6'

PORCH
44' X 8'

WORK BENCH   SHVS.

78'

52'

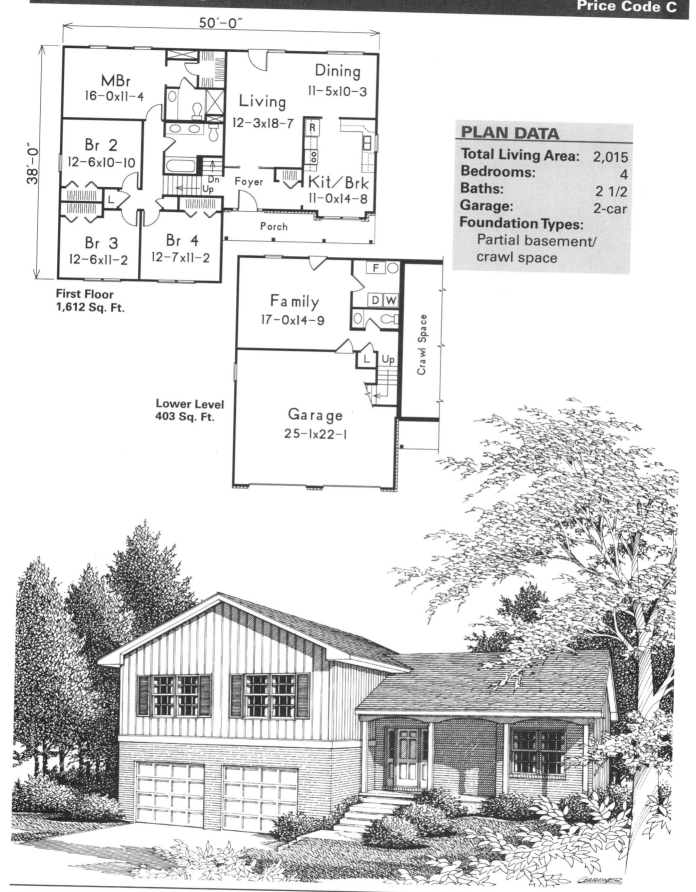

50'-0"

38'-0"

MBr
16-0x11-4

Br 2
12-6x10-10

Br 3
12-6x11-2

Br 4
12-7x11-2

Living
12-3x18-7

Dining
11-5x10-3

Foyer

Dn
Up

Kit/Brk
11-0x14-8

Porch

L

**First Floor
1,612 Sq. Ft.**

Family
17-0x14-9

F

D W

L Up

Crawl Space

Garage
25-1x22-1

**Lower Level
403 Sq. Ft.**

PLAN DATA

Total Living Area: 2,015
Bedrooms: 4
Baths: 2 1/2
Garage: 2-car
Foundation Types:
  Partial basement/
  crawl space

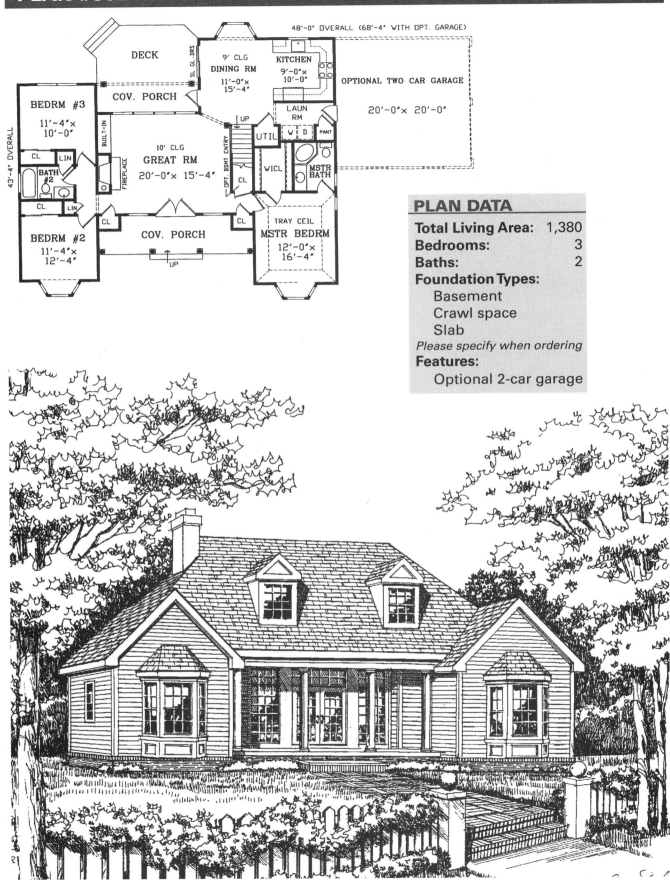

48'-0" OVERALL (68'-4" WITH OPT. GARAGE)

DECK

9' CLG
DINING RM
11'-0"x
15'-4"

KITCHEN
9'-0"x
10'-0"

SL GL DRS

COV. PORCH

OPTIONAL TWO CAR GARAGE

20'-0"x 20'-0"

BEDRM #3
11'-4"x
10'-0"

BUILT-IN

UP

LAUN
RM

43'-4" OVERALL

CL   LIN

BATH
#2

FIREPLACE

10' CLG
GREAT RM
20'-0"x 15'-4"

OPT. BSMT ENTRY

UTIL

W D

PANT

WICL

CL   LIN

CL

MSTR
BATH

BEDRM #2
11'-4"x
12'-4"

CL

COV. PORCH

UP

CL

TRAY CEIL
MSTR BEDRM
12'-0"x
16'-4"

PLAN DATA

Total Living Area: 1,380
Bedrooms: 3
Baths: 2
Foundation Types:
  Basement
  Crawl space
  Slab
Please specify when ordering
Features:
  Optional 2-car garage

First Floor
2,311 Sq. Ft.

Sitting Area

FPL.

TRAY CLG.

Master Suite
17⁹ x 20⁰

PLANT SHELF ABOVE

VAULT

VAULT   VAULT

Vaulted Breakfast

FRENCH DOOR

RADIUS WINDOW

VAULT

Bedroom 2
12² x 11⁶

Bath

Hers

Vaulted M.Bath

SHWR.

PLANT SHELF ABOVE

K.S.

LINEN

His

LINEN   w.   Lgund.
                D.

COATS

STAIRS TO OPT. BSMT.

Pwdr.

STAIRS

RANGE

DW.

REF.

Kitchen

PASS THRU

PANTRY

Vaulted Family Room
16⁰ x 22⁶
15'-0" HIGH CEILING

FPL.

LINEN

Bedroom 3
11⁰ x 11⁰

ARCHED OPENINGS

PLANT SHELF ABOVE

Dining Room
12⁹ x 12⁸
15'-0" HIGH CEILING

Foyer
15'-0" HIGH CEILING

COATS

COVERED PORCH

Vaulted Living Room/
Opt. Bedroom 4
12⁵ x 12⁹

Garage
22⁵ x 21⁰

copyright © 1996 frank betz associates, inc.

61'-0"

65'-4"

Bath

W.i.c.

STAIRS DN.

Opt. Bonus Room
12⁵ x 21⁰

Optional Second Floor
425 Sq. Ft.

PLAN DATA

Total Living Area:	2,311
Bedrooms:	3
Baths:	2 1/2
Garage:	2-car

Foundation Types:
   Basement
   Crawl space
Please specify when ordering
Features:
   Varied ceiling heights

PLAN DATA

Total Living Area:	2,308
Bedrooms:	3
Baths:	2
Garage:	2-car
Foundation Type:	Walk-out basement

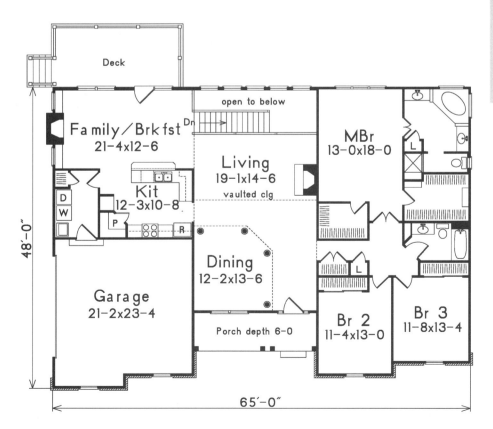

Deck

Family/Brkfst Dn
21-4x12-6

open to below

MBr
13-0x18-0

Living
19-1x14-6
vaulted clg

Kit
12-3x10-8

D
W

P

R

Dining
12-2x13-6

L

Garage
21-2x23-4

Br 2
11-4x13-0

Br 3
11-8x13-4

Porch depth 6-0

48'-0"

65'-0"

PLAN DATA

Total Living Area: 1,197
Bedrooms: 3
Bath: 1
Foundation Types:
　Crawl space standard
　Basement
　Slab

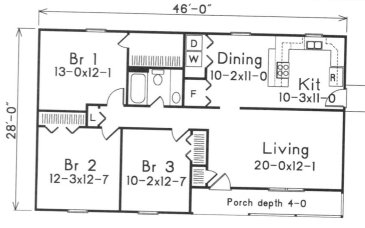

PLAN #562-0296

Price Code A

PLAN DATA

Total Living Area: 1,396
Bedrooms: 3
Baths: 2
Garage: 1-car carport
Foundation Types:
　Basement standard
　Crawl space

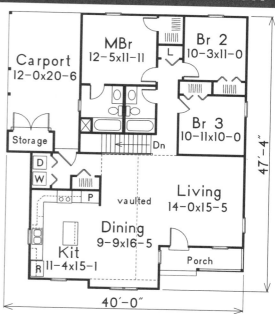

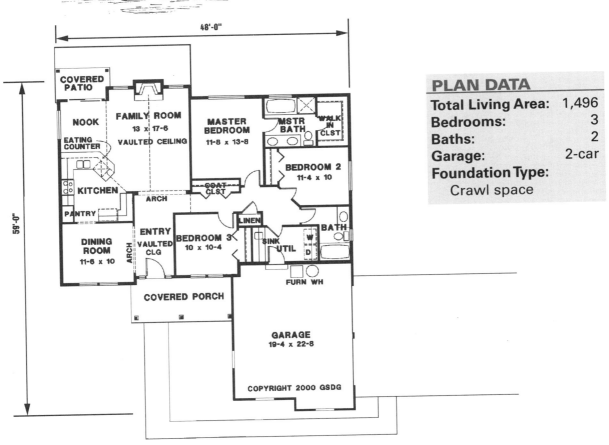

48'-0"

59'-0"

COVERED PATIO

NOOK

FAMILY ROOM
13 x 17-6
VAULTED CEILING

MASTER BEDROOM
11-8 x 13-8

MSTR BATH

WALK IN CLST

EATING COUNTER

KITCHEN

PANTRY

COAT CLST

ARCH

BEDROOM 2
11-4 x 10

DINING ROOM
11-6 x 10

ARCH

ENTRY
VAULTED CLG

BEDROOM 3
10 x 10-4

LINEN

SINK

UTIL

W D

BATH

FURN WH

COVERED PORCH

GARAGE
19-4 x 22-8

COPYRIGHT 2000 GSDG

PLAN DATA

Total Living Area:	1,496
Bedrooms:	3
Baths:	2
Garage:	2-car
Foundation Type:	Crawl space

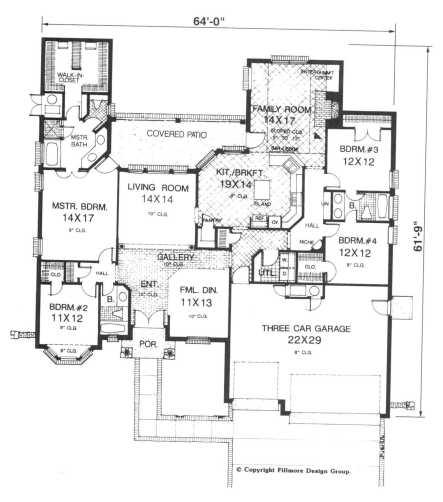

64'-0"

WALK-IN-CLOSET

MSTR. BATH

COVERED PATIO

FAMILY ROOM
14X17
SLOPED CLG.
9' TO 12'
ENTERTAINM'T CENTER
BAR LEDGE

BDRM.#3
12X12

LIVING ROOM
14X14
10' CLG.

KIT./BRKFT.
19X14
8' CLG.
ISLAND

MSTR. BDRM.
14X17
9' CLG.

PANTRY

REF. OV.

LIN.

B.

HALL

NICHE

BDRM.#4
12X12
8' CLG.

GALLERY
10' CLG.

CLO. HALL

ENT.
10' CLG.

FML. DIN.
11X13
10' CLG.

UTL.

W D

CLO.

61'-9"

B.

BDRM.#2
11X12
9' CLG.

THREE CAR GARAGE
22X29
8' CLG.

POR.

8' CLG.

© Copyright Fillmore Design Group.

PLAN DATA

Total Living Area:	2,528
Bedrooms:	4
Baths:	3
Garage:	3-car
Foundation Type:	
Slab	
Features:	
Varied ceiling heights	

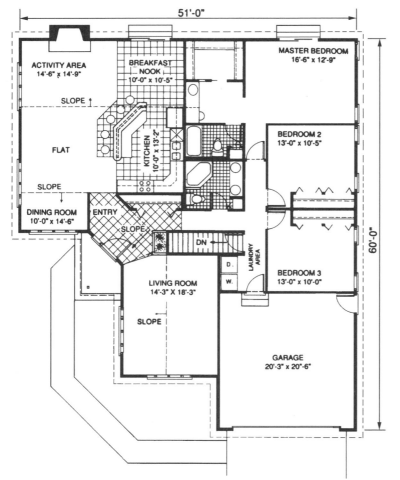

51'-0"

60'-0"

ACTIVITY AREA
14'-6" x 14'-9"

SLOPE ↑

FLAT

SLOPE

DINING ROOM
10'-0" x 14'-6"

BREAKFAST
NOOK
10'-0" x 10'-5"

KITCHEN
10'-0" x 13'-2"

ENTRY

SLOPE

DN

MASTER BEDROOM
16'-6" x 12'-9"

BEDROOM 2
13'-0" x 10'-5"

LAUNDRY
AREA

D.

W.

BEDROOM 3
13'-0" x 10'-0"

LIVING ROOM
14'-3" X 18'-3"

SLOPE

GARAGE
20'-3" x 20'-6"

PLAN DATA

Total Living Area: 2,086
Bedrooms: 3
Baths: 2
Garage: 2-car
Foundation Type:
   Partial basement/
   crawl space

PLAN #562-0277

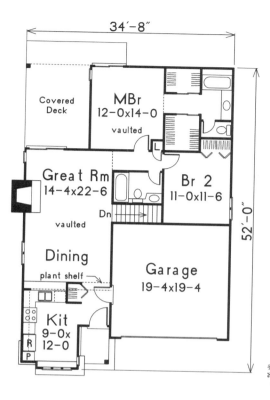

34'-8"

52'-0"

Covered Deck

MBr
12-0x14-0
vaulted

Great Rm
14-4x22-6
vaulted

Dn

Br 2
11-0x11-6

Dining

plant shelf

Garage
19-4x19-4

Kit
9-0x
12-0

R

P

PLAN DATA
Total Living Area: 1,127
Bedrooms: 2
Baths: 2
Garage: 2-car
Foundation Type:
  Basement

PLAN #562-JV-1276-A

PLAN DATA
Total Living Area: 1,296
Bedrooms: 3
Baths: 2
Garage: 2-car
Foundation Type:
  Basement
Features:
  Drive-under garage

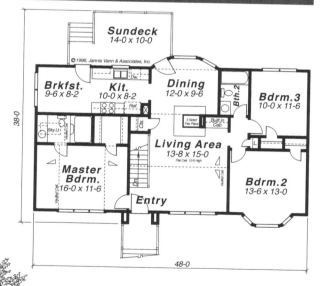

Sundeck
14-0 x 10-0

© 1996, Jannis Vann & Associates, Inc.

Brkfst.
9-6 x 8-2

Kit.
10-0 x 8-2

Dining
12-0 x 9-6

Bth. 2

Bdrm. 3
10-0 x 11-6

Ref.

3 Sided
Fire Place

Built In
Cab

Sky Lt.

Living Area
13-8 x 15-0
Flat Ceil. 12-9 High

Master
Bdrm.
16-0 x 11-6

Entry

Bdrm. 2
13-6 x 13-0

38-0

48-0

53-0

55-4

BEDROOM 2
10'-0" X 15'-0"

BRKFAST RM.
12'-4" X 9'-6"

PORCH

MBEDRM.
13'-6" X 16'-4"

DW

BATH

RG
KITCHEN
REF. PAN.

DINING
10'-6" X 11'-4"

MB.

8" COL.

BEDROOM I
10'-4" X 10'-0"

LIN.

FOYER
10' CEILING

LAU.
W D

STRG.

WH

NOTE:
HVAC IN ATTIC.

PRCH.

GREAT RM.
15'-4" X 19'-0"
10' CEILING

GARAGE
20'-10" X 20'-0"

PLAN DATA

Total Living Area: 1,764
Bedrooms: 3
Baths: 2
Garage: 2-car
Foundation Types:
  Basement
  Walk-out basement
  Crawl space
  Slab
Please specify when ordering
Features:
  10' ceiling in foyer
  and great room

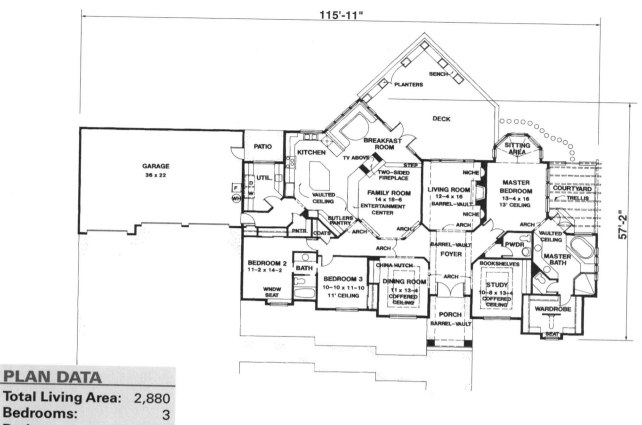

115'-11"

57'-2"

GARAGE
36 x 22

PATIO

KITCHEN

UTIL.

VAULTED
CEILING

BUTLERS
PANTRY

PNTR.

COATS

ARCH

BREAKFAST
ROOM

TV ABOVE

TWO-SIDED
FIREPLACE

FAMILY ROOM
14 x 18-6
ENTERTAINMENT
CENTER

ARCH

ARCH

BENCH

PLANTERS

DECK

STEP

LIVING ROOM
12-4 x 16
BARREL-VAULT

NICHE

NICHE

ARCH

BARREL-VAULT
FOYER

ARCH

SITTING
AREA

MASTER
BEDROOM
13-4 x 16
13' CEILING

ARCH

COURTYARD

TRELLIS

VAULTED
CEILING

PWDR

MASTER
BATH

BEDROOM 2
11-2 x 14-2

BATH

WNDW
SEAT

BEDROOM 3
10-10 x 11-10
11' CEILING

CHINA HUTCH

DINING ROOM
11 x 13-4
COFFERED
CEILING

ARCH

PORCH
BARREL-VAULT

BOOKSHELVES

STUDY
10-8 x 13-4
COFFERED
CEILING

WARDROBE

SEAT

PLAN DATA

Total Living Area:	2,880
Bedrooms:	3
Baths:	2 1/2
Garage:	3-car
Foundation Type:	
Crawl space	
Features:	
Varied ceiling heights	

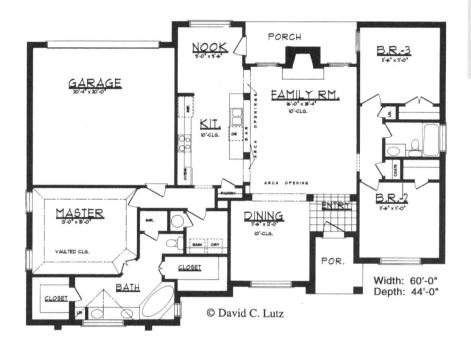

GARAGE
20'-4" x 20'-0"

NOOK
9'-0" x 9'-6"

PORCH

B.R.-3
11'-6" x 11'-0"

KIT.
10'-CLG.

FAMILY RM.
16'-0" x 18'-4"
10'-CLG.

MASTER
13'-0" x 15'-0"
VAULTED CLG.

PANTRY

DINING
11'-6" x 12'-0"
10'-CLG.

ENTRY

B.R.-2
11'-6" x 11'-0"

CLOSET

POR.

BATH

CLOSET

© David C. Lutz

Width: 60'-0"
Depth: 44'-0"

PLAN DATA

Total Living Area: 1,765
Bedrooms: 3
Baths: 2
Garage: 2-car
Foundation Type:
 Slab
Features:
 Varied ceiling heights

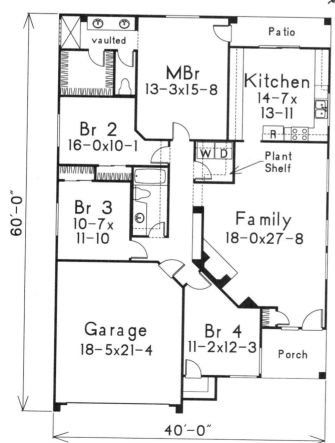

PLAN DATA

Total Living Area:	1,747
Bedrooms:	4
Baths:	2
Garage:	2-car
Foundation Type:	
Slab	

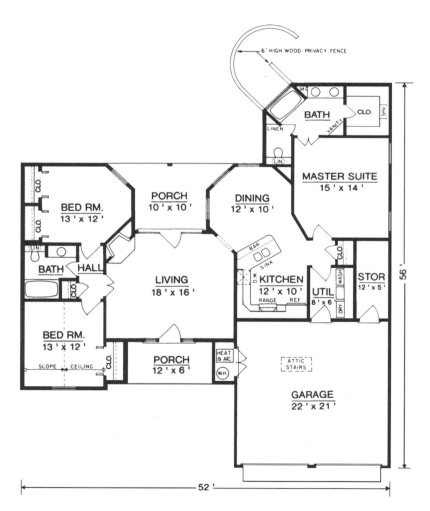

6' HIGH WOOD PRIVACY FENCE

BATH

CLO.

LINEN

LIN

MASTER SUITE
15' x 14'

BED RM.
13' x 12'

PORCH
10' x 10'

DINING
12' x 10'

LIN

BATH   HALL

LIVING
18' x 16'

BAR

CLO.

WASH

STOR
12' x 5'

D.W
SINK

KITCHEN
12' x 10'

UTIL
8' x 6'

DRY

RANGE   REF.

BED RM.
13' x 12'

SLOPE   CEILING

CLO.

PORCH
12' x 6'

HEAT
& A/C

W.H.

ATTIC
STAIRS

GARAGE
22' x 21'

56'

52'

PLAN DATA

Total Living Area:	1,420
Bedrooms:	3
Baths:	2
Garage:	2-car

Foundation Types:
Slab
Crawl space
Please specify when ordering

Features:
- 2" x 6" exterior walls
- 12' ceiling in living room

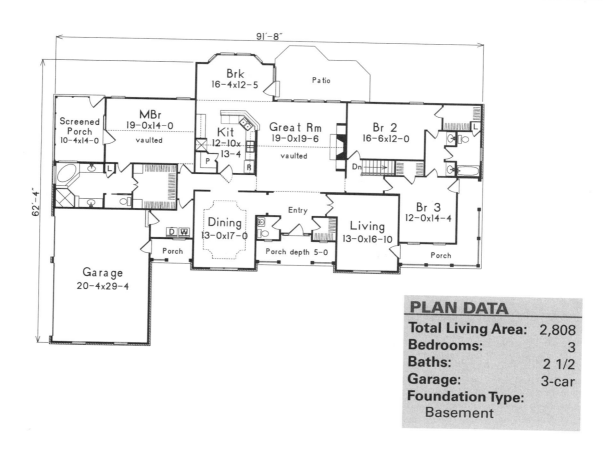

91'-8"

62'-4"

Brk
16-4x12-5

Patio

Screened
Porch
10-4x14-0

MBr
19-0x14-0
vaulted

Kit
12-10x
13-4

Great Rm
19-0x19-6
vaulted

Br 2
16-6x12-0

L

P R

Dn

Br 3
12-0x14-4

L

DW

Dining
13-0x17-0

Entry

Living
13-0x16-10

Porch

Porch depth 5-0

Porch

Garage
20-4x29-4

PLAN DATA

Total Living Area:	2,808
Bedrooms:	3
Baths:	2 1/2
Garage:	3-car
Foundation Type:	
Basement	

PLAN DATA

Total Living Area: 1,996
Bedrooms: 2
Baths: 2
Garage: 3-car
Foundation Types:
   Slab
   Basement
Please specify when ordering
Features:
   Varied ceiling heights

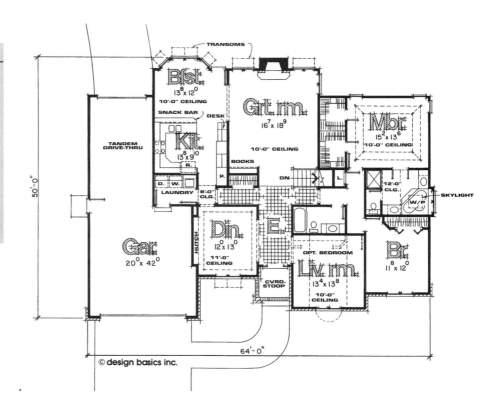

TRANSOMS

Bfst.
13⁸ x 12⁰
10'-0" CEILING

SNACK BAR   DESK

Grt. rm.
16⁷ x 18⁹
10'-0" CEILING

Mbr.
15² x 13⁶
10'-0" CEILING

TANDEM
DRIVE-THRU

Kit.
13⁸ x 9⁰

BOOKS

R.   P.

DN.

L.

D. W.

LAUNDRY

8'-0"
CLG.

12'-0"
CLG.

W/P   SKYLIGHT

50'-0"

Gar.
20⁰ x 42⁰

HUTCH

Dn.
12⁰ x 13⁰
11'-0"
CEILING

OPT. BEDROOM

Liv. rm.
13⁴ x 13⁸
10'-0"
CEILING

Br.
11⁸ x 12⁰

CVRD.
STOOP

© design basics inc.

64'-0"

PLAN DATA

Total Living Area: 1,120
Bedrooms: 3
Baths: 1 1/2
Foundation Types:
  Crawl space standard
  Basement
  Slab

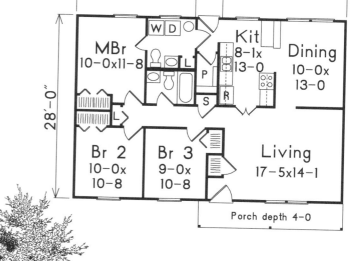

40'-0"

28'-0"

MBr
10-0x11-8

W D

Kit
8-1x
13-0

Dining
10-0x
13-0

Br 2
10-0x
10-8

Br 3
9-0x
10-8

Living
17-5x14-1

Porch depth 4-0

PLAN #562-DL-13663L

Price Code A

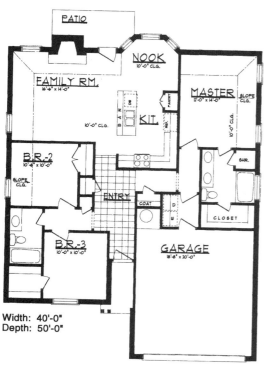

PATIO

NOOK
10'-0" CLG.

FAMILY RM.
16'-8" x 14'-0"

MASTER
12'-0" x 14'-0"
SLOPE CLG.

10'-0" CLG.

10'-0" CLG.

BAR

KIT.

B.R.-2
10'-4" x 10'-0"
SLOPE CLG.

SHR.

ENTRY

COAT

CLOSET

B.R.-3
10'-0" x 10'-0"

GARAGE
18'-8" x 20'-0"

Width: 40'-0"
Depth: 50'-0"

PLAN DATA

Total Living Area: 1,366
Bedrooms: 3
Baths: 2
Garage: 2-car
Foundation Type:
  Slab
Features:
  Varied ceiling heights

PLAN DATA

Total Living Area: 2,513
Bedrooms: 4
Baths: 2 full, 2 half
Garage: 2-car
Foundation Type: Basement

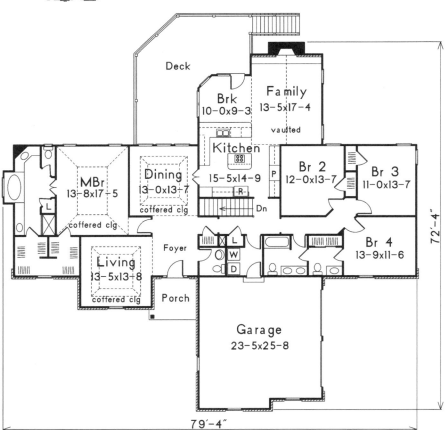

Deck

Brk
10-0x9-3

Family
13-5x17-4
vaulted

Kitchen
15-5x14-9

Br 2
12-0x13-7

Br 3
11-0x13-7

MBr
13-8x17-5
coffered clg

Dining
13-0x13-7
coffered clg

Dn

P

R

Br 4
13-9x11-6

Living
13-5x13-8
coffered clg

Foyer

L
W
D

Porch

Garage
23-5x25-8

72'-4"

79'-4"

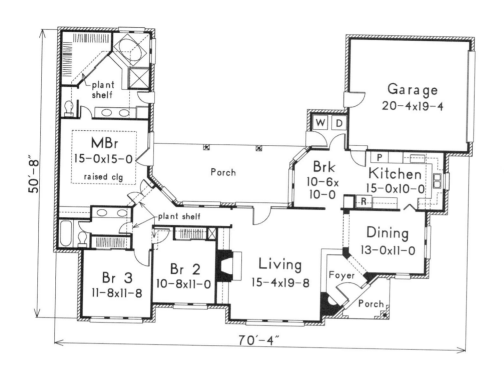

50'-8"

plant
shelf

MBr
15-0x15-0
raised clg

Porch

Garage
20-4x19-4

W D

P

Brk
10-6x
10-0

Kitchen
15-0x10-0

R

plant shelf

Dining
13-0x11-0

Br 3
11-8x11-8

Br 2
10-8x11-0

Living
15-4x19-8

Foyer

Porch

70'-4"

PLAN DATA

Total Living Area:	1,996
Bedrooms:	3
Baths:	2
Garage:	2-car
Foundation Types:	
Slab standard	
Crawl space	

PLAN DATA

Total Living Area: 1,785
Bedrooms: 3
Baths: 2
Garage: 2-car
Foundation Types:
  Basement
  Crawl space
  Slab
Please specify when ordering
Features:
  - 11' ceilings in living, dining and kitchen area
  - Open floor plan is wheelchair accessible

Width: 58'-0"
Depth: 57'-0"

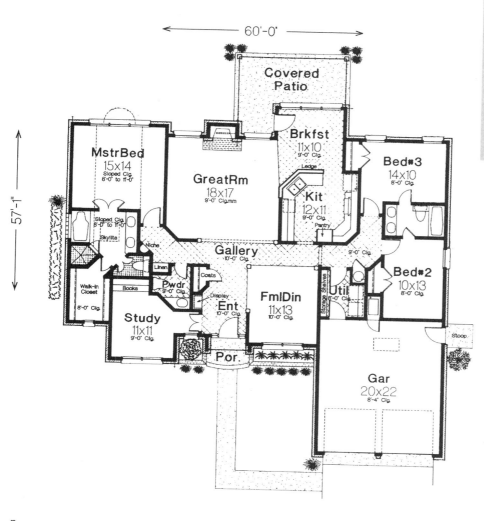

60'-0"

57'-1"

Covered Patio

MstrBed
15x14
Sloped Clg.
8'-0" to 11'-0"

GreatRm
18x17
9'-0" Clg.mm

Brkfst
11x10
9'-0" Clg.

Bed#3
14x10
8'-0" Clg.

Sloped Clg.
8'-0" to 11'-0"

Skylite

Niche

Ledge

Kit
12x11
9'-0" Clg.

Pantry

Walk-In Closet
8'-0" Clg.

Linen

Coats

Pwdr
9'-0" Clg.

Books

Display

Gallery
10'-0" Clg.

Storage Shelves

9'-0" Clg.

Bed#2
10x13
8'-0" Clg.

Util
9'-0" Clg.

Study
11x11
9'-0" Clg.

Ent
10'-0" Clg.

FmlDin
11x13
10'-0" Clg.

Por.

Stoop

Gar
20x22
8'-4" Clg.

PLAN DATA

Total Living Area:	2,061
Bedrooms:	3
Baths:	2 1/2
Garage:	2-car

Foundation Types:
  Crawl space
  Slab
Please specify when ordering

Features:
  Varied ceiling heights

PLAN DATA

Total Living Area:	1,429
Bedrooms:	3
Baths:	2
Garage:	2-car
Foundation Type:	
Basement	
Features:	
Drive-under garage	

Bfst 11 x 9

Grt. rm. 14 x 17

Mbr 11 x 16 9'-0" CLG.

Kit 11 x 10

Dn 12 x 11

Br 11 x 11

Br 11 x 10

COVERED PORCH

© design basics inc.

First Floor

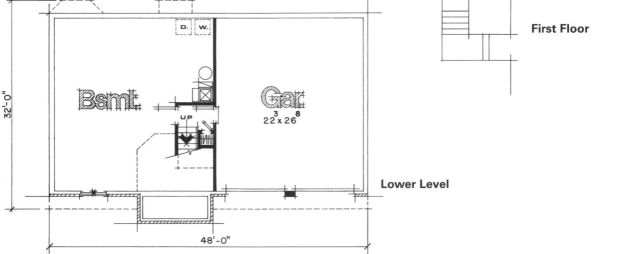

Bsmt

Gar 22 x 26

32'-0"

48'-0"

Lower Level

PLAN DATA

Total Living Area: 1,941
Bedrooms: 3
Baths: 2
Garage: 2-car
Foundation Types:
  Basement
  Walk-out basement
  Crawl space
  Slab
Please specify when ordering
Features:
  Varied ceiling heights

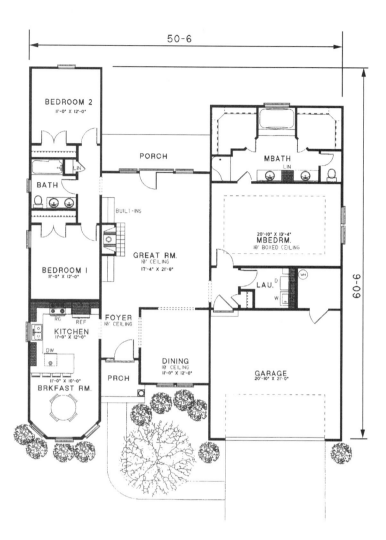

© HOME DESIGN SERVICES, INC.

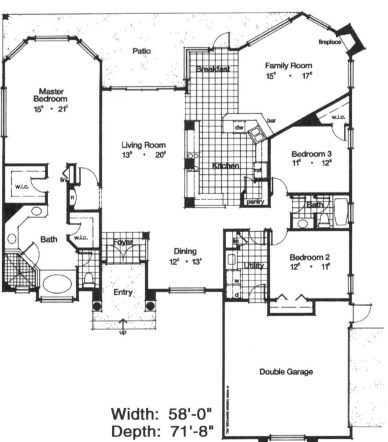

Width: 58'-0"
Depth: 71'-8"

PLAN DATA

Total Living Area:	2,278
Bedrooms:	3
Baths:	2
Garage:	2-car
Foundation Type:	
Slab	

B.R.-3
11'-3" x 11'-0"
SLOPE CLG.
8'   10'

PORCH
10'-CLG.

MASTER
VAULED CLG.
13'-6" x 17'-0"

STORAGE

BATH
10'-CLG.

SHOWER

LINEN

SEAT

CLOSET

LIVING
10'-CLG.
13'-6" x 13'-0"

FAMILY
15'-0" x 17'-0"
STEP UP CLG.

TWO BAY FIRE PLACE

MEDIA CTR.

LINEN

STORAGE

B.R.-4
10'-0" x 11'-0"
SLOPE CLG.
8'   10'

NOOK
11'-8" x 10'-0"
9'-CLG.

ENTRY

DINING
10'-CLG.

OVENS

DW

BAR

KITCH.

B.R.-2
CATH CLG.
11'-3" x 11'-3"

REF.

PANTRY

UTIL. RM.

DRY / WASHER

W H

STORAGE

GARAGE
21'-6" x 21'-8"
8'-CLG.

© David C. Lutz

Width: 59'-1"
Depth: 70'-5"

PLAN DATA

Total Living Area:	2,382
Bedrooms:	4
Baths:	2
Garage:	2-car
Foundation Type:	Slab

Features:
- Garage with storage
- Varied ceiling heights

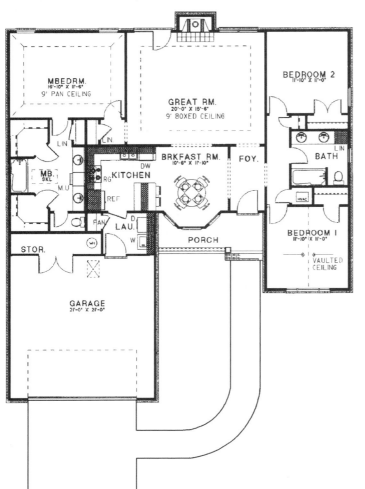

50-0

MBEDRM.
16'-10" X 11'-6"
9' PAN CEILING

GREAT RM.
20'-0" X 15'-6"
9' BOXED CEILING

BEDROOM 2
11'-10" X 11'-0"

56-0

LIN.

MB.
9 KL

M.U

LIN.

DW

KITCHEN

RG

REF

PAN.

BRKFAST RM.
10'-8" X 11'-10"

FOY.

BATH

LIN.

LAU.

D

W

PORCH

STOR.

WH

HVAC

BEDROOM I
11'-10" X 11'-0"

VAULTED
CEILING

GARAGE
21'-0" X 21'-0"

PLAN DATA

Total Living Area: 1,538
Bedrooms: 3
Baths: 2
Garage: 2-car
Foundation Types:
  Basement
  Walk-out basement
  Crawl space
  Slab
Please specify when ordering
Features:
  Varied ceiling heights

PLAN DATA

Total Living Area:	2,434
Bedrooms:	4
Baths:	3 1/2
Garage:	3-car
Foundation Type:	
Slab	
Features:	
Varied ceiling heights	

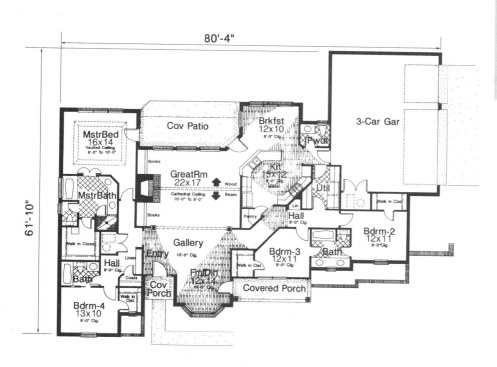

PLAN DATA

Total Living Area:	1,635
Bedrooms:	3
Baths:	2
Garage:	2-car

Foundation Types:
- Basement
- Crawl space
- Slab

Please specify when ordering

Features:
- Varied ceiling heights

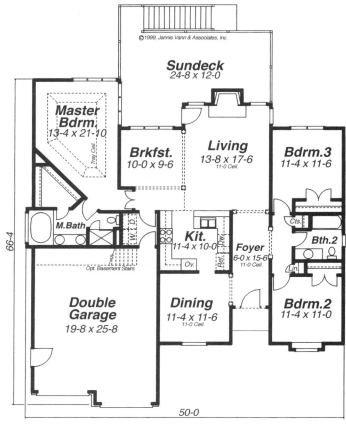

© 1999, Jannis Vann & Associates, Inc.

Sundeck 24-8 x 12-0

Master Bdrm. 13-4 x 21-10 *Tray Ceil.*

Brkfst. 10-0 x 9-6

Living 13-8 x 17-6 11-0 Ceil.

Bdrm.3 11-4 x 11-6

M.Bath

W. D.

Kit. 11-4 x 10-0

Foyer 6-0 x 15-6 11-0 Ceil.

Cts.

Bth.2

Lin.

Opt. Basement Stairs Ov. Ref.

Double Garage 19-8 x 25-8

Dining 11-4 x 11-6 11-0 Ceil.

Bdrm.2 11-4 x 11-0

66-4

50-0

Width: 64'-4"
Depth: 66'-0"

PLAN DATA

Total Living Area: 2,380
Bedrooms: 4
Baths: 3
Garage: 2-car
Foundation Type:
  Slab
Features:
  Varied ceiling heights

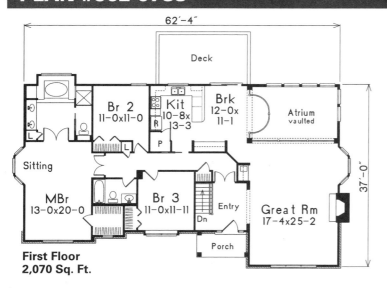

62'-4"

Deck

Br 2
11-0x11-0

Kit
10-8x
13-3

Brk
12-0x
11-1

Atrium
vaulted

Sitting

MBr
13-0x20-0

Br 3
11-0x11-11

Entry

Dn

Great Rm
17-4x25-2

Porch

37'-0"

**First Floor
2,070 Sq. Ft.**

PLAN DATA

Total Living Area:	2,070
Bedrooms:	3
Baths:	2
Garage:	2-car
Foundation Type:	
Walk-out basement	
Features:	
Drive-under garage	

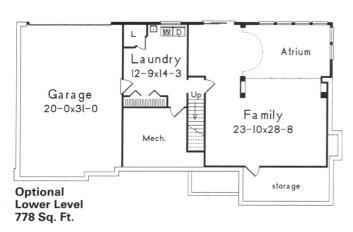

Laundry
12-9x14-3

Atrium

Garage
20-0x31-0

Up

Mech.

Family
23-10x28-8

storage

**Optional
Lower Level
778 Sq. Ft.**

Rear View

PLAN #562-0687

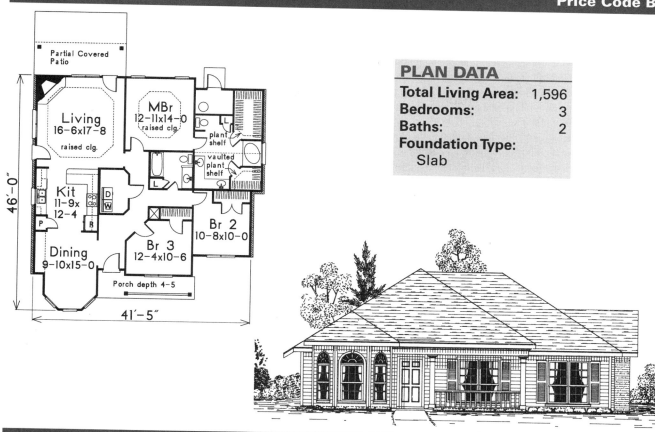

Partial Covered Patio

Living 16-6x17-8 *raised clg.*

MBr 12-11x14-0 *raised clg.*

plant shelf

vaulted plant shelf

L

L

Kit 11-9x 12-4

D W

P

R

Dining 9-10x15-0

Br 3 12-4x10-6

Br 2 10-8x10-0

Porch depth 4-5

46'-0"

41'-5"

PLAN DATA
Total Living Area: 1,596
Bedrooms: 3
Baths: 2
Foundation Type:
  Slab

PLAN #562-0226

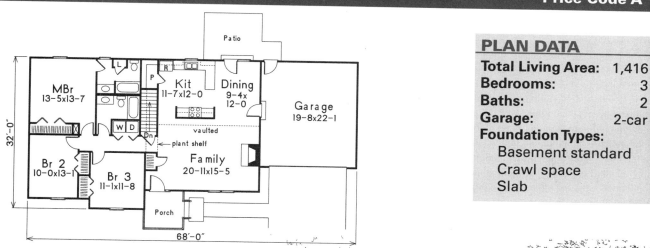

Patio

MBr 13-5x13-7

L

P R

Kit 11-7x12-0

Dining 9-4x 12-0

Garage 19-8x22-1

W D

Dn

vaulted

plant shelf

Br 2 10-0x13-1

Br 3 11-1x11-8

Family 20-11x15-5

Porch

32'-0"

68'-0"

PLAN DATA
Total Living Area: 1,416
Bedrooms: 3
Baths: 2
Garage: 2-car
Foundation Types:
  Basement standard
  Crawl space
  Slab

PLAN #562-1223-1 & 2

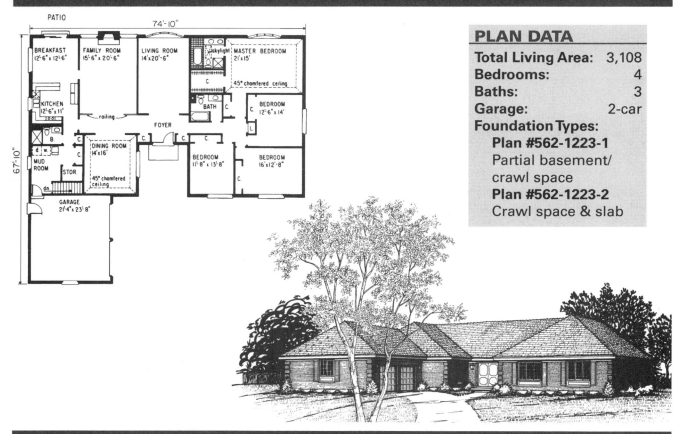

PLAN DATA
Total Living Area: 3,108
Bedrooms: 4
Baths: 3
Garage: 2-car
Foundation Types:
  Plan #562-1223-1
  Partial basement/
  crawl space
  Plan #562-1223-2
  Crawl space & slab

PLAN #562-0689

PLAN DATA
Total Living Area: 1,539
Bedrooms: 3
Baths: 2
Garage: 2-car carport
Foundation Type:
  Slab

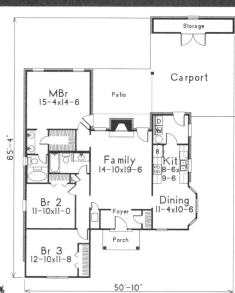

PLAN DATA

Total Living Area:	1,490
Bedrooms:	2
Baths:	2
Garage:	3-car
Foundation Type:	
Basement	

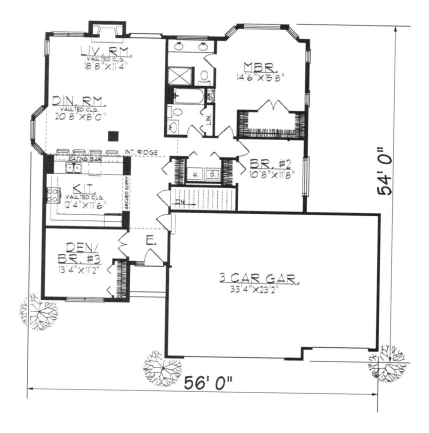

LIV. RM.
VAULTED CLG.
18'8"X11'4"

DIN. RM.
VAULTED CLG.
20'8"X8'0"

MBR.
14'6"X15'8"

EATING BAR

INT. RIDGE

KIT.
VAULTED CLG.
12'4"X11'6"

BR. #2
10'8"X11'8"

LIN.

W.   D.

DEN/
BR. #3
13'4"X11'2"

E.

3 CAR GAR.
33'4"X23'2"

54' 0"

56' 0"

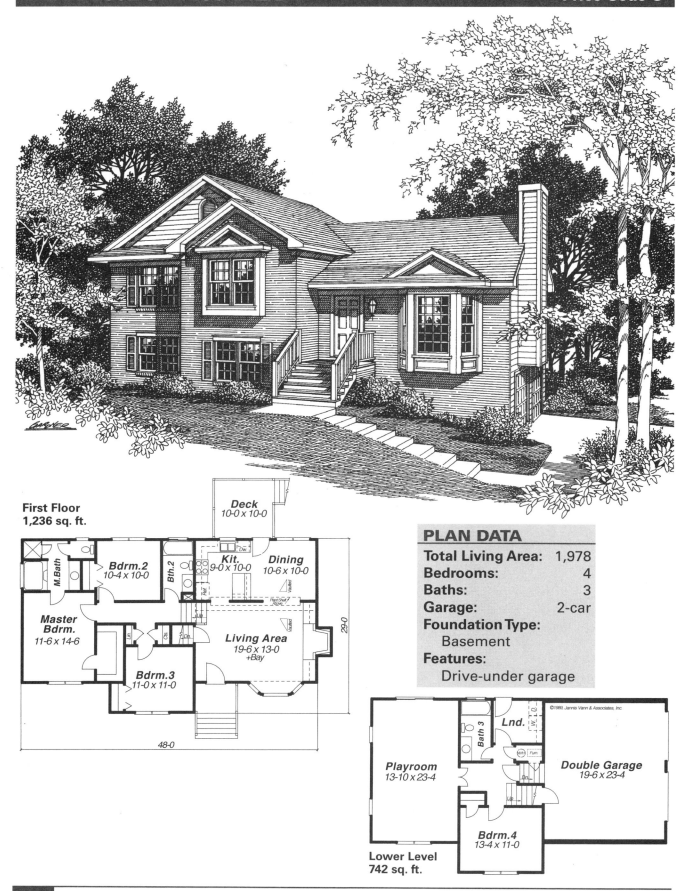

**First Floor
1,236 sq. ft.**

Deck
10-0 x 10-0

M.Bath

Bdrm.2
10-4 x 10-0

Bth.2

Kit.
9-0 x 10-0

Dining
10-6 x 10-0

Master
Bdrm.
11-6 x 14-6

Living Area
19-6 x 13-0
+Bay

Bdrm.3
11-0 x 11-0

29-0

48-0

PLAN DATA

Total Living Area:	1,978
Bedrooms:	4
Baths:	3
Garage:	2-car
Foundation Type:	
Basement	
Features:	
Drive-under garage	

Bath 3

Lnd.

©1989 Jannis Vann & Associates, Inc.

Playroom
13-10 x 23-4

Double Garage
19-6 x 23-4

Bdrm.4
13-4 x 11-0

**Lower Level
742 sq. ft.**

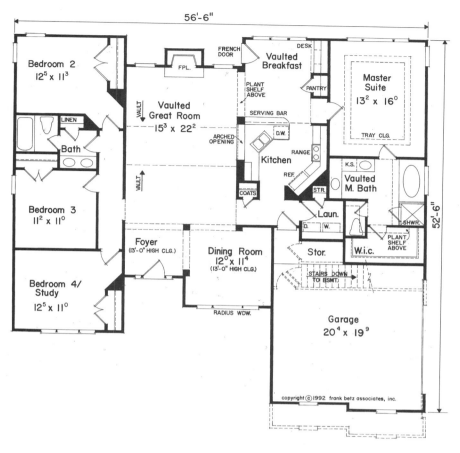

56'-6"

Bedroom 2
12⁵ x 11³

FRENCH DOOR

FPL.

Vaulted Breakfast

DESK

Master Suite
13² x 16⁰

LINEN

VAULT

Vaulted Great Room
15³ x 22²

PLANT SHELF ABOVE

SERVING BAR

PANTRY

Bath

D.W.

ARCHED OPENING

Kitchen

RANGE

TRAY CLG.

VAULT

REF.

K.S.

Bedroom 3
11² x 11⁰

COATS

STR.

Vaulted M. Bath

Laun.

52'-6"

D. W.

Foyer
(13'-0" HIGH CLG.)

Dining Room
12⁰ x 11⁴
(13'-0" HIGH CLG.)

Stor.

SHWR.

W.i.c.

PLANT SHELF ABOVE

Bedroom 4/
Study
12⁵ x 11⁰

STAIRS DOWN TO BSMT.

RADIUS WDW.

Garage
20⁴ x 19⁹

copyright ©1992 frank betz associates, inc.

PLAN DATA

Total Living Area: 1,945
Bedrooms: 4
Baths: 2
Garage: 2-car
Foundation Types:
   Basement
   Crawl space
   Slab
Please specify when ordering

PLAN DATA

Total Living Area: 3,556
Bedrooms: 4
Baths: 3 1/2
Garage: 3-car
Foundation Type:
  Slab
Features:
  Varied ceiling heights

Width: 85'-0"
Depth: 85'-0"

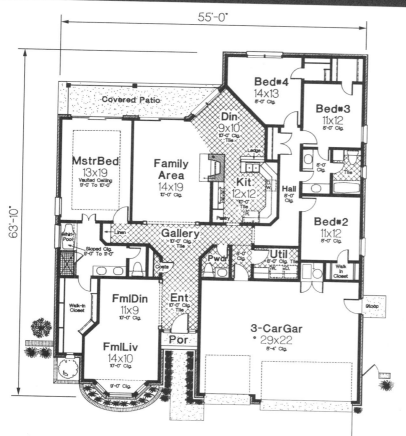

55'-0"

63'-10"

Covered Patio

MstrBed
13x19
Vaulted Ceiling
9'-0" To 10'-0"

Family
Area
14x19
10'-0" Clg.

Din
9x10
10'-0" Clg.
Tile

Bed#4
14x13
8'-0" Clg.

Bed#3
11x12
8'-0" Clg.

Kit
12x12
10'-0" Clg.
Tile

Hall
8'-0" Clg.

Tile

Bed#2
11x12
8'-0" Clg.

Whirl Pool

Sloped Clg.
9'-0" To 11'-0"

Gallery
10'-0" Clg.
Tile

Linen

Pwdr

Util
8'-0" Clg. Tile

Walk In Closet

Closet

Walk-in Closet

FmlDin
11x9
10'-0" Clg.

Ent
10'-0" Clg.
Tile

Por

3-CarGar
29x22
8'-4" Clg.

Stoop

FmlLiv
14x10
10'-0" Clg.

9'-0" Clg.

PLAN DATA

Total Living Area: 2,370
Bedrooms: 4
Baths: 2 1/2
Garage: 3-car
Foundation Type:
    Slab
Features:
    Varied ceiling heights

PLAN DATA

Total Living Area:	2,115
Bedrooms:	3
Baths:	2
Garage:	2-car

Foundation Types:
- Basement
- Crawl space
- Slab

Please specify when ordering

Features:
- 12' ceiling in family room
- 14' ceiling in dining room

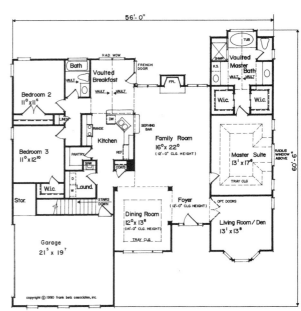

PLAN #562-0798

Price Code C

Width: 56'-0"
Depth: 60'-8"

PLAN DATA

Total Living Area:	2,128
Bedrooms:	4
Baths:	2
Garage:	2-car

Foundation Types:
- Crawl space
- Slab

Please specify when ordering

Features:
- 10' ceiling in living room

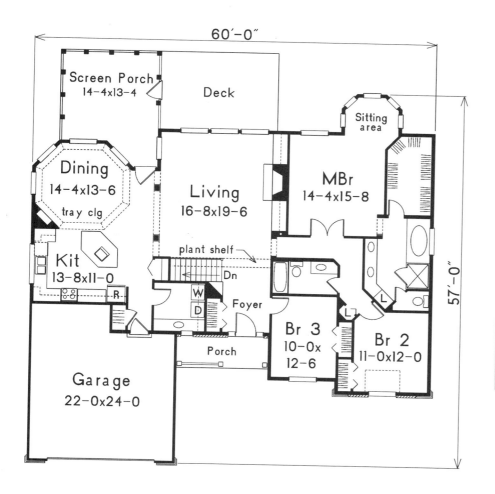

60'-0"

Screen Porch
14-4x13-4

Deck

Sitting area

Dining
14-4x13-6

tray clg

Living
16-8x19-6

MBr
14-4x15-8

plant shelf

Kit
13-8x11-0

Dn

Foyer

W
D

R

Br 3
10-0x
12-6

Br 2
11-0x12-0

L

L

Porch

Garage
22-0x24-0

57'-0"

PLAN DATA

Total Living Area: 2,003
Bedrooms: 3
Baths: 2
Garage: 2-car
Foundation Type:
  Basement
Features:
  10' ceiling in living
  room

PLAN #562-DB3010

Price Code A

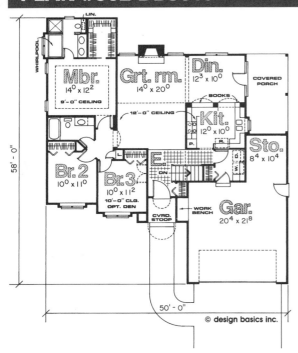

© design basics inc.

PLAN DATA
Total Living Area: 1,422
Bedrooms: 3
Baths: 2
Garage: 2-car
Foundation Type:
  Basement
Features:
  Varied ceiling heights

PLAN #562-JV-1716-A

Price Code B

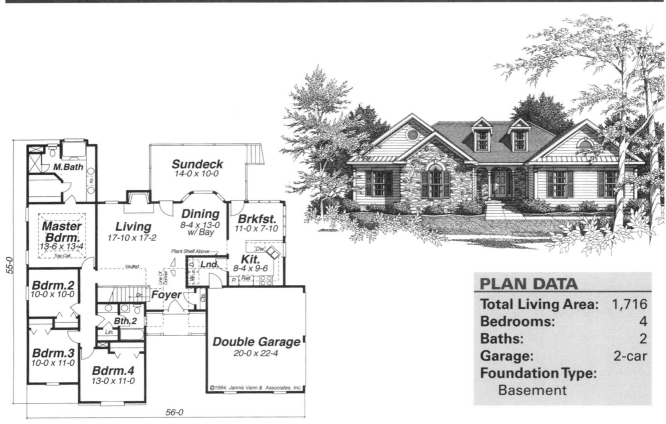

©1994, Jannis Vann & Associates, Inc.

PLAN DATA
Total Living Area: 1,716
Bedrooms: 4
Baths: 2
Garage: 2-car
Foundation Type:
  Basement

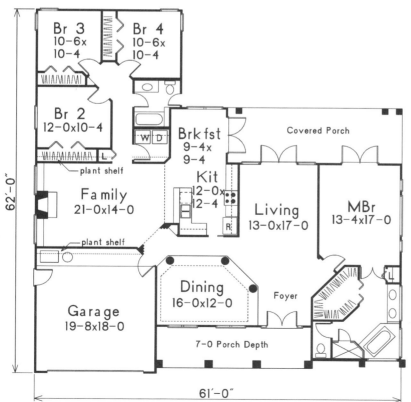

Br 3
10-6x
10-4

Br 4
10-6x
10-4

Br 2
12-0x10-4

plant shelf

W D

Brkfst
9-4x
9-4

Covered Porch

Kit
12-0x
12-4

Family
21-0x14-0

Living
13-0x17-0

MBr
13-4x17-0

plant shelf

R

Dining
16-0x12-0

Foyer

Garage
19-8x18-0

7-0 Porch Depth

L

62'-0"

61'-0"

PLAN DATA

Total Living Area: 2,153
Bedrooms: 4
Baths: 2
Garage: 2-car
Foundation Type:
 Slab
Features:
 Varied ceiling heights

PLAN DATA

Total Living Area: 1,941
Bedrooms: 4
Baths: 2 1/2
Garage: 2-car
Foundation Type:
  Walk-out basement

Deck

Dining
10-8x12-0
vaulted

Skylts

Dn

plant shelf   vaulted

plant shelf

Great Room
16-0x15-9

MBr
12-5x15-0

Kit
10-4x11-4
vaulted

Porch

Garage
18-4x20-4

46'-8"

46'-0"

First Floor
996 Sq. Ft.

46'-0"

24'-4"

Br 3
9-9x10-4

Atrium
9-6x7-7

up

Br 2
12-3x11-6

Family
16-0x15-5

Bar

Br 4
9-9x10-1

Storage
18-0x9-3

Lower Level
945 Sq. Ft.

PLAN DATA

Total Living Area: 1,477
Bedrooms: 3
Baths: 2
Garage: 2-car
Foundation Type:
  Basement
Features:
  Garage with storage

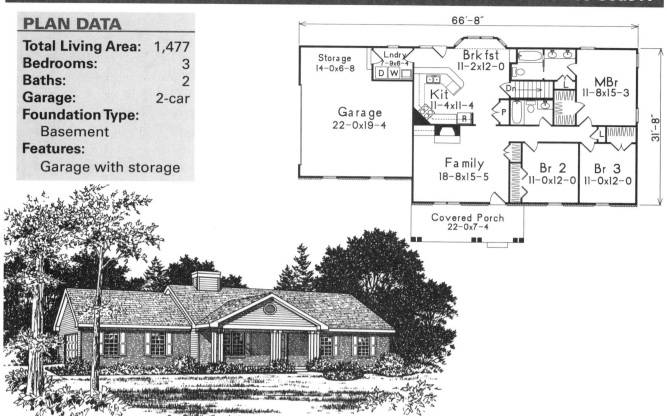

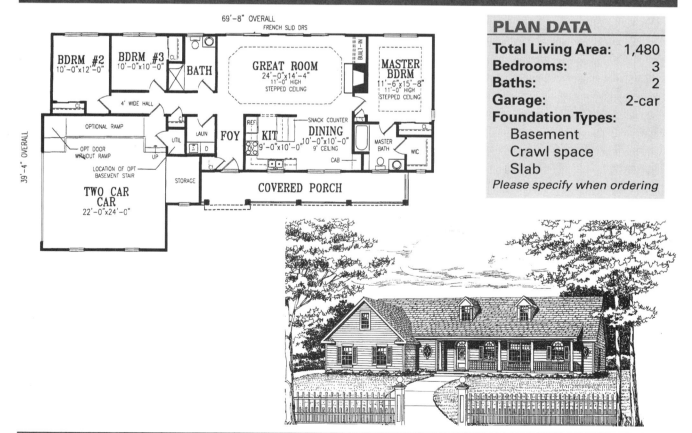

PLAN DATA

Total Living Area: 1,480
Bedrooms: 3
Baths: 2
Garage: 2-car
Foundation Types:
  Basement
  Crawl space
  Slab
Please specify when ordering

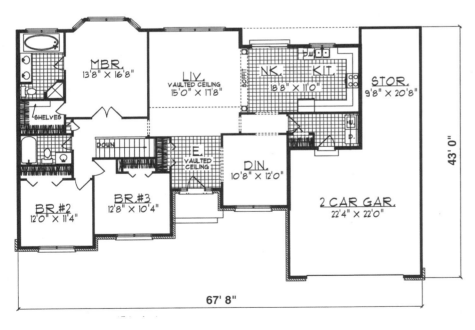

MBR.
13'8" X 16'8"

LIV.
VAULTED CEILING
15'0" X 17'8"

NK.
18'8" X 11'0"

KIT.

STOR.
9'8" X 20'8"

SHELVES

DOWN

E.
VAULTED CEILING

DIN.
10'8" X 12'0"

2 CAR GAR.
22'4" X 22'0"

BR. #2
12'0" X 11'4"

BR. #3
12'8" X 10'4"

43' 0"

67' 8"

PLAN DATA

Total Living Area: 1,763
Bedrooms: 3
Baths: 2
Garage: 2-car
Foundation Type:
    Basement

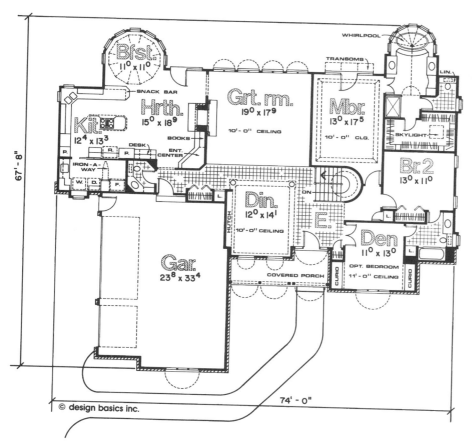

Bfst.
11⁰ x 11⁰

WHIRLPOOL

TRANSOMS

LIN.

SNACK BAR

Hrth.
15⁰ x 18⁹

Grt. rm.
19⁰ x 17⁹

Mbr.
13⁰ x 17⁵

Kit.
12⁴ x 13³

10'-0" CEILING

10'-0" CLG.

SKYLIGHT

BOOKS

DESK

ENT. CENTER

R.

P.

Br.2
13⁰ x 11⁰

IRON-A-WAY

W. D. F.

L

Din.
12⁰ x 14¹

ON

HUTCH

10'-0" CEILING

E

Gar.
23⁸ x 33⁴

Den
11⁰ x 13⁰

OPT. BEDROOM
11'-0" CEILING

CURIO

CURIO

L

COVERED PORCH

67'-8"

74'-0"

© design basics inc.

PLAN DATA

Total Living Area: 2,512
Bedrooms: 3
Baths: 2 1/2
Garage: 3-car
Foundation Type:
  Basement
Features:
  Varied ceiling heights

G. McDonald

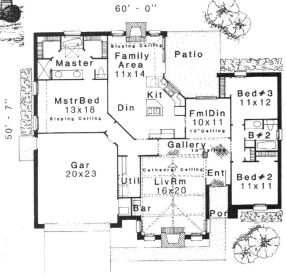

60' - 0''

50' - 7''

Master

MstrBed
13x18
Sloping Ceiling

Gar
20x23

Util

Bar

Family
Area
11x14

Sloping Ceiling

Din

Kit

Patio

FmlDin
10x11
10'Ceiling

Gallery
10'Ceiling

Cathedral Ceiling

LivRm
16x20

Ent

Por

Bed #3
11x12

B #2

Bed #2
11x11

PLAN DATA

Total Living Area:	1,980
Bedrooms:	3
Baths:	2
Garage:	2-car
Foundation Type:	
Slab	

Screen Porch
12-8 x 12-0

Sundeck
15-0 x 12-0

Brkfst.
12-0 x 9-6

Master
Bdrm.
13-6 x 20-0

Kit.
12-0 x 10-2

Living
15-0 x 20-0
Vaulted Ceil.

Vaulted Ceil.

Bdrm.2
14-10 x 12-6

Linen

Bath 2

M.Bath

Dining
11-8 x 11-0

Foyer

Lnd.

Bdrm.3
15-0 x 21-8

Double Garage
21-4 x 21-8

© 1992 Jannis Vann & Associates, Inc.

62-0

68-0

PLAN DATA

Total Living Area:	1,982
Bedrooms:	3
Baths:	2 1/2
Garage:	2-car
Foundation Types:	
Basement	
Crawl space	
Slab	
Please specify when ordering	

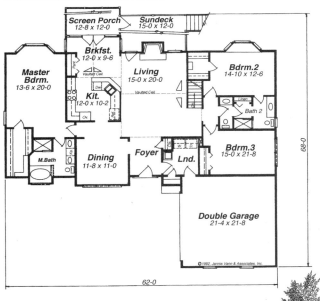

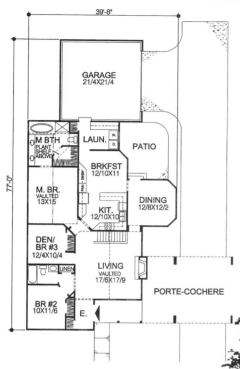

PLAN DATA

Total Living Area:	1,631
Bedrooms:	3
Baths:	2
Garage:	2-car
	1-car carport
Foundation Type:	
Basement	

PLAN #562-JFD-10-1840-2

Price Code C

PLAN DATA

Total Living Area:	1,840
Bedrooms:	3
Baths:	2 1/2
Garage:	2-car
Foundation Type:	
Basement	

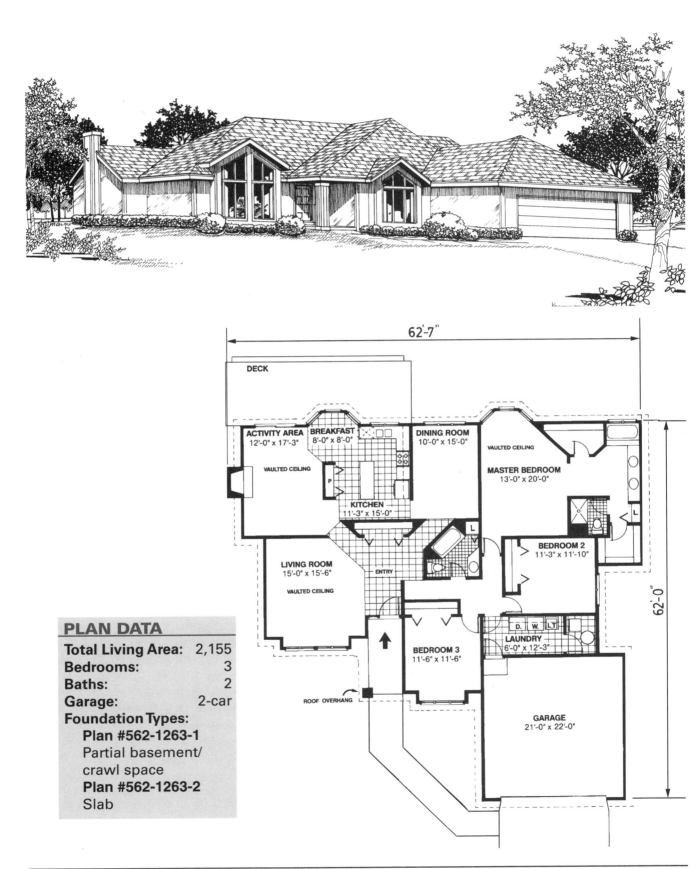

DECK

62'-7"

62'-0"

ACTIVITY AREA
12'-0" x 17'-3"

VAULTED CEILING

BREAKFAST
8'-0" x 8'-0"

DINING ROOM
10'-0" x 15'-0"

VAULTED CEILING

MASTER BEDROOM
13'-0" x 20'-0"

P

KITCHEN
11'-3" x 15'-0"

BEDROOM 2
11'-3" x 11'-10"

L

LIVING ROOM
15'-0" x 15'-6"

VAULTED CEILING

ENTRY

D. W. LT

LAUNDRY
6'-0" x 12'-3"

BEDROOM 3
11'-6" x 11'-6"

ROOF OVERHANG

GARAGE
21'-0" x 22'-0"

PLAN DATA

Total Living Area: 2,155
Bedrooms: 3
Baths: 2
Garage: 2-car
Foundation Types:
   Plan #562-1263-1
   Partial basement/
   crawl space
   Plan #562-1263-2
   Slab

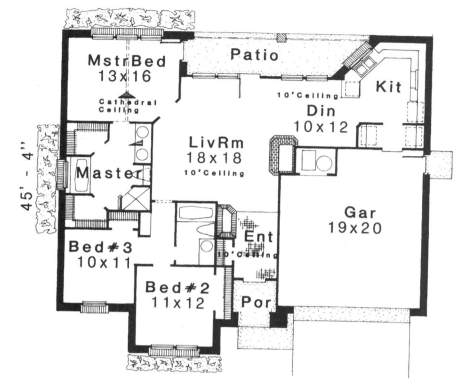

50' - 0''

45' - 4''

MstrBed
13 x 16

Cathedral
Ceiling

Patio

Kit

10'Ceiling

Din
10 x 12

LivRm
18 x 18
10'Ceiling

Master

Gar
19 x 20

Bed #3
10 x 11

Ent
10'Ceiling

Bed #2
11 x 12

Por

PLAN DATA

Total Living Area:	1,417
Bedrooms:	3
Baths:	2
Garage:	2-car

Foundation Type:
Slab

Features:
Varied ceiling heights

SOCRATES

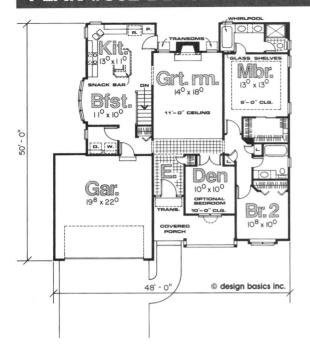

PLAN DATA

Total Living Area: 1,479
Bedrooms: 2
Baths: 2
Garage: 2-car
Foundation Types:
  Basement
  Slab
Please specify when ordering

PLAN DATA

Total Living Area: 2,057
Bedrooms: 3
Baths: 2
Garage: 2-car
Foundation Types:
  Basement
  Crawl space
  Slab
Please specify when ordering
Features:
  Varied ceiling heights

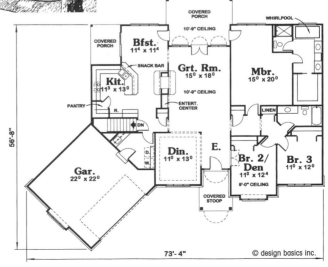

PLAN DATA

Total Living Area: 2,155
Bedrooms: 3
Baths: 2 1/2
Garage: 3-car
Foundation Type:
  Crawl space
Features:
  Varied ceiling heights

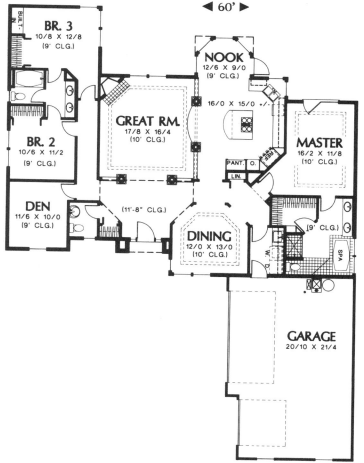

◄ 60' ►

BR. 3
10/8 X 12/8
(9' CLG.)

BUILT-IN

NOOK
12/6 X 9/0
(9' CLG.)

GREAT RM.
17/8 X 16/4
(10' CLG.)

16/0 X 15/0 +/-

MASTER
16/2 X 11/8
(10' CLG.)

BR. 2
10/6 X 11/2
(9' CLG.)

PANT. O.

LIN.

DEN
11/6 X 10/0
(9' CLG.)

(11'-8" CLG.)

(9' CLG.)

DINING
12/0 X 13/0
(10' CLG.)

SPA

▲
79'
▼

GARAGE
20/10 X 21/4

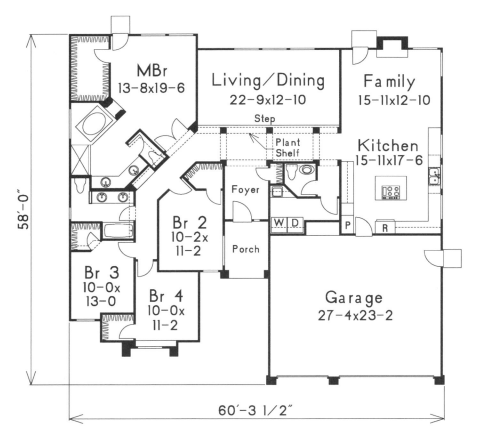

MBr
13-8x19-6

Living/Dining
22-9x12-10

Family
15-11x12-10

Step

Plant Shelf

Kitchen
15-11x17-6

Foyer

Br 2
10-2x
11-2

W D

Porch

P

R

Br 3
10-0x
13-0

Br 4
10-0x
11-2

Garage
27-4x23-2

58'-0"

60'-3 1/2"

PLAN DATA

Total Living Area:	2,255
Bedrooms:	4
Baths:	2 1/2
Garage:	3-car
Foundation Type: Slab	

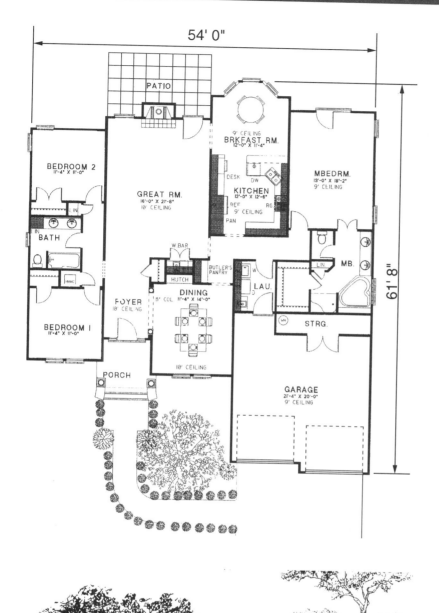

54' 0"

61' 8"

PATIO

9' CEILING
BRKFAST RM.
12'-0" X 11'-4"

BEDROOM 2
11'-4" X 11'-0"

GREAT RM.
16'-0" X 21'-8"
10' CEILING

MBEDRM.
13'-0" X 18'-2"
9' CEILING

DESK   DW

KITCHEN
12'-0" X 12'-6"
9' CEILING

REF   RG.
PAN

BATH
IN   LIN

W.BAR

BUTLER'S PANTRY

HUTCH

LIN.   **MB.**

FOYER
10' CEILING

DINING
8" COL.   11'-4" X 14'-0"

W   LAU.   D

BEDROOM 1
11'-4" X 11'-0"

10' CEILING

WH   **STRG.**

PORCH

GARAGE
21'-4" X 20'-0"
9' CEILING

PLAN DATA

Total Living Area:	1,963
Bedrooms:	3
Baths:	2
Garage:	2-car

Foundation Types:
   Basement
   Walk-out basement
   Crawl space
   Slab
Please specify when ordering
Features:
   Varied ceiling heights

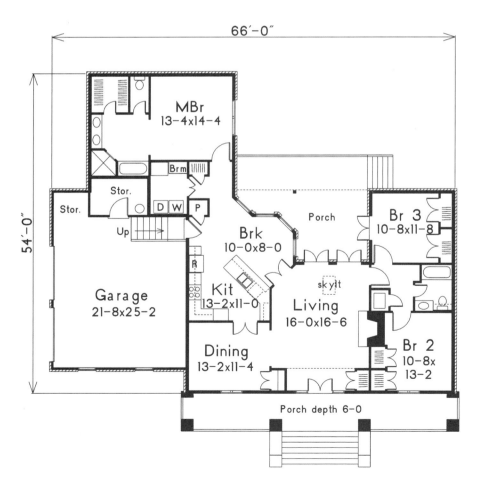

66'-0"

54'-0"

MBr
13-4x14-4

Brm

Stor.

Stor.

D W P

Up

Porch

Br 3
10-8x11-8

Brk
10-0x8-0

R

skylt

Garage
21-8x25-2

Kit
13-2x11-0

Living
16-0x16-6

Br 2
10-8x
13-2

Dining
13-2x11-4

Porch depth 6-0

PLAN DATA

Total Living Area: 1,800
Bedrooms: 3
Baths: 2
Garage: 2-car
Foundation Types:
  Crawl space standard
  Slab
Features:
  - 2" x 6" exterior walls
  - 12' ceilings in
    kitchen, eating area,
    dining and living
    rooms

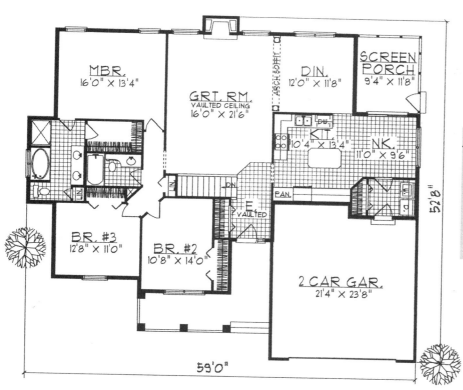

MBR.
16'0" X 13'4"

GRT. RM.
VAULTED CEILING
16'0" X 21'6"

DIN.
12'0" X 11'8"

SCREEN PORCH
9'4" X 11'8"

KIT.
10'4" X 13'4"

NK.
11'0" X 9'6"

PAN.

BR. #3
12'8" X 11'0"

BR. #2
10'8" X 14'0"

E.
VAULTED

DN.

2 CAR GAR.
21'4" X 23'8"

52'8"

59'0"

PLAN DATA

Total Living Area:	1,806
Bedrooms:	3
Baths:	2
Garage:	2-car
Foundation Type:	
Basement	

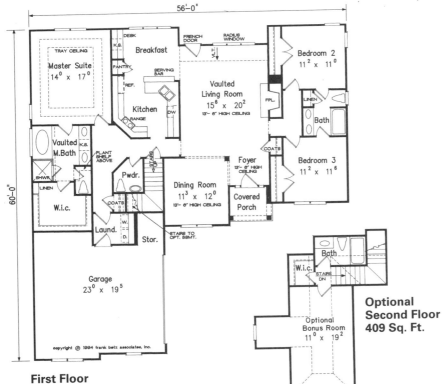

First Floor
1,845 Sq. Ft.

56'-0"

TRAY CEILING

Master Suite
14⁰ x 17⁰

Breakfast

DESK

K.B.

PANTRY

REF.

Kitchen

SERVING BAR

DW

RANGE

FRENCH DOOR

RADIUS WINDOW

Vaulted Living Room
15⁶ x 20²
13'- 6" HIGH CEILING

Bedroom 2
11² x 11⁰

FPL.

LINEN

Bath

Vaulted M.Bath

K.B.

PLANT SHELF ABOVE

SHWR.

LINEN

W.i.c.

Pwdr.

COATS

Laund.

W.
D.

Stor.

COATS

Dining Room
11³ x 12⁰
13'- 6" HIGH CEILING

Foyer
13'- 6" HIGH CEILING

Covered Porch

Bedroom 3
11² x 11⁶

STAIRS TO OPT. BSMT.

W.

Garage
23⁰ x 19⁵

copyright © 1994 frank betz associates, inc.

60'-0"

Optional Second Floor
409 Sq. Ft.

Bath

W.i.c.

STAIRS DN

Optional Bonus Room
11⁰ x 19²

PLAN DATA

Total Living Area:	1,845
Bedrooms:	3
Baths:	2 1/2
Garage:	2-car

Foundation Types:
   Basement
   Crawl space
Please specify when ordering
Features:
   Varied ceiling heights

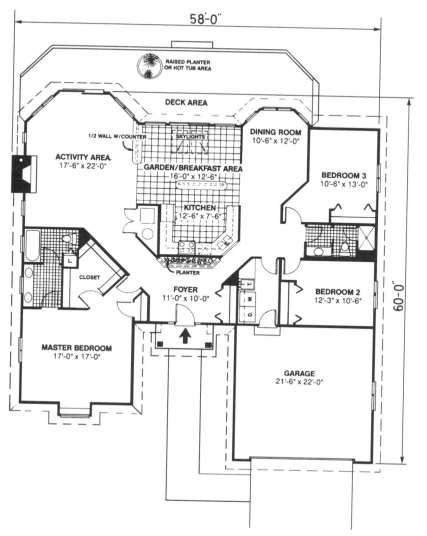

58'-0"

60'-0"

RAISED PLANTER
OR HOT TUB AREA

DECK AREA

1/2 WALL W/COUNTER

SKYLIGHTS

DINING ROOM
10'-6" x 12'-0"

ACTIVITY AREA
17'-6" x 22'-0"

GARDEN/BREAKFAST AREA
16'-0" x 12'-6"

BEDROOM 3
10'-6" x 13'-0"

KITCHEN
12'-6" x 7'-6"

CLOSET

PLANTER

FOYER
11'-0" x 10'-0"

BEDROOM 2
12'-3" x 10'-6"

MASTER BEDROOM
17'-0" x 17'-0"

GARAGE
21'-6" x 22'-0"

PLAN DATA

Total Living Area:	2,190
Bedrooms:	3
Baths:	2
Garage:	2-car
Foundation Types:	
Basement	
Slab	

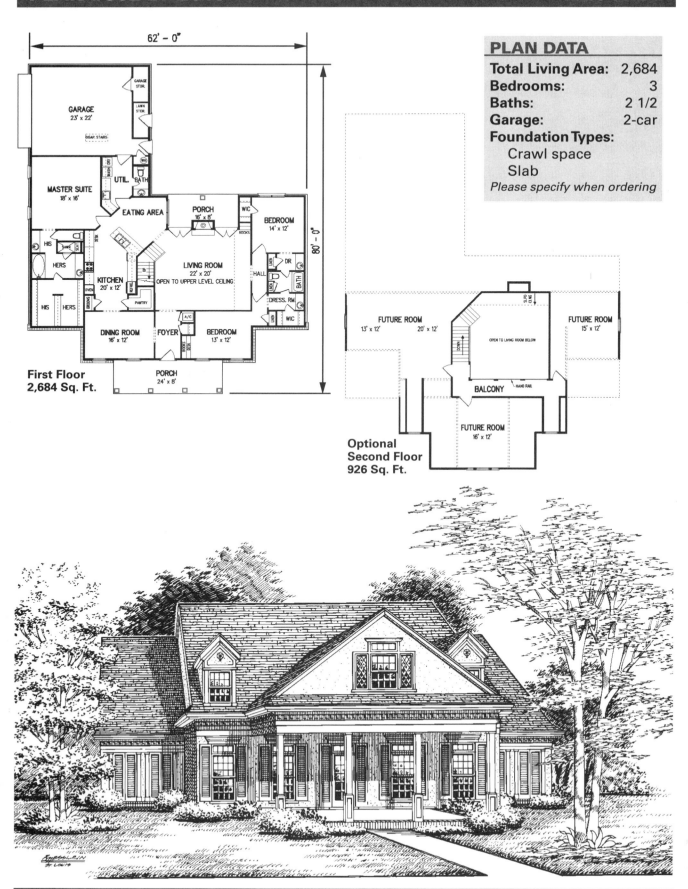

PLAN DATA

Total Living Area: 2,684
Bedrooms: 3
Baths: 2 1/2
Garage: 2-car
Foundation Types:
Crawl space
Slab
Please specify when ordering

62' - 0"

80' - 0"

GARAGE
23' x 22'

GARAGE STOR.

LAWN STOR.

DISAP. STAIRS

MASTER SUITE
18' x 16'

UTIL.

BATH

EATING AREA

PORCH
16' x 8'

WIC

BEDROOM
14' x 12'

HIS

HERS

KITCHEN
20' x 12'

LIVING ROOM
22' x 20'
OPEN TO UPPER LEVEL CEILING

HALL

DR

BATH

HIS

HERS

PANTRY

DRESS. RM.

WIC

DINING ROOM
16' x 12'

FOYER

BEDROOM
13' x 12'

A/C

First Floor
2,684 Sq. Ft.

PORCH
24' x 8'

FUTURE ROOM
13' x 12'

FUTURE ROOM
20' x 12'

OPEN TO LIVING ROOM BELOW

FUTURE ROOM
15' x 12'

BALCONY

HAND RAIL

FUTURE ROOM
16' x 12'

Optional
Second Floor
926 Sq. Ft.